Affectionately Yours,
George Washington

By The Same Author

ONE SMALL CANDLE
THE PILGRIMS' FIRST YEAR IN AMERICA
NOW WE ARE ENEMIES
BEAT THE LAST DRUM

Fiction

KING OF THE HILL
THE GOD OF LOVE
ALL GOOD MEN

Affectionately Yours,
George Washington

A Self-Portrait
in
Letters of Friendship

c. 1

---

edited by Thomas J. Fleming

W · W · *Norton & Company, Inc.*
NEW YORK

"Letters of friendship require no study, the communications are easy and allowances are expected and made. . . . To corrispond with those I love is among my highest gratifications."

CONTENTS

Affectionately Yours,
George Washington

INTRODUCTION

*T*here are over twenty-five thousand separate documents in the collected writings of George Washington. A high percentage of these come under the general heading of official papers, letters Washington wrote in his various public capacities—Colonel of the Virginia Militia, Commander in Chief of the Revolutionary Army, President of the United States. They include army orders of the day, state papers, communications to Congress. These documents, often written by an aide, a secretary, or a talented ghost such as James Madison or Alexander Hamilton, show little of the human being, George Washington. Too often they perpetuate the image which prompted one historian to call Washington "the man in the white marble toga." There was an almost awesome austerity in Washington's official life, especially the years of his Presidency. His political enemy, Thomas Jefferson, writing after Washington's death, admitted that "his integrity was most pure, and his justice the most inflexible I have ever known, no motives of interest or consanguinity or friendship or hatred being able to bias his decision." Samuel Eliot Morison, in a brilliant paper published many years ago, traced this side of Washington's character to his youthful friendship with the Fairfaxes, English aristocrats who, like others of their class in the eighteenth century, were fired by the stern virtues of the ancient Romans as summed up in Joseph Addison's tragedy Cato and the stoic philosophy of the younger Seneca.

But there is another George Washington, a warm and fascinating human being who lived within this official statue. This Washington suffered the pangs of adolescent passion, fell in love with his best friend's wife, wept on the deathbed of his stepdaughter Patsy Custis, and after leading a revolution and founding a na-

11

tion which would transform the civilized world could say, "I had rather be at Mount Vernon with a friend or two about me than to be attended at the seat of government by the officers of state and the representatives of every power in Europe."

This George Washington is best revealed in what he called "letters of friendship." Washington was never a first-rate conversationalist. He suffered all his life from the feeling that he had received an inferior education. But even Jefferson admitted that he wrote a first-rate letter, no small compliment from the author of the Declaration. Thus the rationale for this book. No one can do a better job of recapturing the human side of George Washington for our generation than the man himself.

The text follows the Centennial Edition of Washington's writings edited by John C. Fitzpatrick. This edition reproduces the letters exactly as Washington wrote them, even attempting, whereever possible, to eliminate the minor revisions that Washington himself made thirty years later. There are times when this makes for somewhat difficult reading. In his early letters, Washington was not particularly interested in correct spelling or good syntax. But the real man is more interesting than an improved version.

At certain points, always indicated or summarized, passages that relate to local business transactions, improvements to the Mount Vernon farm, and similar minor details have been deleted. Also omitted, where it seemed advisable, are routine salutations and closings. Finally, it should be made clear that these are not all Washington's letters of friendship but a selection based on a personal judgment of which ones give us the best insight into the man. The reader who wishes to make further explorations can consult the thirty-nine-volume Collected Writings of George Washington.

CHAPTER ONE

Boy Into Soldier

George Washington's first letters are updated. They are entered in a small memorandum book that contains the diary of his "Journey over the Mountains, 1748," an expedition on which he served as assistant surveyor, laying out tracts in the vast five million acres of Virginia that the British crown had granted to the Fairfax family. There were many Fairfaxes in Virginia. Washington's brother Lawrence married Ann, daughter of William Fairfax, who served as the family's agent in the colony and owned a handsome house, Belvoir, just up the river from Mount Vernon. Fairfax's son, George William, was seven years older than Washington and was his companion on this journey which gave the gangling sixteen-year-old his first glimpse of the frontier.

He describes his adventure in a lively letter to his cousin Richard Washington.

DEAR RICHARD: The receipt of your kind favor of the 2d of this Instant afforded me unspeakable pleasure as I am convinced I am still in the Memory of so Worthy a friend a friendship I shall ever be proud of Increasing you gave me the more pleasure as I receiv'd it amongst a parcel of Barbarian's and an uncooth set of People the like favour often repeated would give me Pleasure altho I seem to be in a Place where no real Satis: be had since you receid my Letter in October Last I have not sleep'd above three Nights or four in a bed but after walking a good deal all the Day lay down before the fire upon a Little Hay Straw Fodder or bairskin which ever is to be had with Man Wife and Children like a Parcel of Dogs or Catts and happy's he that gets the Birth nearest the fire there's nothing would make it pass of tolerably but a good Reward a Dubbleloon is my constant gain every Day that the Weather will permit my going

13

out and sometime Six Pistoles the coldness of the Weather will not allow my making a long stay as the Lodging is rather too cold for the time of Year I have never had my cloths of but lay and sleep in them like a Negro except the few Nights I have lay'n in Frederick Town.

On his return from this trip, George continued his work as a surveyor and spent most of his off hours at Belvoir or nearby Mount Vernon. In the Virginia of his day, the name Fairfax meant what Rockefeller means to us. The best society in the colony swirled through Belvoir, and George Washington participated in it eagerly. The Fairfaxes, including dour, misanthropic Lord Fairfax himself, who had come from England in 1747, treated the overgrown adolescent with extraordinary kindness, which he remembered for the rest of his life. But the belles of this highly sociable plantation society were not so kind. As a third son, Washington's inheritance was meager—a few hundred acres of a second-rate plantation near Fredericksburg. When it came to charm and polish, he was miles behind other well-to-do young Virginians who went to school in England. The result was a series of romantic rebuffs which George laments in the following letter to another cousin, Robin Washington.

DEAR FRIEND ROBIN: As its the greatest mark of friendship and esteem Absent Friends can shew each other in Writing and often communicating their thoughts to his fellow Companions makes me endeavor to signalize myself in acquainting you from time to time and at all times my situation and employments of Life and could wish you would take half the Pains of contriving me a letter by any oppertunity as you may be well assured of its meeting with a very welcome reception my Place of Residence is at present at His Lordships where I might was my heart disengag'd pass my time very pleasantly (agreeably) as theres a very agreeable Young Lady Lives in the same House (Colo. George Fairfax's Wife's sister) *

* Probably Elizabeth Eary.

but as that's only adding Fuel to fire it makes me the more uneasy for by often and unavoidably being in Company with her revives my former Passion for your Low Land Beauty whereas was I to live more retired from young Women I might in some measure eliviate my sorrows by burying that chast and troublesome Passion in the grave of oblivion or etarnall forgetfulness for as I am very well assured that's the only antidote or remedy that I ever shall be releivd by or only recess than can administer any cure or help to me as I am well convinced was I ever to attempt any thing I should only get a denial which would be only adding grief to uneasiness.

He sings a similar sad song to another friend, whom we know only as John.

DEAR FRIEND JOHN: As its the greatest mark of friendship and esteem you can shew to an absent Friend In often Writing to him so hope youl not deny me that Favour as its so ardently wish'd and Desired by me. its the greatest pleasure I can yet forsee of having in fairfax to hear from my friends Particularly yourself was my affections disengaged I might perhaps form some pleasures in the conversasion of an agreeable young Lady as there is one now Lives in the same house with me (but as that only serves to make me more dull by putting me oftener in Remembrance of the other) but as that is only nourishment to my former Affa for by often seeing her brings the other into my remembrance where as perhaps was she not often (unavoidably) presenting herself to my view I might in some measure eliviate my sorrows by burrying the other in the grave of oblivion I am well convinced my heart stands in defiance of all others but only he thats given it (for much) care enough to dread a second assault and from a different Quarter tho I well know let it have as many attacks as it will from others they cant be more fierce than it has been I could wish to know whether you have taken your intended trip downwards or not if you wish what Success as also to know how my friend Lawrence drives on in his art of courtship as I fancy you mgt. both nearly guess how it will respectively go with each of you.

He writes a fourth letter after three rebuffs to a Fredericksburg belle and makes the mistake of praising another girl. But in his eagerness for "transactions in your parts," he reveals a lively interest in news about people and places dear to him that was to continue throughout his life.

DEAR SALLY: This comes to Fredericksburg fair in hopes of meeting with a speedy Passage to you if your not there which hope you'l get shortly altho I am almost discouraged from Writing to you as this is my fourth to you since I receivd any from yourself I hope you'l not make the Old Proverb good out of sight out of Mind as its one of the greatest Pleasures I can yet foresee of. having in Fairfax in often hearing from you hope you'l not deny it me

I pass the time of much more aggreeabler than what I imagined I should as there's a very agreeable Young Lady lives in the said house where I reside (Colo. George Fairfax's wife Sister) that in a great measure cheats my sorrow and dejectedness tho not so as to draw my thoughts altogether from you Parts I could wish to be with you down there with all my heart but as it is a thing almost Impractakable shall rest my self where I am with hopes of shortly having some minutes of your transactions in your Parts which will be very welcomely received by your

Washington spent three years working as a surveyor and playing at Belvoir and Mount Vernon. Then a combination of family tragedy and international politics catapulted him onto the world stage. His brother Lawrence died of consumption when Washington was twenty. He left George the Mount Vernon estate, and the Fairfaxes helped him obtain Lawrence's job as one of the colony's four militia officers with the rank of major. In this capacity Washington volunteered to carry a message from Virginia's governor, Robert Dinwiddie, to the commander of a French fort on the southern shore of Lake Erie. Dinwiddie warned the French to stop encroaching on English territory. The French refused the warning and claimed that the territory—nothing less than the entire Ohio valley—belonged to France. On this thousand-mile journey through the winter woods, Washington found ample evidence of French preparations for war. He hurried back to Virginia with the news and was soon out on the frontier again, a lieutenant colonel leading a ragbag regiment of militia. Within a few days he fought a skirmish with a French patrol that proved to be the opening shot in one of history's greatest conflicts, the Seven Years' War. The impetuous young lieutenant colonel describes the fight in a vivid letter to his younger brother, John Augustine Washington.

Camp at Great Meadow, May 31, 1754

Since my last arrived at this place, where three days ago we had an engagement with the French, that is, a party of our men with one of theirs. Most of our men were out upon other detachments, so that I had scarcely 40 men remaining under my command, and about 10 or 12 Indians; nevertheless we obtained a most signal victory. The battle lasted about 10 or 15 minutes, with sharp firing on both sides, till the French gave ground and ran, but to no great purpose. There were 12 killed of the French, among whom was Mons. de Jumonville, their commander, and 21 taken prisoners, among whom are Mess. La Force and Drouillon, together with two cadets. I have sent them to his honour the Governor, at Winchester, under a guard of 20 men, conducted by Lieutenant West. We had but one man killed, and two or three wounded. Among the wounded on our side was Lieutenant Waggener, but no danger, it is hoped, will ensue. We expect every hour to be attacked by superior force, but, if they forbear one day longer, we shall be prepared for them. We have already got entrenchments, are about a pallisado which I hope will be finished today. The Mingoes [Ohio Valley Iroquois] have struck the French and I hope will give a good blow before they have done. I expect 40 odd of them here tonight, which, with our fort and some reinforcements from Col. Fry, will enable us to exert our noble courage with spirit.

P.S. I fortunately escaped without any wound, for the right wing, where I stood, was exposed to and received all the enemy's fire, and it was the part where the man was killed, and the rest wounded. I heard the bullets whistle, and, believe me, there is something charming in the sound.

The bullets soon lost their charming sound. Four weeks later Washington was attacked by a much superior force of French and Indians. Although he fought from the protection of a small stockade named Fort Necessity, the French, firing from behind rocks and trees, soon demoralized his amateur soldiers and Washington was forced to sign a humiliating surrender. The parley was carried on at midnight in a rainstorm, and Washington's interpreter spoke very inadequate French. He therefore missed a key word in the surrender document, which had Washington confessing that he had "assassinated" the leader of the patrol he had wiped out a few weeks before. This made Washington a political liability to the devious Governor Dinwiddie, who soon decided to get rid of the young man. He did so in a neat maneuver, reorganizing the Virginia regiment into independent companies and announcing that henceforth the highest rank any officer could hold would be that of captain. His pride smarting over this de facto demotion (and over several public criticisms of his strategy at Fort Necessity), Washington resigned and went home to Mount Vernon. He stayed there six months, and it is probably during this period that he became involved in an even more frustrating experience: he fell in love with the wife of his best friend.   .

This was Sally Fairfax, who had married George William Fairfax, Washington's companion of frontier surveying days. Extremely well educated for a Virginia woman of the period, Sally was tall, cool, witty, and by reputation impudent and flirtatious. It is easy to see how such a woman could have been perfect consolation for a reticent, unhappy warrior. Washington remained at Mount Vernon for about six months, sharing bachelor quarters with his brother Jack (John Augustine). The two men dined frequently at Belvoir, called upon Sally to make them patent medicines for minor ills, and sent over cloth and measurements that she turned into shirts. Imperceptibly over these months Washington fell in love with this charming young woman who was only two years older than he.

There is not an iota of evidence that he yielded to the passion. As a man of honor he tried instead to bury it deep within himself, and therefore undoubtedly welcomed an opportunity to escape from Sally's tantalizing presence. It came with the arrival of General Edward Braddock at the head of a glistening British army. Braddock had orders to drive the French off the Virginia frontier and seize Fort Duquesne at the forks of the Ohio (present-day Pittsburgh) and secure this vast territory for England. He invited Washington to join his staff as an aide and the young man accepted eagerly. He rode away, scattering numerous letters to his friends. The following went to Sally Fairfax.

Bullskin, April 30, 1755.

DEAR MADAM: In order to engage your corrispondence, I think it expedient just to deserve it; which I shall endeavour to do by embracing the earliest, and every oppertunity of writing to you.

It will be needless to expatiate on the pleasures that communication of this kind will afford me, as it shall suffice to say; a corrispondance with my Friends is the greatest satisfaction I expect to enjoy, in the course of the Campaigne, and that none of my friends are able to convey more real delight than you can to whom I stand indebted for so many obligations.

If an old proverb can claim my belief I am certainly [?] share of success; for surely no man ever made a worse beginning, than I have; out of 4 Horses which we brought from home, one was kill'd outright, and the other 3 render'd unfit for use; so that I have been detain'd here three days already, and how much longer I may continue to be so, the Womb of time must discover.

I must beg my Compliments to Miss. Hannah,* Miss Dent,** and any other's that think me worthy of their enquirys.

I am Madam Yr. most Obedt. Servt.

* Hannah Fairfax was Sally's sister-in-law.
** Elizabeth Dent, a frequent Belvoir guest, joined Sally in signing a lively letter welcoming Washington home on his previous return from the battlefront.

A letter to his brother Jack gives a glimpse of how quickly he won a place on Braddock's staff.

Winchester, May 6, 1755

DEAR JACK: A very fatiegueing Ride, and long round brought me to the General (the day I parted with you) at Frederick Town; a small Village 15 Miles below the blue Ridge in Maryland from thence we proceeded to this place, where we have halted since Saturday last, and shall depart from Wills Creek tomorrow.

I find there is no probability of Marching the Army from Wills Creek till the latter end of this Month, or the first of next; so that you may imagine time will hang heavy upon my hands. I meet with a familiar complaisance in this Family, especially from the General, who I hope to please without difficulty, for I may say it can scarce be done with as he uses, and requires less ceremony than you can well conceive.

I have order'd the Horse Gist to Bullskin [the Washington farm in Frederick County] and my own here, if serviceable; other¬ wise you must have them carr'd down when Countess is sent up: I have conceive'd a good Op'n of Gist, therefore, I hope you will not let him want for proper usage, if he sh'd be s't instead of the Greys; which will be the case if they are able to perform the Journey.

I hope you'll have frequent oppert'ys to expatiate upon the State of my Affairs, w'ch you adm'r to such degree of satisf'n to a Person in my situation. At present I have nothing to add but my comp'ts to all friends, particularly the good Family at Belvoir who I hope to hear are in good health.

To his mother, Washington wrote in more restrained fashion. She had embarrassed him by descending on Mount Vernon and doing everything in her power to dissuade him from risking his life on the frontier once more.

Winchester, May 6, 1755.

HONOUR'D MADAM: I came to this place last Saturday, and shall set out to morrow with the General for Wills Creek; where I fear we shall wait some time for a sufficient number of Waggons to transport us over the Mountains.

I am very happy in the General's Family, and I am treated with a complaisant Freedom which is quite agreeable; so that I have no occasion to doubt the satisfaction I propos'd in making the Campaigne.

As we have met with nothing yet worth relating I shall only beg my Love to my Brother's and Sister's; and Compliments to Friends.

    I am, Honour'd Madam,

        Yr. most Dutiful and Obedt. Son,

Another letter to Sally Fairfax reveals the range of this flirtatious belle's ambition. When General Braddock arrived on the scene, there was fierce competition between the first ladies of Virginia to see who could claim the famous old war dog as an exclusive social prize. Sally evidently tried and lost and ordered Washington to find out why. This obviously caused him no end of diplomatic trouble, but like everything else he did, he doggedly saw the matter through, hoping some lively letters would be his reward. In this he was disappointed. Around this time Lord Fairfax developed a great coolness toward the family of George William Fairfax. Several students of the subject have speculated that part of the trouble may have been caused by Sally's flirtation with Washington or some other equally available young Virginian. Lord Fairfax was something of a misogynist, having been jilted in his only try at marriage. He therefore tended to have a rather pathological dislike for any signs of instability in a woman. Fear of a rupture with the man who had it in his power to disinherit her husband may well have contributed to Sally's caution in her dealings with Washington.

                Fort Cumberland, May 14, 1755.

DEAR MADAM: I have at last, with great pains and difficulty, discovered the Reason why Mrs. Wardrope is a greater favourite of Genl. Braddock's than Mrs. Fairfax; and met with more respect at the late review in Alexandria.

The cause I shall communicate, after rallying you for neglecting the means that introduced her to his favour which to say truth were in a present of delicious Cake, and potted Wood cocks; that wrought such wonders upon the Heart of the General as upon those of the gentlemen that they became instant Admirers, not only the charms, but the Politeness of this Fair Lady.

We have a favourable prospect of halting here three Weeks or a Month longer for Waggons, Horses and Forage; so that it is easy to conceive my situation will be very pleasant and agreeable, when I dreaded this (before I came out) more than every other Incident that might happen in the Campaigne.

I hope you will favour me with your corrispondance since you see my willing desirousness [?—the word is unclear] to deserve the Honour, and of approving myself, Your most Obedt. and most Humble Servt.

Among his friends and relations, Washington never put on airs. He knew that in comparison to the Fairfaxes and others he was a very minor member of the Virginia gentry. His frank ambition to rise in the world was one of the most engaging aspects of this enterprising young man.

Fort Cumberland, May 14, 1755.
DEAR BROTHER: As wearing Boots is quite the Mode, and mine in a declining State; I must beg the favour of you to procure me a pair that is good, and neat, and send them to Major Carlyle, who I hope will contrive them as quick as my necessity requires.

I see no prospect of moving from this place; as we have neither Horses nor Waggons enough, and no forage for them to subsist upon but what is expected from Philadelphia; therefore, I am well convinced that the trouble and difficulty we must encounter in passing the Mountain for want of proper conveniences, will equal all the other Interruptions of the Campaigne; for I conceive the March of such a Train of Artillery in these Roads to be a tremendous undertaking: As to any danger from the Enemy I look upon it as trifling, for I believe they will be oblig'd to exert their utmost

Force to repel the attacks to the Northward, where Governour Shirley and other's with a body of 8,000 Men, will annoy their Settlements, and attempt their Forts.

The Gen'l. has appointed me one of his aids de Camps, in which Character I shall serve this Campaigne, agreeably enough, as I am thereby freed from all commands but his, and give Order's to all, which must be implicitly obey'd.

I have now a good oppertunity, and shall not neglect it, of forming an acquaintance, which may be serviceable hereafter, if I can find it worth while pushing my Fortune in the Military way.

I have wrote to my two female corrispondents [Sarah Carlyle and Sally Fairfax, who were sisters-in-law] by this oppertunity, one of which letters I have inclosed to you, and beg y'r deliverance off. I shall expect a succinct acc't of all that happened since my departure.

I amy, dear Jack, etc.

The next letter continues his reports of his travels, but then moves to a revealing passage, advising Jack on his relations with the Fairfax family, including George's candid appraisal of the social position of the Washingtons.

Winchester, May 28, 1755.
DEAR JACK: I came to this place last Night, and was greatly disappointed at not finding the Cavalry according to promise; I am oblig'd to wait till it does arrive, or till I can procure a Guard from the Militia, either of which I suppose will detain me two days; as you may, with almost equal success, attempt to raize the Dead to life again, as the force of this County; and that from Wills Creek cannot be expected in less than the forementioned time without they are now upon their March.

The Droughth in this County, if possible, exceeds what we see below; so that, it is very reasonably conjectur'd they won't make Corn to suffice the People; and as for Tobacco, they decline all thoughts of making any.

The Inhabitants of this place abound in News, but as I apprehend it is founded upon as much truth as some I heard in my way down, I think it advisable to forego the recital till a little better authority confirms the report, and then you may expect to have a succinct acct.

I shou'd be glad to hear you live Harmony and good fellowship with the family at Belvoir, as it is in their power to be very serviceable upon many occassion's to us, as young beginner's. I wou'd advise your visiting often as one step towards it; the rest, if any more is necessary, your own good sense will sufficient dictate; for to that Family I am under many obligations, particularly to the old Gentleman [William Fairfax].

Mrs. Fairfax and Mrs. Spearing * express'd an inclination to hear whether I liked this place (with my charge safe), you may therefore acquaint them that I met with no other Interruption than the difficulty of gettg. Horses after I found her's for want of Shoes grew lame, I was oblig'd to get a fresh horse every 15 or 20 Miles, which render'd the journey tiresome. I shou'd have receiv'd greater relief from the fatigues of my journey, and my time wou'd have been spent much more agreeably, had I halted below, rather than at this vile post but I little imagin'd I shou'd have occasion to wait for a Guard who ought to have waited for me; if either must have waited at all. My Compliments attend my Friends who I wish health and happiness to, very sincerely; I am Dear Jack, your most Affectionate Brother

To this letter Washington added a long postscript asking Jack to investigate the possibilities of his being elected to the Virginia House of Burgesses, either from his own county or from another county in which he owned land. He carefully listed all the potential candidates and told Jack that Major John Carlyle, husband of Sally's sister-in-law, Sarah Fairfax, had hinted that he ought to run. Jack proved to be less than astute as a campaign manager. He advised Washington to run and he was soundly trounced.

But this was still in the future. Washington was in the pres-

* Mrs. Ann Spearing, another signer of the aforementioned letter of welcome that went from Belvoir to Washington.

ent ever more deeply involved in Edward Braddock's problems as the choleric general struggled to lead his army through the wilderness. In the following letter to William Fairfax, Washington tells how he has been frequently forced to defend American honor from the general's wrathful attacks. There were good reasons for Braddock's temper. The colonists had repeatedly defaulted on their promises and contracts for provisions, wagons, and horses. Without the aid of a Pennsylvania politician named Benjamin Franklin, the entire campaign might have collapsed.

Camp at Wills Creek, June 7, 1755.

HONBLE. SIR: I arriv'd with my charge safe in Camp the 30th of last Month, after waiting a Day and a piece in Winchester expecting the Calvalry to Escort me up; in which I was Disappointed, and oblig'd to make use of a small Guard of the Militia of Frederick.

The General, by frequent breaches of Contracts, has lost all degree of patience; and for want of that consideration and moderation which shou'd be used by a Man of Sense upon these occassion's, will I fear, represent us in a light we little deserve; for instead of blameing the Individuals as he ought, he charges all his Disappointments to a publick Supineness; and looks upon the Country, I believe, as void of both Honour and Honesty; we have frequent disputes on this head, which are maintained with warmth on both sides, especially on his, who is incapable of Arguing with't; or giving up any point he asserts, let it be ever so incompatible with Reason.

There is a Line of Communication to be open'd from Pensylvania to the French Fort Duquisne along w'ch we are to receive, after a little time, all our Convoys of Provisions, &c.; 2d. will move from hence. We have no certain accts. of the French on Ohio; but have advises by Letter from Governor Morris [Robert Hunter Morris, Governor of Pennsylvania] that a Body of three hund'd past Oswego, and that a still larger body was hourly expected; so that I apprehend we shall not take possession of Fort Duquisne so quietly as was imagin'd.

The Inclos'd is to my good Friend Mrs. Carlyle, who I hope

will not suffer our former corrispondance to drop; my Sincere wishes and Compliments attends all enquiring Friends: and I am, etc.

While defending American honor, Washington also had to cope with his mother, who pursued him into the wilderness with two rather silly requests. The Dutchman is no doubt a Pennsylvania German that she hoped to obtain to oversee her plantation.

Camp at Wills Creek, June 7, 1755.
HONOUR'D MADAM: I was favour'd with yours by Mr. Dick, and am sorry it is not in my power to provide you with either a Dutch man, or the Butter as you desire, for we are quite out of that part of the Country where either are to be had, as there are few or no Inhabitants where we now lie Encamp'd, and butter cannot be had here to supply the wants of the Camp.

I was sorry it was not in my power to call upon you as I went to, or came from Williamsburg to'ther Day, which I shou'd have done if the business I went upon, which was for money, wou'd have suffer'd me to have made an hour's delay.

I hope you will spend the chief part of your time at Mount Vernon as you say, where I am certain everything will be order'd as much for your satisfaction as possible, in the situation we are in.

There is a Detachment of 500 Men March'd from this towards the Aligany, to prepare the Roads &c. and it is imagin'd the main body will move now in abt. 5 days time.

As nothing else that is remarkable, occur's to me, I shall conclude, after begging my love and Compliments to all Friends Dear Madam Yr. Most Affect. and Dutiful Son

From Fort Cumberland deep in the wilderness, Washington wrote once more to Sally, delicately treading along the brink of intimacy.

Fort Cumberland at Willes Creek, June 7, 1755.
DEAR MADAM: When I had the pleasure to see you last, you ex-

press'd an Inclination to be informed of my safe arrival at Camp with the charge that was entrusted to my care; but at the same time desir'd it might be communicated in a letter to some body of your acquaintance. This I took as a Gentle rebuke and polite manner of forbidding me corrisponding with you and conceive this opinion is not illy founded when I sifted it thus. I have hither to found it impracticable to engage one moment of your attention. If I am right in this I hope you will excuse my present presumption and lay the imputation to lateness at my successful arrival. If on the contrary these are fearfull apprehensions only, how easy is it to remove my suspicion, enliven my dull hours, and make me happier than the Day is long, by honouring me with a corrispondance which you did once partly promise.

Please to make my Complts. to Miss Hannah, and to Mr. Bryan,* to whom I shall do myself the pleasr. of writing so soon as I hear he is return'd from Westmorcland.

I am Madam Your most Obedt. etc.

The British foray into the Western forests ended in the incredible disaster history has called Braddock's defeat. Attacked by a howling mob of French and Indians, the redcoats panicked, fired blindly into their own ranks, and refused to obey a single order. Washington was the only one of Braddock's aides unwounded by the opening volleys. Although he had been prostrate with fever for ten days, he rode furiously around the chaotic battlefield delivering the general's orders. Four bullets passed through his clothes, two horses were shot out from under him. Yet he was one of the few who kept his head, and when Braddock fell, mortally wounded, Washington helped organize a rear guard which carried the dying general off the battlefield and preserved the fragments of the army from pursuit. He stayed on horseback for most of the next forty-eight hours, a remarkable tribute to his astonishing vitality.

Braddock's defeat was one of the emotional turning points of George Washington's life. Never again would he worship England

* Bryan Fairfax; he was a half brother of George William Fairfax, and was four years younger than Washington.

as the repository of wisdom and military skill. His letters reflect the shock of what he had witnessed.

His first, to his brother Jack, refuted the rumor that he had been slain.

> *Fort Cumberland,* July 18, 1755.
> DEAR JACK: As I have heard since my arriv'l at this place, a circumstantial acct. of my death and dying speech, I take this early oppertunity of contradicting both, and of assuring you that I now exist and appear in the land of the living by the miraculous care of Providence, that protected me beyond all human expectation; I had 4 Bullets through my Coat, and two Horses shot under me, and yet escaped unhurt.
>
> We have been most scandalously beaten by a trifling body of men; but fatigue and want of time prevents me from giving any of the details till I have the happiness of seeing you at home; which I now most ardently wish for, since we are drove in thus far. A weak and Feeble state of Health, obliges me to halt here for 2 or 3 days, to recover a little strength, that I may thereby be enabled to proceed homeward with more ease; You may expect to see me there on Saturday or Sunday Se'night, which is as soon as I can well be down as I shall take my Bullskin Plantation's in my way. Pray give my Compl'ts to all my F'ds. I am Dr. Jack, y'r most Affect. Broth'r

The next, to his mother, gives more details of the disaster.

> *(Fort Cumberland,* July 18, 1755)
> HONOUR'D MAD'M: As I doubt not but you have heard of our defeat, and perhaps have it represented in a worse light (if possible) than it deserves; I have taken this earliest oppertunity to give you some acct. of the Engagement, as it happen'd within 7 miles of the French Fort, on Wednesday the 9th. Inst.
>
> We March'd on to that place with't any considerable loss, having only now and then a stragler pick'd up by the French Scoutg. Ind'nd. When we came there, we were attack'd by a Body

of French and Indns. whose number, (I am certain) did not exceed 300 Men; our's consisted of abt. 1,300 well arm'd Troops; chiefly of the English Soldiers, who were struck with such a panick, that they behav'd with more cowardice than it is possible to conceive; The Officers behav'd Gallantly in order to encourage their Men, for which they suffer'd greatly; there being near 60 kill'd and wounded; a large proportion out of the number we had! The Virginia Troops shew'd a good deal of Bravery, and were near all kill'd; for I believe out of 3 Companys that were there, there is scarce 30 Men left alive; Capt. Peyrouny and all his Officer's down to a Corporal was kill'd; Capt. Polson shar'd near as hard a Fate; for only one of his was left: In short the dastardly behavior of those they call regular's expos'd all others that were inclin'd to do their duty to almost certain death; and at last, in dispight of all the efforts of the Officer's to the Contrary, they broke and run as Sheep pursued by dogs; and it was impossible to rally them.

The Genl. was wounded; of w'ch he died 3 Days after; Sir Peter Halket was kill'd in the Field where died many other brave Officer's; I luckily escap'd with't a wound, tho' I had four Bullets through my Coat, and two Horses shot under me; Captns. Orme and Morris two of the Genls. Aids de Camp, were wounded early in the Engagem't which render'd the duty hard upon me, as I was the only person then left to distribute the Genl's Orders which I was scarcely able to do, as I was not half recover'd from a violent illness, that confin'd me to my Bed, and a Waggon, for above 10 Days; I am still in a weak and Feeble cond'n; which induces me to halt here, 2 or 3 Days in hopes of recov'g. a little Strength, to enable me to proceed homewards; from whence, I fear I shall not be able to stir till towards Sept., so that I shall not have the pleasure of seeing you till then, unless it be in Fairfax; please to give my love to Mr. Lewis and my Sister * and Compts. to Mr. Jackson ** and all other Fds. that enquire after me. I am, Hon'd Madam Yr. most dutiful Son.

* Fielding Lewis, who married Washington's sister Elizabeth (Betty).
** Probably Robert Jackson, one of the witnesses to the will of Augustine Washington, George's father.

P.S. You may acqt. Priscilla Mullican that her Son Charles is very well, hav'g only rec'd a slight w'd in his Foot, w'ch will be cur'd with't detrimt. to him, in a very small time.

We had abt. 300 Men kill'd and as many, and more, wounded.

The remnants of Braddock's army retreated all the way to Philadelphia, leaving the Virginia frontier naked to the scalping knives of the now blood-maddened Indians. The panicky Virginia Assembly turned to George Washington for protection, asking him to take command of a regiment with the commission of colonel. He accepted reluctantly, knowing it was almost impossible to defend three hundred miles of forested frontier with a mere seven hundred men.

Once more his mother offered a hundred objections to his going, and he replied somewhat curtly. .

Mount Vernon, August 14, 1755.
HONOR'D MADAM: If it is in my power to avoid going to the Ohio again, I shall, but if the Command is press'd upon me by the genl. voice of the Country, and offer'd upon such terms as can't be objected against, it wou'd reflect eternal dishonour upon me to refuse it; and that, I am sure must, or ought, to give you greater cause of uneasiness than my going in an honourable Com'd.; for upon no other terms I will accept of it if I do at all; at present I have no proposals or any mention made abt. it only from private hands. I am etc.

To his Cousin Charles Lewis, Washington had no pretensions about his military ability.

Mount Vernon, August 14, 1755.
DEAR SIR: I return most unfeigned thanks for your hearty demonstrations of Friendship, in kind congratulation's on my safe return, and I wish dear Charles, it was more in my power than it is to answer the favourable opinion my Friends have conceiv'd of my abilitys, let them not be deceiv'd, I am unequal to the Task, and do as-

sure you it requires more experience than I am master of to conduct an affair of the importance that this is now arisen to.

If I do go, I shou'd think myself happy in havg. you of our party, if you have reconcil'd it perfectly to yourself and Family, otherwise I think you wou'd be blameable to involve them in so much uneasiness as your absence will necessaryly give; I have wrote fully to your Broth'r Wnr. to whom I must refer you for further particular's I am Dr. Charles, etc.

For the next two years Washington was to fight a maddening, frustrating frontier war. His correspondence was almost totally official. Long weary reports about minor skirmishes, rather silly arguments with the governor about how many batmen he was legally permitted to have, struggles with mutinous troops, deserters. The war, meanwhile, swept north as the British struck at the heart of French power in Canada. Washington was left behind, the commander of a minor theater. He watched with dismay and his disillusionment with a military career slowly deepened. He began writing long letters to his agent in London ordering expensive furnishings for Mount Vernon—draperies and rugs and bedspreads—not the sort of thing a bachelor would ordinarily think about.

In March 1758, while on his way home from a visit to Williamsburg, Colonel Washington stopped for the night at "the White House," the residence of Martha Dandridge Custis. A widow of seven months, Martha was one of Virginia's wealthiest young women. We have no record of her meeting Colonel Washington before this overnight visit, but she owned a splendid six-chimney house in Willamsburg and it is more than probable that she had already met Virginia's most distinguished young soldier. At any rate they knew each other well enough to become engaged a few months later.

Washington, meanwhile, committed himself to one more campaign in the western wilderness, serving as the commander of a Virginia brigade accompanying another British army marching to avenge Braddock's defeat. On July 20, 1758, he wrote the following note to his fiancé. Douglas Southall Freeman, Washington's premier biographer, has expressed concern because there are some aspects of the letter that made him suspect its authenticity. Washington, for instance, never used the word "courier" at this time. The letter may have been edited somewhat by the previous keepers of the Washington papers. Other parts of it, however, particularly the reference to friendship (in deliberate contrast to love) is a note that Washington struck in his references to Martha throughout his life. This by no means implies that Washington downgraded their relationship. On the contrary, Washington's experience had convinced him that passionate love was a very transitory thing, fickle and undependable, whereas friendship in the Roman use of the word was life's noblest emotion. A century before Washington's birth, the great English thinker Francis Bacon echoed the prevailing opinion when he wrote, "A man cannot speak to his son but as a father, to his wife but as a husband, whereas a friend may speak as the case requires." That the reticent young Washington found he could speak so frankly to Martha Custis is no small compliment to her good sense and charm.

July 20, 1758

We have begun our march for the Ohio. A courier is starting for Williamsburg, and I embrace the opportunity to send a few words to one whose life is now inseparable from mine. Since that happy hour when we made our pledges to each other, my thoughts have been continually going to you as another Self. That an all-powerful Providence may keep us both in safety is the prayer of your ever faithful and affectionate friend.

The news of Washington's engagement had long since reached Sally Fairfax's sharp ears. Sally, who obviously knew all too well what was going on inside Washington, must have twitted him about complaints he had been making to numerous Virginians about the British general's choice of a route to the Ohio. She suggested, perhaps with a touch of irony, that since Washington had professed himself a "votary of love" he was really impatient to possess Martha Custis. This produced in Washington

*nothing less than an emotional explosion. The text here follows the
original manuscript, recently rediscovered in Harvard's Houghton
Library, and printed here with their permission. As James Thomas
Flexner, Washington's most recent biographer, points out, the
strange punctuation does much to intimate Washington's turmoil.*

Camp at Fort Cumberland, 12. Sept. 1758
DEAR MADAM: Yesterday I was honourd with your short, but very
agreable favour of the first Inst^t.—how joyfully I catch at the
happy occasion of renewing a Corrispondance which I feard was
disrelished on your part, I leave to time, that never failing Expositor
of all things—and to a Monitor equally as faithful in my own
Breast to Testifie.—In silence I now express my joy.—Silence
which in some cases—I wish the present-speaks more Intelligably
than the sweetest Eloquence.—

If you allow that any honour can be derivd from my opposition
to our present System of management you destroy the merit of it
entirely in me by attributing my anxiety to the annimating prospect
of possessing Mrs. Custis.——When——I need not name it.—
guess yourself.—Should not my own Honour and Country's welfare
be the excitement? Tis true, I profess myself a Votary of Love—I
acknowledge that a Lady is in the Case—and further I confess, that
this Lady is known to you.—Yes Madam as well as she is to one
who is too sensible of her Charms to deny the Power, whose Influence he feels and must ever submit to. I feel the force of her
amiable beauties in the recollection of a thousand tender passages
that I could wish to obliterate, till I am bid to revive them.—but
experience alas! sadly reminds me how Impossible this is.—and
evinces an Opinion which I have long entertaind, that there is a
Destiny, which has the Sovereign controul of our Actions-not to be
resisted by the strongest efforts of Human Nature.—

You have drawn me my dear Madam, or rather have I drawn
myself, into an honest confession of a Simple Fact—misconstrue
not my meaning-'tis obvious—doubt in [it?] not, not expose it,—
the World has no business to know the object of my Love,—declared in this manner to-you when I want to conceal it——One

thing above all things in this World I wish to know and only one person of your Acquaintance can solve me that or guess my meaning.—but adieu to this, till happier times, if I ever shall see them.—the hours at present are melancholy dull.—neither the rugged Toils of War, nor the genteler conflict of A———— B———s [Assembly Balls] is in my choice. -I dare believe you are as happy as you say-I wish I was happy also—Mirth, good humour, ease of Mind and. ——what else? cannot fail to render you so, and consummate your Wishes.— ——— [?]

If one agreeable Lady could almost wish herself a fine Gentleman for the sake of another; I apprehend, that many fine Gentleman will wish themselves finer, e'er Mrs. Spotswood is possest. -She has already become a reigning toast in this Camp; and many there are in it, who intends (fortune favoring) to make honourable Scar's speak the fullness of their Merit, and be a messenger of their Love to Her.—

I cannot easily forgive the unseasonable haste of my last express, if he deprived me thereby of a single word you intended to add.—the time of the present messenger is, as the last might have been, entirely at your disposal.—I cannot expect to hear from my Friends more than this once, before the Fate of the Expedition will some how or other be determined, I therefore beg to know when you set out for Hampton, & when you expect to return to Belvoir again—and I should be glad to hear also of your speedy departure, as I shall thereby hope for your return before I get down; the disappointment of seeing [the failure to see] your family would give me much concern.— ——— [?] From anything I can yet see 'tis hardly possible to say when we shall finish. I don't think there is a probability of it till the middle of November.—Your Letter to Captn Gist I forwarded by a safe hand the moment it came to me. -his answer shall be carefully transmitted.

Col.° Mercer to whom I delivered your message and Compliments, joins me very heartily in wishing you and the Ladies of Belvoir the perfect enjoyment of every Happiness this World affords. —be assured that I am D Madam with the most unfeigned regard, your Most Obedient & Most Obliged H^{ble} Servt

Four months later, Washington's military career ended, when the British-American army drove the French from Fort Duquesne and Washington himself hoisted the British flag at that key junction of the Allegheny and the Monongahela. On January 6, 1759, he married Martha Custis at the "White House" and took her home to Mount Vernon.

CHAPTER TWO

A Domesticated Hero

*F*or the next sixteen years Wash-
ington was content to be master of Mount Vernon, stepfather to
Jacky and Patsy Custis, Martha's two children, and member of the
Virginia House of Burgesses. He worked from dawn or even before
(he frequently rose at 4 A.M.) to dusk supervising his own and the
Custis estates, which involved over twenty-nine thousand scattered
acres and some six hundred Negroes, not to mention overseers,
white artisans, and other personnel. Most of his correspondence
during these years concerns business matters—sales of tobacco in
England, orders for clothing, wine, house furnishings, even a coach.
But military friendships still loomed large, and he was always ready
and eager to lend a helping hand to a former comrade in arms. In
1760, Captain Robert MacKenzie, one of his junior officers, wrote
him asking for a letter of recommendation to the British commander-in-chief in North America, General Amherst. Washington's reply is full of both honest friendship and realism. Washington was well aware that he had been nothing more than the commander of a minor theater of war.

> *Mount Vernon*, November 20, 1760.
> DEAR SIR: Had your Letter of the 17th of August come to my
> hands before the 18th. Inst., I should not have given you the
> trouble of perusing my answer to it at this late Season. I am sorry
> you shoud think it necessary to introduce a request that is founded
> upon Reason and equity with an Apology, to me; had you claimed
> that as a Right, which you seem rather to ask as a favour I shoud
> have thought myself wanting in that justice which is the distin-
> guishing Characteristick of an Honest Man to have with-held it
> from you.

But to answer your purposes and at the same time to avoid the Imputation of Impertinence, I am I confess, a little more at a loss to determine. That Genl. Amherst may have heard of such a Person as I am, is probable; And this I dare venture to say is the Ultimate knowledge he has of me; how then shoud I appear to him in an Epistalory way and to set down and write a Certificate of your behaviour carries an Air of formality that seems more adapted to the soldiery than Officers. I must therefore beg the favour of you to make what use you please of this Letter.

For Sir, with not more pleasure than truth, I can declare to you, and the World, that while I had the honour of Commanding the Regiment, your conduct both as an Officer and Gentleman were unexceptionable good; and in every Instance, as far as I was capable of discerning, such, as to have merited applause from better judges. Since my time Colo. Byrd has been witness to your Behaviour and his Letter Recommendatory must I am perswaded do you more Service than my sanguine endeavours can. Altho he, nor no other Person, is more sensible of your worth nor more Inclind to contribute their best Offices towards the Completion of your wishes than etc.

Washington was on friendly terms with all those he called his "kin." But Martha's brother-in-law, Burwell Bassett, was among his favorites. Washington often stayed overnight at the Bassett estate, Eltham, in New Kent County near Williamsburg, and one suspects, from the joshing tone of this letter, that when he did, a good time was had by all.

Mount Vernon, August 28, 1762.

DEAR SIR: I was favoured with your Epistle wrote on a certain 25th of July when you ought to have been at Church, praying as becomes every good Christian Man who has as much to answer for as you have; strange it is that you will be so blind to truth that the enlightning sounds of the Gospel cannot reach your Ear, nor no Examples awaken you to a sense of Goodness; could you but behold with what religious zeal I hye me to Church on every Lords day, it would do your heart good, and fill it I hope with equal fervency; but heark'ee; I am told you have lately introduced into your Family, a certain production which you are lost in admiration of, and spend so much time in contemplating the just proportion of its parts, the ease, and conveniences with which it abounds, that it is thought you will have little time to animadvert upon the prospect of your crops &c; pray how will this be reconciled to that anxious care and vigilance, which is so escencially necessary at a time when our growing Property, meaning the Tobacco, is assailed by every villainous worm that has had an existence since the days of Noah (how unkind it was of Noah now I have mentioned his name to suffer such a brood of vermin to get a birth in the Ark) but perhaps you may be as well of as we are; that is, have no Tobacco for them to eat and there I think we nicked the Dogs, as I think to do you if you expect any more; but not without a full assurance of being with a very sincere regard etc.

The Stamp Act, Parliament's first attempt to tax the colonies internally, required Americans to use stamps on all legal and commercial paper, pamphlets, newspapers, almanacs, cards, and dice. It infuriated the colonists and led to riots and political agitation. Washington's reaction to it appears in a letter to Martha's English relative Francis Dandridge, which also throws some interesting light on Washington's marriage.

Mount Vernon, September 20, 1765.
SIR: If you will permit me after six years silence, the time I have been married to your Niece, to pay my respects to you in this Epistolary way I shall think myself happy in beginning a corrispondance which cannot but be attended with pleasure on my side.

I shoud hardly have taken the liberty Sir, of Introducing myself to your acquaintance in this manner, and at this time, least you shoud think my motives for doing of it arose from sordid views had not a Letter which I receivd sometime this Summer from Robt. Cary & Co. given me Reasons to believe that such an advance on my side woud not be altogether disagreeable on yours before this I rather apprehended that some disgust at the News of your Nieces Marriage with me, and why I coud not tell, might have been the cause of your silence upon that event, and discontinuing a corrispondance which before then you had kept up with her; but if I could only flatter myself, that you woud in any wise be entertaind with the few occurances that it might be in my power to relate from hence I shoud endeavour to attone for my past remisness, in this respect, by future punctuality.

At present few things are under notice of my observation that can afford you any amusement in the recital. The Stamp Act Imposed on the Colonies by the Parliament of Great Britain engrosses the conversation of the Speculative part of the Colonists, who look upon this unconstitutional method of Taxation as a direful attack upon their Liberties, and loudly exclaim against the Violation; what may be the result of this and some other (I think I may add) ill judgd Measures, I will not undertake to determine; but this I may venture to affirm, that the advantage accrueing to the Mother Country will fall greatly short of the expectations of the Ministry; for certain it is, our whole Substance does already in a manner flow to Great Britain and that whatsoever contributes to lessen our Importation's must be hurtful to their Manufacturers. And the Eyes of our People, already beginning to open, will perceive, that many Luxuries which we lavish our substance to Great Britain for, can well be dispensd with whilst the necessaries of Life are (mostly) to be had within ourselves. This consequently will introduce frugality, and be a necessary stimulation to Industry. If Great Britain therefore Loads her Manufactures with heavy Taxes, will it not facilitate these Measures? they will not compel us I think to give our Money for their exports, whether we will or no, and certain I am none of their Traders will part from them without a valuable consideration. Where then is the Utility of these Restrictions?

As to the Stamp Act, taken in a single view, one, and the first bad consequences attending it I take to be this. Our Courts of Judicature must inevitably be shut up; for it is impossible (or next of kin to it) under our present Circumstances that the Act of Parliam't can be complyd with were we ever so willing to enforce the execution; for not to say, which alone would be sufficient, that we have not Money to pay the Stamps, there are many other Cogent Reasons to prevent it; and if a stop be put to our judicial proceedings I fancy the Merchants of G. Britain trading to the Colonies will not be among the last to wish for a Repeal of it.

I live upon Potomack River in Fairfax County, about ten Miles below Alexandria and many miles distant from any of my Wifes Relations; who all reside upon York River, and who we seldom see more than once a year, not always that. My wife who is very well and Miss Custis (Children of her former Marriage) all join in making a tender of their Duty and best respects to yourself and the Aunt. My Compliments to your Lady I beg may also be made acceptable and that you will do me the justice to believe that I am, etc.

As trouble with England deepened, George William Fairfax and Sally decided to return to the motherland. Sally seems to have been the prime mover. She had now centered her ambitions on obtaining the family title for her husband. In 1773 they were preparing to leave and Fairfax asked Washington if he would supervise his estate in their absence. Washington's answer is again evidence of his complete honesty, as well as loyalty to an old friend.

Mount Vernon, January 19, 1773.
DEAR SIR: If you are done with my Compass and Plotting Instruments, I should be glad to receive them by the bearer, as I measure all my Fields, and am now Inclosing a new one, and do not know where to lay the Rails that are to Fence it, till I find how much of the Field will give me the quantity of Land I want to Inclose.

As I wrote to you in haste the morning of the day Lord Sterlg. yourself &ca. were to dine here (in answer to your Letter of the 1st. Inst.) I might not perhaps have expressed my meaning so clearly as I wishd to have done, in respect to the several matters therein containd; and therefore cannot help again repeating, that, if you think, engaged as I often am in Company, with my own business, and the business of others, I can be as serviceable to you in your absence, as another who may have more leisure, but not more Inclination, I shall undertake it with chearfulness. My only diffidence arose from an apprehension that, I had it not in my power to give that attention to your business which the nature of the case might require; and that I might in fact, do you a disservice by undertaking more than I could perform; but upon perusing your Letter more attentively, I find that, as you only require that I should have an eye to the conduct of your Steward or manager, and to remit his Collections; I can do it with very little difficulty; and will, if you think proper to repose this Trust in me, discharge it to the best of my judgment.

Our Compliments are presented to yourself, and Mrs. Fairfax who we hope to hear is better. One of the Letters herewith sent was found upon the Road in Stafford and brought from thence a day or two ago by By L: Washington * I am, etc,

Jack Custis was one of Washington's major worries during these years. He was almost pathetically anxious to have Jack obtain the education he himself never received. But Martha was a compulsively doting mother and there was an indolent streak in Jack which not even Washington could overcome. Washington hired numerous tutors and scolded and pleaded, but Jack's mind remained centered on "guns, horses, dogs, and equipage." Then from his tutor came an even more alarming report, "an astonishing propensity for the fair sex." In 1773, without telling either his mother or his stepfather, Jack, then nineteen, became engaged to an Annapolis belle named Nellie Calvert. Washington was forced to write a frank though embarrassed letter to the girl's father, in which he did his best to both approve and postpone the match.

Mount Vernon, April 3, 1773.
DEAR SIR: I am now set down to write to you on a Subject of Importance, and of no small embarrassment to me. My Son in Law

---

* Cousin Lund Washington, superintendent of Mount Vernon and its farms from 1775 to 1785. The son of Townsend and Elizabeth (Lund) Washington, he was five years younger than George Washington.

and Ward, Mr. Custis, has, as I have been informed, paid his Addresses to your Second Daughter, and having made some progress in her Affections has required her in Marriage. How far a union of this Sort may be agreeable to you, you best can tell, but I should think myself wanting in Candor was I not to acknowledge, that, Miss Nellie's amiable qualifications stands confess'd at all hands; and that, an alliance with your Family, will be pleasing to his.

This acknowledgment being made you must permit me to add Sir, that at this, or in any short time, his youth, inexperience, and unripened education, is, and will be insuperable obstacles in my eye, to the completion of the Marriage. As his Guardian, I conceive it to be my indispensable duty (to endeavor) to carry him through a regular course of Education, many branches of which, sorry I am to add, he is totally deficient of; and to guard his youth to a more advanced age before an Event, on which his own Peace and the happiness of another is to depend, takes place; not that I have any doubt of the warmth of his Affections, nor, I hope I may add, any fears of a change in them; but at present, I do not conceive that he is capable of bestowing that due attention to the Important consequences of a marriage State, which is necessary to be done by those, who are Inclin'd to enter into it; and of course, am unwilling he should do it till he is. If the Affection which they have avowd for each other is fixed upon a Solid Basis, it will receive no diminution in the course of two or three years, in which time he may prosecute his Studies, and thereby render himself more deserving of the Lady, and useful to Society; If unfortunately, (as they are both young) there should be an abatement of Affection on either side, or both, it had better precede, than follow after, Marriage.

Delivering my Sentiments thus, will not, I hope, lead you into a belief that I am desirous of breaking off the Match; to postpone it, is all I have in view; for I shall recommend it to the young Gentleman with the warmth that becomes a man of honour, (not withstanding he did not vouchsafe to consult either his Mother or me, on the occasion) to consider himself as much engaged to your Daughter as if the indissoluble Knot was tied; and, as the surest means of effecting this, to stick close to his Studies, (in which I flatter myself you will join me) by which he will, in a great measure, avoid those little Flirtations with other Girls which may, by dividing the Attention, contribute not a little to divide the Affection.

It may be expected of me perhaps to say something of Fortune, But, to discend to particulars, at this time, may seem rather premature. In general therefore I shall inform you that Mr. Custis's Estate consists of about 15,000 Acres of Land, good part of it adjoining the City of Williamsburg, and none 40 Miles from it; several Lotts in the said City; between two and three hundred Negroes; and about Eight or ten thousand Pounds upon Bond, and in the hands of his Merchants. This Estate he now holds Independent of his Mother's Dower, which will be an acquisition to it at her Death, and upon the whole such an one as you will readily acknowledge ought to entitle him to a handsome Portion in a Wife; But, as I should never require a Child of my own to make a Sacrifice of himself to Interest, so, neither do I think it incumbent on me to recommend it as a Guardian; but as I know you are full able, I should hope, and expect, if we were now upon the point of Settling these Preliminaries, that you would also be willing to do something genteel by your Daughter.

At all times when you, Mrs. Calvert, or the young Ladies can make it convenient to favor us with a visit we should be happy in seeing you at this place. Mrs. Washington and Miss Custis join me in respectful Compliments and I am, dear Sir, etc.

Washington took Jack to New York and enrolled him as a student at Kings College (which revolutionary ardor would soon rechristen Columbia). A few weeks later, a sad event at Mount Vernon nullified this laborious and expensive effort to make Jack an educated man. Patsy Custis, who had suffered for years from a form of epilepsy, succumbed in the midst of a seizure. In the following letter, Washington relates the mournful news to Burwell Bassett.

Mount Vernon, June 20, 1773.

DEAR SIR: It is an easier matter to conceive, than to describe the distress of this Family; especially that of the unhappy Parent of our Dear Patsy Custis, when I inform you that yesterday removed the Sweet Innocent Girl entered into a more happy and peaceful abode than any she has met with in the afflicted Path she hitherto has trod.

She rose from Dinner about four o'clock in better health and spirits than she appeared to have been in for some time; soon after which she was seized with one of her usual Fits, and expired in it, in less than two minutes without uttering a word, a groan, or scarce a sigh. This sudden, and unexpected blow, I scarce need add has almost reduced my poor Wife to the lowest ebb of Misery; which is encreas'd by the absence of her son, (whom I have just fixed at the College in New York from whence I returned the 8th Inst) and want of the balmy consolation of her Relations; which leads me more than ever to wish she could see them, and that I was Master of Arguments powerful enough to prevail upon Mrs. Dandridge [Frances Jones Dandridge, Martha Washington's mother] to make this place her entire and absolute home. I should think as she lives a lonesome life (Betsey [Elizabeth Dandridge, Martha's sister] being married) it might suit her well, and be agreeable, both to herself and my Wife, to me most assuredly it would.

I do not purpose to add more at present, the end of my writing being only to inform you of this unhappy change.

Our Sincere Affections are offered to Mrs. Bassett, Mrs. Dandridge, and all other Friends, and I am very sincerely.

As a result of Patsy's death, all of Washington's plans for Jack fell apart. Martha could not endure the thought of her only child being so far from home and Jack was permitted to abandon his studies and return to Mount Vernon. He promptly married dark-eyed Nellie while Washington looked on in silent frustraton.

During these same years, Washington was engaged in very delicate negotiation with the British Government for bounty lands promised him and the soldiers of his regiment in return for their

service on the frontier. One of his former officers, a dissolute character named George Muse, who had been accused of cowardice at
Fort Necessity, suddenly sent a letter accusing Washington of trying to cheat him out of his fair share of the grant. Nothing infuriated Washington more than being accused of dishonesty. His reply
to Muse, while it is entirely lacking in affection and friendship, is
included because it gives an unforgettable look at Washington
with his dander up.

Mount Vernon, January 29, 1774.
SIR: Your impertinent Letter of the 24th. ulto., was delivered to
me yesterday by Mr. Smith. As I am not accustomed to receive
such from any Man, nor would have taken the same language from
you personally, without letting you feel some marks of my resentment; I would advise you to be cautious in writing me a second of
the same tenour; for though I understand you were drunk when
you did it, yet give me leave to tell you, that drunkness is no excuse
for rudeness; and that, but for your stupiduty and sottishness you
might have known, by attending to the public Gazettes, (particularly Rinds of the 14th. of January last) that you had your full
quantity of ten thousand acres of Land allowed you; that is, 9073
acres in the great Tract. . . .

In the remainder of the letter, Washington stated further reasons for his lack of sympathy: most of the claimants had not been
given the full amount of land entitled to them, Washington himself being short by almost five hundred acres. Moreover, on the
basis of personal merit, Muse deserved no more land, nor was it
Washington's affair in any case but rather that of the government.
Finally Washington suggested that Muse was fortunate to have received any land at all.

Meanwhile, relations between America and England drifted
toward a new low, and in retaliation Parliament passed the Boston
Port Bill, closing the harbor to commercial traffic. Virginia stood
firmly beside Massachusetts and when the Royal Governor, Lord
Dunmore, dissolved the Assembly, Washington was among the

twenty-five delegates who met privately at the Raleigh Tavern and passed the rebellious Virginia Resolutions.

A few weeks later, Washington found himself engaged in a debate with George William Fairfax's younger brother Bryan, an equally close friend. A sensitive, intellectual man, Bryan was Loyalist in sentiment although he could see the justice of many American complaints. In this exchange Washington clearly demonstrates that he has given careful thought to the politics of revolution.

Mount Vernon, July 4, 1774.

DEAR SIR: John has just delivered to me your favor of yesterday, which I shall be obliged to answer in a more concise manner, than I could wish, as I am very much engaged in raising one of the additions to my house, which I think (perhaps it is fancy) goes on better whilst I am present, than in my absence from the workmen.

I own to you, Sir, I wished much to hear of your making an open declaration of taking a poll for this county, upon Colonel West's publicly declining last Sunday; and I should have written to you on the subject, but for information then received from several gentlemen in the churchyard, of your having refused to do so, for the reasons assigned in your letter; upon which, as I think the country never stood more in need of men of abilities and liberal sentiments than now, I entreated several gentlemen at our church yesterday to press Colonel Mason to take a poll, as I really think Major Broadwater, though a good man, might do as well in the discharge of his domestic concerns, as in the capacity of a legislator. And therefore I again express my wish, that either you or Colonel Mason would offer. I can be of little assistance to either, because I early laid it down as a maxim not to propose myself, and solicit for a second.

As to your political sentiments, I would heartily join you in them, so far as relates to a humble and dutiful petition to the throne, provided there was the most distant hope of success. But have we not tried this already? Have we not addressed the Lords, and remonstrated to the Commons? And to what end? Did they deign to look at our peitions? Does it not appear, as clear as the sun in its meridian brightness, that there is a regular, systematic plan formed to fix the right and practice of taxation upon us? Does not the uniform conduct of Parliament for some years past confirm this? Do not all the debates, especially those just brought to us, in the House of Commons on the side of government, expressly declare that America must be taxed in aid of the British funds, and that she has no longer resources with in herself? Is there any thing to be expected from petitioning after this? Is not the attack upon the liberty and property of the people of Boston, before restitution of the loss to the India Company was demanded, a plain and self-evident proof of what they are aiming at? Do not the subsequent bills (now I dare say acts), for depriving the Massachusetts Bay of its charter, and for transporting offenders into other colonies or to Great Britain for trial, where it is impossible from the nature of the thing that justice can be obtained, convince us that the administration is determined to stick at nothing to carry its point? Ought we not, then, to put our virtue and fortitude to the severest test?

With you I think it a folly to attempt more than we can execute, as that will not only bring disgrace upon us, but weaken our cause; yet I think we may do more than is generally believed, in respect to the nonimportation scheme. As to the withholding of our remittances, that is another point, in which I own I have my doubts on several accounts, but principally on that of justice; for I think, whilst we are accusing others of injustice, we should be just ourselves; and how this can be, whilst we owe a considerable debt, and refuse payment of it to Great Britain, is to me inconceivable. Nothing but the last extremity, I think, can justify it. Whether this is now come, is the question.

I began with telling you, that I was to write a short letter. My paper informs me I have done otherwise. I shall hope to see you to-morrow, at the meeting of the county in Alexandria, when these points are to be considered. I am, dear Sir, your most obedient and humble servant.

A month later, Washington continued the debate.

Mount Vernon, August 24, 1774.

DEAR SIR: Your letter of the 5th instant came to this place, forwarded by Mr. Ramsay, a few days after my return from Williamsburg, and I delayed acknowledging it sooner, in the hopes that I should find time, before I began my other journey to Philadelphia, to answer it fully, if not satisfactorily; but, as much of my time has been engrossed since I came home by company, by your brother's sale and the business consequent thereupon, in writing letters to England, and now in attending to my own domestic affairs previous to my departure as above, I find it impossible to bestow so much time and attention to the subject matter of your letter as I could wish to do, and therefore, must rely upon your good nature and candor in excuse for not attempting it. In truth, persuaded as I am, that you have read all the political pieces, which compose a large share of the *Gazette* at this time, I should think it, but for your request, a piece of inexcusable arrogance in me, to make the least essay towards a change in your political opinions; for I am sure I have no new lights to throw upon the subject, or any other arguments to offer in support of my own doctrine, than what you have seen; and could only in general add, that an innate spirit of freedom first told me, that the measures, which administration hath for some time been, and now are most violently pursuing, are repugnant to every principle of natural justice; whilst much abler heads than my own hath fully convinced me, that it is not only repugnant to natural right, but subversive of the laws and constitution of Great Britain itself, in the establishment of which some of the best blood in the kingdom hath been spilt. Satisfied, then, that the acts of a British Parliament are no longer governed by the principles of justice, that it is trampling upon the valuable rights of Americans, confirmed to them by charter and the constitution they themselves boast of, and convinced beyond the smallest doubt, that these measures are the result of deliberation, and attempted to be carried into execution by the hand of power, is it a time to trifle, or risk our cause upon petitions, which with difficulty obtain access, and afterwards are thrown by with the utmost contempt? Or should we, because heretofore unsuspicious of design, and then unwilling to enter into disputes with the mother country, go on to bear more, and forbear to enumerate our just causes of complaint? For my own part, I shall not undertake to say where the line between Great Britain and the colonies should be drawn; but I am clearly of opinion, that one ought to be drawn, and our rights clearly ascertained. I could wish, I own, that the dispute had been left to posterity to determine, but the crisis is arrived when we must assert our rights, or submit to every imposition, that can be heaped upon us, till custom and use shall make us as tame and abject slaves, as the blacks we rule over with such arbitrary sway.

I intended to have wrote no more than an apology for not writing; but I find I am insensibly running into a length I did not expect, and therefore shall conclude with remarking, that, if you disavow the right of Parliament to tax us, (unrepresented as we are,) we only differ in respect to the mode of opposition, and this difference principally arises from your belief, that they—the Parliament, I mean,—want a decent opportunity to repeal the acts; whilst I am as fully convinced, as I am of my own existence, that there has been a regular, systematic plan formed to enforce them, and that nothing but unanimity in the colonies (a stroke they did not expect) and firmness, can prevent it. It seems from the best advices from Boston, that General Gage is exceedingly disconcerted at the quiet and steady conduct of the people of the Massachusetts Bay, and at the measures pursuing by the other governments; as I dare say he expected to have forced those oppressed people into compliance, or irritated them to acts of violence before this, for a more colorable pretense of ruling that and the other colonies with a high hand. But I am done.

I shall set off on Wednesday next for Philadelphia, whither, if you have any commands, I shall be glad to oblige you in them; being, dear Sir, with real regard, &c.

P.S. Pray what do you think of the Canada Bill?

The Canada Bill or Quebec Act was not part of the so-called "intolerable" or coercive acts punishing the port of Boston but it was regarded as equally malicious by the colonists. It provided for a highly centralized administration in the French tradition with scarcely a trace of democratic procedures. The Catholic Church was given a privileged position. Worst of all, the act extended Canada's boundaries to the Ohio River, annihilating the claims of Massachusetts and—more important to Washington—Virginia to this rich area.

Washington went to Philadelphia as one of Virginia's representatives at the First Continental Congress. In the midst of this historic convention, Washington wrote a serious letter to his old friend and former subordinate officer in the Virginia Regiment, Captain Robert MacKenzie, who was now serving with the 43rd Regiment of Foot, part of the British Army occupying Boston. MacKenzie had written an earlier letter to Washington in which he gave a highly pro-British version of the state of affairs in Massachusetts.

Philadelphia, October 9, 1774.

DEAR SIR: Your letter of the 13th. ultimo from Boston gave me pleasure, as I learnt thereby, that you were well, and might be expected at Mount Vernon in your way to or from James River, in the course of the winter.

When I have said this, permit me with the freedom of a friend (for you know I always esteemed you) to express my sorrow, that fortune should place you in a service, that must fix curses to the latest posterity upon the diabolical contrivers, and, if success (which, by the by, is impossible) accompanies it, execrations upon all those, who have been instrumental in the execution.

I do not mean by this to insinuate, that an officer is not to discharge his duty, even when chance, not choice, has placed him in a disagreeable situation; but I conceive, when you condemn the conduct of the Massachusetts people, you reason from effects, not causes; otherwise, you would not wonder at the people, who are every day receiving fresh proofs of a systematic assertion of an arbitrary power, deeply planned to overturn the laws and constitution of their country, and to violate the most essential and valuable rights of mankind, being irritated, and with difficulty restrained from acts of the greatest violence and intemperance. For my own part, I confess to you candidly, that I view things in a very different point of light to the one in which you seem to consider them; and though you are led to believe by venal men, for such I must take the liberty of calling those new-fangled counsellors, which fly to and surround you, and all others, who, for honorary or pecuniary gratifications, will lend their aid to overturn the constitution, and introduce a system of arbitrary government, although you are taught, I say, by discoursing with such men, to believe, that the people of Massachusetts are rebellious, setting up for independency, and what not, give me leave, my good friend, to tell you, that you are abused, grossly abused, and this I advance with a degree of confidence and boldness, which may claim your belief, having better opportunities of knowing the real sentiments of the people you are among, from the leaders of them, in opposition to the present measures of the administration, than you have from those whose business it is, not to disclose truths, but to misrepresent facts in order to justify as much as possible to the world their own conduct; for give me leave to add, and I think I can announce it as a fact, that it is not the wish or interest of that government, or any other upon this continent, separately or collectively, to set up for independency; but this you may at the same time rely on, that none of them will ever submit to the loss of those valuable rights and privileges, which are essential to the happiness of every free state, and without which, life, liberty, and property are rendered totally insecure.

These, Sir, being certain consequences, which must naturally result from the late acts of Parliament relative to America in general, and the government of Massachusetts Bay in particular, is it to be wondered at, I repeat, that men, who wish to avert the impending blow, should attempt to oppose it in its progress, or prepare for their defence, if it cannot be diverted? Surely I may be allowed to answer in the negative; and again give me leave to add as my opinion, that more blood will be spilt on this occasion, if the ministry are determined to push matters to extremity, than history has ever yet furnished instances of in the annals of North America, and such a vital wound given to the peace of this great country, as time itself cannot cure, or eradicate the remembrance of.

But I have done. I was involuntarily led into a short discussion of this subject by your remarks on the conduct of the Boston people, and your opinion of their wishes to set up for independency. I am as well satisfied as I can be of my existence that no such thing is desired by any thinking man in all North America; on the contrary, that it is the ardent wish of the warmest advocates for liberty, that peace and tranquility, upon constitutional grounds, may be restored, and the horrors of civil discord prevented.

I am very glad to hear that my friend Stewart was well when you left London. I have not had a letter from him these five years, nor heard of him I think for two. I wish you had mentioned his employment, poor Mercer! I often hear from him; much cause has he, I fear, to lament his having fallen into the accursed state of attendance and dependance. I remain with very great esteem, dear Sir.

Robert Stewart and George Mercer had been fellow campaigners of Washington's frontier war days. As Washington once did, Stewart desired a British army commission and went to London in search of it. Washington offered him a three hundred-pound loan to help him buy one. Mercer, on the other hand, had suffered a fate all too common among Virginia planters: bankruptcy. He had gone to London in 1763 to help plead Virginia's claims to the Ohio Territory. Without his supervision, his estates deteriorated and in 1771-72 he was forced to mortgage much of his land. In 1774 his estate was sold at public auction for "upwards of 14,000 pounds," which went to his creditors.

In spite of the peacemaking efforts of the First Continental Congress, the drift to war continued. George III clung to a policy of punishment and repression. Parliament vacillated. In Virginia men began forming independent companies. More than a few

wrote to George Washington asking him to assume command of
them. Then came the explosion everyone dreaded—gunfire at Lex-
ington erupted into an all-day running battle with two brigades of
British troops. After discussing business matters, Washington brings
George William Fairfax, now in England, up to date.

Philadelphia, May 31, 1775.

DEAR SIR: . . . Before this Letter can reach you, you must, undoubtedly, have received an Account of the engagement in the
Massachusetts Bay between the Ministerial Troops (for we do not,
nor cannot yet prevail upon ourselves to call them the King's
Troops) and the Provincials of that Government; But as you may
not have heard how that affair began, I enclose you the several
Affidavits that were taken after the Action.

General Gage acknowledges, that the detachment under Lieutenant Colonel Smith was sent out to destroy private property; or,
in other Words, to destroy a Magazine which self preservation
obliged the Inhabitants to establish. And he also confesses, in
effect at least, that his Men made a very precipitate retreat from
Concord, notwithstanding the reinforcement under Lord Percy,
the last of which may serve to convince Lord Sandwich (and others
of the same sentiment) that the Americans will fight for their Liberties and property, however pusilanimous, in his Lordship's Eye,
they may appear in other respects.

From the Accounts I have been able to collect of that affair;
indeed from every one, I believe the fact, stripped of all colouring,
to be plainly this, that if the retreat had not been as precipitate as
it was (and God knows it could not well have been more so) the
Ministerial Troops must have surrendered, or been totally cut off:
For they had not arrived in Charlestown (under cover of their
Ships) half an hour, before a powerful body of Men from Marble-
head and Salem were at their heels, and must, if they had happened to have been up one hour sooner, inevitably intercepted
their retreat to Charlestown. Unhappy it is though to reflect, that a
Brother's Sword has been sheathed in a Brother's breast, and that,

the once happy and peaceful plains of America are either to be drenched with Blood, or Inhabited by Slaves. Sad alternative! But can a virtuous Man hesitate in his choice?

I am, With sincere Regard and Affectionate compliments to Mrs. Fairfax, Dear Sir, etc.

Washington wrote this letter from Philadelphia, where the second Continental Congress was in session. Two weeks later he accepted command of the army of raw militiamen besieging the British around Boston. From this moment Washington began a new life. He did not even have time to go home and say farewell to those who had made his peaceful years in Virginia so rich in contentment. His first thought was of Martha, and he wrote her a tender letter that underscored the words of his honest reply to Congress, "I do not think myself equal to the command I am honored with."

Philadelphia, June 18, 1775.

MY DEAREST: I am now set down to write to you on a subject, which fills me with inexpressible concern, and this concern is greatly aggravated and increased, when I reflect upon the uneasiness I know it will give you. It has been determined in Congress, that the whole army raised for the defence of the American cause shall be put under my care, and that it is necessary for me to proceed immediately to Boston to take upon me the command of it.

You may believe me, my dear Patsy, when I assure you, in the most solemn manner that, so far from seeking this appointment, I have used every endeavor in my power to avoid it, not only from my unwillingness to part with you and the family, but from a consciousness of its being a trust too great for my capacity, and that I should enjoy more real happiness in one month with you at home, than I have the most distant prospect of finding abroad, if my stay were to be seven times seven years. But as it has been a kind of destiny, that has thrown me upon this service, I shall hope that my undertaking it is designed to answer some good purpose. You might, and I suppose did perceive, from the tenor of my letters, that I was apprehensive I could not avoid this appointment, as I did not pretend to intimate when I should return. That was the case. It was utterly out of my power to refuse this appointment, without exposing my character to such censures, as would have reflected dishonor upon myself, and given pain to my friends. This, I am sure, could not, and ought not, to be pleasing to you, and must have lessened me considerably in my own esteem. I shall rely, therefore, confidently on that Providence, which has heretofore preserved and been bountiful to me, not doubting but that I shall return safe to you in the fall. I shall feel no pain from the toil or the danger of the campaign; my unhappiness will flow from the uneasiness I know you will feel from being left alone. I therefore beg, that you will summon your whole fortitude, and pass your time as agreeably as possible. Nothing will give me so much sincere satisfaction as to hear this, and to hear it from your own pen. My earnest and ardent desire is, that you would pursue any plan that is most likely to produce content, and a tolerable degree of tranquillity; as it must add greatly to my uneasy feelings to hear, that you are dissatisfied or complaining at what I really could not avoid.

As life is always uncertain, and common prudence dictates to every man the necessity of settling his temporal concerns, while it is in his power, and while the mind is calm and undisturbed, I have, since I came to this place (for I had not time to do it before I left home) got Colonel Pendleton to draft a will for me, by the directions I gave him, which will I now enclose. The provision made for you in case of my death will, I hope, be agreeable.

I shall add nothing more, as I have several letters to write, but to desire that you will remember me to your friends, and to assure you that I am, with the most unfeigned regard, my dear Patsy, your affectionate, &c.

To his brother Jack he wrote in a similar vein, but with more realistic frankness. The "political motive" of Congress refers to need for a southerner to command the largely New England army before Boston, as proof of American unity.

Philadelphia, June 20, 1775.

DEAR BROTHER: I am now to bid adieu to you, and to every kind of domestick ease, for a while. I am Imbarked on a wide Ocean, boundless in its prospect, and from whence, perhaps, no safe harbour is to be found. I have been called upon by the unanimous Voice of the Colonies to take Command of the Continental Army. An honour I neither sought after, nor desired, as I am thoroughly convinced, that it requires greater Abilities, and much more experience, than I am Master of, to conduct a business so extensive in its nature, and arduous in the execution; but the partiallity of the Congress, joined to a political motive, really left me without a Choice; and I am now Commissioned a General and Commander in chief of all the Forces now raisd, or to be raisd, for the defence of the United Colonies. That I may discharge the Trust to the Satisfaction of my Imployers, is my first wish; that I shall aim to do it, there remains as little doubt of; how far I may succeed is another point; but this I am sure of, that in the worst event I shall have the consolation of knowing (if I act to the best of my judgment) that the blame ought to lodge upon the appointers, not the appointed, as it was by no means a thing of my own seeking, or proceeding from any hint of my friends.

I am at liberty to inform you, that the Congress, in a Committee, (which will I dare say, be agreed to when reported) have consented to a Continental Currency; have ordered two millions of Dollars to be struck for payment of the Troops, &c. and have voted 15,000 Men as a Continental Army, which number will be augmented, as the strength of the British Troops will be greater than was expected at the time of passing that vote. General Ward, General Lee, General Schuyler and General Putnam are appointed Major Generals under me; the Brigadier Generals are not yet appointed. Major Gates Adjutant General. I expect to set out to-morrow for Boston and hope to be joined there in a little time by Ten Companies of Riflemen from this Province, Maryland and Virginia; For other Articles of Intelligence, I shall refer you to the Papers, as the Printers are diligent in collecting every thing that is stirring.

I shall hope that my Friends will visit and endeavor to keep up the spirits of my Wife as much as they can, as my departure will, I know, be a cutting stroke upon her; and on this account alone, I have many very disagreeable sensations. I hope you and my sister (although the distance is great) will find as much leisure this Summer, as to spend a little time at Mount Vernon.

My sincere regards attend you both as also the little ones and I am your most affectionate Brother.

A week later he wrote the following note, which suggests that Martha had come a long way toward replacing the unattainable Sally Fairfax in George Washington's heart.

Philadelphia, June 23, 1775.

MY DEAREST: As I am within a few minutes of leaving this city, I would not think of departing from it with out dropping you a line, especially as I do not know whether it may be in my power to write again till I get to the camp at Boston. I go fully trusting in that providence, which has been more bountiful to me than I deserve and in full confidence of a happy meeting with you some time in the fall. I have no time to add more as I am surrounded with company to take leave of me. I return an unalterable affection for you which neither time or distance can change my best love to Jack and Nelly and regard for the rest of the family; conclude me with the utmost truth and Sincerety, Yr. entire.

CHAPTER THREE

Patriot Into General

Washington's correspondence now became crowded with reports to Congress, addresses to legislatures, replies to soldiers seeking commissions. But in the midst of his official letters he still found time to pen startling frank opinions of the ragbag army he found waiting for him outside Boston. Among his favorite correspondents was his brother Jack.

> *Camp at Cambridge, about 5 miles*
> *from Boston,* July 27, 1775.

DEAR BROTHER: On the 2nd Inst. I arrived at this place, after passing through a great deal of delightful Country, covered with grass, (although the Season has been dry) in a very different manner to what our Lands in Virginia are.

I found a mixed multitude of People here, under very little discipline, order, or Government. I found the enemy in possession of a place called Bunker's Hill, on Charles Town Neck, strongly Intrenched, and Fortifying themselves; I found part of our Army on two Hills, (called Winter and Prospect Hills) about a Mile and a quarter from the enemy on Bunker's Hill, in a very insecure state; I found another part of the Army at this Village; and a third part at Roxbury, guarding the Entrance in and out of Boston. My whole time, since I came here, has been Imployed in throwing up Lines of Defence at these three several places; to secure, in the first Instance, our own Troops from any attempts of the Enemy; and, in the next, to cut off all Communication between their troops and the Country; For to do this, and to prevent them from penetrating into the Country with Fire and Sword, and to harass them if they do, is all that is expected of me; and if effected, must totally overthrow the designs of Administration, as the whole Force of Great

Britain in the Town and Harbour of Boston can answer no other end, than to sink her under the disgrace and weight of the expense. Their Force, including Marines, Tories, &c., are computed, from the best accounts I can get, at about 12,000 Men; ours, including Sick absent, &c., at about 16,000; but then we have a Cemi Circle of Eight or Nine Miles, to guard to every part of which we are obliged to be equally attentive; whilst they, situated as it were in the Center of the Cemicircle, can bend their whole Force (having the entire command of the Water), against any one part of it with equal facility; This renders our Situation not very agreeable, though necessary; however, by incessant labour (Sundays not excepted), we are in a much better posture of defence than when I first came. The Inclosed, though rough, will give you some small idea of the Situation of Boston, and Bay on this side; as also of the Post they have Taken in Charles Town Neck, Bunker's Hill, and our Posts.

By very authentick Intelligence lately received out of Boston (from a Person who saw the returns), the number of Regulars (including I presume the Marines) the morning of the Action on Bunker's Hill amounted to 7533 Men; their killed and wounded on that occasion amounted to 1043, whereof 92 were Officers. Our loss was 138 killed, 36 Missing, and 276 Wounded.

The Enemy are sickly, and scarce of Fresh provisions, Beef, which is chiefly got by slaughtering their Milch Cows in Boston, sells from one shilling to 18d. Sterling per lb.; and that it may not get cheaper, or more plenty, I have drove all the Stock, within a considerable distance of this place, back into the Country, out of the Way of the Men of war's Boats; In short, I have, and shall continue to do, every thing in my power to distress them. The Transports are all arrived and their whole Reinforcement is Landed, so that I can see no reason why they should not if they ever attempt it, come boldly out and put the matter to Issue at once; if they think themselves not strong enough to do this, they surely will carry their Arms (having Ships of War and Transports ready) to some other part of the Continent, or relinquish the dispute; the last of which the Ministry, unless compelled will never agree to do.

Our Works, and those of the Enemy are so near and quite open between that we see every thing that each other is doing. I recollect nothing more worth mentioning. I shall therefore conclude with my best wishes, and love to my Sister and Family, and Compliments to any enquiring Friends, your most affectionate brother.

Another favorite Correspondent was his cousin Lund Washington, who had agreed to manage Mount Vernon in his absence.

Camp at Cambridge, August 20, 1775.

DEAR LUND: Your letter by Captn. Prince came to my hands last night; I was glad to learn by it that all are well. the acct. given of the behaviour of the Scotchmen at Port Tobacco and Piscataway surprized and vexed me. Why did they Imbark in the cause? What do they say for themselves? What does other say of them? are they admitted into Company? or kicked out of it? What does their Countrymen urge in Justification of them? they are fertile in invention, and will offer excuses where excuses can be made. I cannot say but I am curious to learn the reasons why men who had subscribed, and bound themselves to each other and their Country, to stand forth in defence of it, should lay down their arms the first moment they were called upon. . . .

Spinning should go forward with all possible dispatch, as we shall have nothing else to depend upon if these disputes continue another year. I can hardly think that Lord Dunmore can act so low, and unmanly a part, as to think of siezing Mrs. Washington by way of revenge upon me; howev'r, as I suppose she is, before this time gone over to Mr. Calvert's, and will soon after retng., go down to New Kent, she will be out of his reach for 2 or 3 months to come, in which time matters may, and probably will, take such a turn as to render her removal either absolutely necessary, or quite useless. I am nevertheless exceedingly thankful to the Gentlemen of Alexandria for their friendly attention to this point and desire you will if there is any sort of reason to suspect a thing of this kind provide a Kitchen for her in Alexandria, or some other place of safety elsewhere for her and my Papers.

The People of this government [Massachusetts] have obtained a Character which they by no means deserved; their officers generally speaking are the most indifferent kind of People I ever saw. I have already broke one Colo. and five Captains for Cowardice and for drawing more Pay and Provisions than they had Men in their Companies; there is two more Colos. now under arrest, and to be tried for the same offences; in short they are by no means such Troops, in any respect, as you are led to believe of them from the accts. which are published, but I need not make myself Enemies among them, by this declaration, although it is consistent with truth. I dare say the Men would fight very well (if properly Officered) although, they are an exceeding dirty and nasty people; had they been properly conducted at Bunkers Hill (on the 17th of June) or those that were there properly supported, the Regulars would have met with a shameful defeat, and a more considerable loss than they did, which is now known to be exactly 1057 killed and wounded; it was for their behaviour on that occasion that the above Officers were broke, for I never spared one that was accused of Cowardice but brot 'em to immediate Tryal.

Our Lines of Defence are now completed, as near so at least as can be; we now wish them to come out, as soon as they please, but they (that is the Enemy) discover no Inclination to quit their own Works of Defence; and as it is almost impossible for us to get to them, we do nothing but watch each other's motions all day at the distance of about a Mile, every now and then picking out a stragler when we can catch them without their Intrenchments, in return, they often Attempt to Cannonade our Lines to no other purpose than the waste of a considerable quantity of Powder to themselves which we should be very glad to get.

What does Doctr. Craik say to the behaviour of his Countrymen, and Townspeople? Remember me kindly to him, and tell him that I should be very glad to see him here if there was anything worth his acceptance; but the Massachusetts People suffer nothing to go by them that they can lay hands upon. . . .

Washington's reference to Doctor James Craik underscores his sense of isolation in Massachusetts. He obviously yearned for the company of at least one close friend to whom he could unburden himself. Educated in Edinburgh, Craik had served with Washington on Braddock's expedition and thereafter was his personal physician.

Washington's carping attitude toward New England diminished slowly and ultimately vanished from his letters. Some historians feel the turning point came on the day one of his aides rushed into headquarters and announced that they had miscounted the American army's supply of powder—instead of 430 barrels there were only 38. New Hampshire General John Sullivan, who was conferring with Washington when he received the news said, "He was so struck he did not utter a word for half an hour." In this long silence Washington may well have taken stock of himself and the chaotic army he was fated to lead and realized both needed correction if a unified America was somehow to be achieved.

Toward the end of the summer Washington wrote another letter to his brother Jack. He was in a much more sanguine mood and obviously had more control both of himself and the military situation.

Camp at Cambridge, September 10, 1775.
DEAR BROTHER: So little has happened since the date of my last, that I should scarce have given you the trouble of reading this Letter, did I not imagine that it might be some satisfaction to you to know that we are well and in no fear or dread of the Enemy. Being, in our own opinion at least, very securely Intrenched, and wishing for nothing more than to see the Enemy out of their strong holds, that the dispute may come to an Issue.

The inactive state we lye in is exceedingly disagreeable, especially as we can see no end to it, having had no advices lately from Great Britain to form a judgment upon.

In taking possession about a fortnight ago, of a Hill within point blank (Cannon) shott of the Enemy's Lines on Charles Town Neck we expected to bring on a general Action, especially as we had been threatened by reports from Boston several days before, that they (that is the Enemy) intended an Attack upon our Intrenchments, nothing, however, followed but a severe Cannonade for a day or two, and a Bombardment afterwards for the like time; which, however, did us no other damage, than to kill two or three men, and wound as many more. Both are now at an end, as they found that we disregarded their Fire and continued our Works 'till we had got them compleated.

Unless the Ministerial Troops in Boston are waiting for reinforcements, I cannot devise what they are staying there after; and why (as they affect to despise the Americans,) they do not come forth, and put an end to the contest at once. They suffer greatly for want of fresh Provisions, notwithstanding they have pillaged several Islands of a good many Sheep and Cattle. They are also scarce of Fuel, unless, (according to the acct. of one of their Deserters,) they mean to pull down Houses for Firing. In short, they are, from all accts. suffering all the Inconveniences of a Siege. It is true, by having the entire Command of the Sea, and a powerful Navy; and moreover, as they are now beginning to take all Vessells indiscriminately, we cannot stop their Supplies through that Channel; but their Succours in this way hath not been so powerful as to enable them to give the Common Soldiers much fresh meat as yet. By an Acct. from Boston of the 4th Inst. the Cattle lately brought in there, sold at publick auction from Fifteen to £34.10 Sterg. [a 1775 pound was worth about $50 in modern money] apiece; and the Sheep from 30/to 36/ each; and that Fowls and every other Species of Fresh Provisions went in proportion. The expence of this, one would think, must soon tire them were it not that they intend to fix all the Expence of this War upon the Colonies, if they can, I suppose we shall add.

Washington closed with a description of the two-pronged American assault on Canada. One army, led by Philip Schuyler, was moving up Lake Champlain; a second, led by Benedict Arnold, up the Kennebec River to seize Quebec. During these same crowded days, Washington was gradually making new friends. One of the

men *he liked best was thirty-four-year-old Joseph Reed, a Philadelphia attorney whom he met during sessions of the Continental Congress. Reed joined Washington's staff and soon became the most
trusted officer in his family. But Reed's keen interest in Philadelphia
politics led to frequent trips home, which made life difficult for
Washington, who was having trouble finding competent aides. His
troubles redoubled when one of his best staff men, Edmund Randolph (future attorney general of the United States), was forced to
return to Virginia because of the death of his uncle, Peyton Randolph. Washington communicates this problem and others to
Reed, in Philadelphia.*

Cambridge, November 8, 1775.

DEAR SIR: The shipwreck of a vessel, said to be from Philadelphia
to Boston, near Plymouth, with one hundred and twenty pipes
of wine, one hundred and eighteen of which are saved; another,
from Boston to Halifax, near Beverly, with about two hundred and
forty pounds' worth of dry goods; the taking of a wood-vessel bound
to Boston by Captain Adams; and the sudden departure of Mr.
Randolph, (occasioned by the death of his uncle,) are all the occurrences worth noticing, which have happened since you left this.

I have ordered the wine and goods to this place for sale; as also
the papers. The latter may unfold secrets, that may not be pleasing
to some of your townsmen, and which, so soon as known, will be
communicated.

I have been happy enough to convince Captain Macpherson,
as he says, of the propriety of returning to the Congress. He sets
out this day, and I am happy in his having an opportunity of laying
before them a scheme for the destruction of the naval force of
Great Britain. A letter and journal of Colonel Arnold's [Benedict
Arnold], to the 13th ultimo, are come to hand, a copy of which I
enclose to the Congress, and by application to Mr. Thomson
[Charles Thomson, secretary of the Continental Congress] you can
see. I think he is in Quebec. If I hear nothing more of him in five
days, I shall be sure of it.

I had like to have forgotten what sits heaviest upon my mind, the new arrangement of officers. Although we have not enough to constitute the new corps, it hath employed the general officers and myself ever since Thursday last, and we are nearly as we begun.

Connecticut wants no Massachusetts man in their corps; Massachusetts thinks there is no necessity [for a Rhode-Islander] to be introduced amongst them; and New Hampshire says, it's very hard, that her valuable and experienced officers (who are willing to serve) should be discarded, because her own regiments, under the new establishment, cannot provide for them. In short, after a four days' labor, I expect that numbers of officers, who have given in their names to serve, must be discarded from Massachusetts, (where the regiments have been numerous, and the number in them small) and Connecticut, completed with a fresh recruit of officers from its own government. This will be departing, not only from the principles of common justice, but from the letter of the resolve agreed on at this place; but, at present, I see no help for it. We are to have another meeting upon the matter this day, when something must be hit upon, as time is slipping off. My compliments to Mrs. Reed and to all inquiring friends. I am, with sincerity and truth, dear Sir, your affectionate humble servant.

P.S. I had just finished my letter when a blundering Lieutenant of the blundering Captain Coit, who had just blundered upon two vessels from Nova Scotia, came in with the account of it, and before I could rescue my letter, without knowing what he did, picked up a candle and sprinkled it with grease; but these are kind of blunders which one can readily excuse.

A few weeks later, Reed, like some of the others, began talking of resigning. Washington wrote him the following letter, which gives a striking picture of the problems he had simply trying to organize his own headquarters. The letter ends with another concern—Martha Washington's first trip north to join her husband in winter camp. So timid and fearful about many things, Martha proved herself a veritable spartan woman during the war, traveling almost a thousand miles(round trip) over abominable roads, to be at her husband's side each year when the campaign season closed.

Camp at Cambridge, November 20, 1775.
DEAR SIR: . . . That hint contained in the last of your letters, respecting. your continuance in my family, in other words, your wish that I could dispense with it, gives me pain. You already, my dear Sir, knew my sentiments on this matter; you cannot but be sensible of your importance to me; at the same time I shall again repeat, what I have observed to you before, that I can never think of promoting my convenience at the expense of your interest and inclination. That I feel the want of you, yourself can judge, when I inform you, that the peculiar situation of Mr. Randolph's affairs obliged him to leave this soon after you did; that Mr. Baylor [Virginian George Baylor, who was only twenty-three], contrary to my expectation, is not in the slightest degree a penman, though spirited and willing; and that Mr. Harrison [Robert Hanson Harrison of Maryland], though sensible, clever, and perfectly confidential, has never yet moved upon so large a scale, as to comprehend at one view the diversity of matter, which comes before me, so as to afford that ready assistance, which every man in my situation must stand more or less in need of. Mr. Moylan,* it is true, is very obliging; he gives me what assistance he can; but other business must necessarily deprive me of his aid in a very short time. This is my situation; judge you, therefore, how much I wish for your return, especially as the armed vessels, and the capital change (in the state of this army) about to take place, have added an additional weight to a burden, before too great for me to stand under with the smallest degree of comfort to my own feelings. My mind is now fully disclosed to you, with this assurance sincerely and affectionately of accompanying it, that whilst you are disposed to continue with me, I shall think myself too fortunate and happy to wish for a change.

Dr. [John] Morgan, (as director of the hospital,) is exceedingly wanted at this place, and ought not to delay his departure for the camp a moment, many regulations being delayed, and accounts postponed, till his arrival. I have given G. S. and Col. P. a hint of the prevailing reports in Connecticut, without intimating from

* Stephen Moylan, born in Cork, Ireland, where his brother was Roman Catholic Archbishop. He was muster-master general of the Continental Army at this time.

what quarter they came (for indeed I received them through different channels) in order to put them upon their guard; they both deny the charge roundly, and wish for an opportunity of vindication. I thought as this information had come to my ears in different ways, it was best to speak to these gentlemen in terms expressive of my abhorrence of such conduct, and of the consequences that might flow from it, and think it will have a good effect. The method you have suggested, of the advanced pay, I very much approve of, and would adopt, but for the unfortunate cramped state of our treasury, which keeps us for ever under the hatches. Pray urge the necessity of this measure to such members as you may converse with, and the want of cash to pay the troops for the months of October and November; as also to answer the demands of the commissary, quartermaster, and for contingencies. To do all this, a considerable sum will be necessary. Do not neglect to put that wheel in motion, which is to bring us the shirts, medicines, &c. from New York; they are much wanting here, and cannot be had, I should think, upon better terms than on a loan from the best of Kings, so anxiously disposed to promote the welfare of his American subjects.

Dr. Church * is gone to Governor Trumbull, to be disposed of in a Connecticut gaol, without the use of pen, ink, or paper, to be conversed with in the presence of a magistrate only, and in the English language. So much for indiscretion, the Doctor will say. Your accounts of our dependence upon the people of Great Britain, I religiously believe. It has long been my political creed, that the ministry durst not have gone on as they did, but under the firmest persuasion that the people were with them. The weather has been unfavorable, however, for the arrival of their transports; only four companies of the seventeenth regiment and two of the artillery are yet arrived, by our last advices from Boston.

Our rascally privateersmen go on at the old rate, mutinying if they cannot do as they please. Those at Plymouth, Beverly, and Portsmouth, have done nothing worth mentioning in the prize

* Dr. Benjamin Church, a prominent Boston physician, was arrested as a British spy shortly after Washington took command of the army.

way, and no accounts are yet received from those farther eastward.

Arnold, by a letter which left him the 27th ultimo, had then only got to the Chaudiere Pond, and was scarce of provisions. His rear division, under the command of the *noble* Colonel Enos, had, without his privity or consent, left him with three companies; and his expedition, (inasmuch as it is to be apprehended, that Carleton, [Sir Guy Carleton, British commander in chief in Canada], with the remains of such force as he had been able to raise, would get into Quebec before him,) I fear, in a bad way. For further particulars I refer you to Mr. Hancock who has enclosed to him copies of Arnold's and Enos's letters. The last-named person is not yet arrived at this camp.

I think you for your frequent mention of Mrs. Washington. I expect she will be in Philadelphia about the time this letter may reach you, on her way hither. As she and her conductor, (who I expect will be Mr. Custis, her son,) are perfect strangers to the road, the stages, and the proper places to cross Hudson's River, (by all means avoiding New York,) I shall be much obliged in your particular instructions and advice to her. I do imagine, as the roads are bad and the weather cold, her stages must be short, especially as I expect her horses will be pretty much fatigued; as they will, by the time she gets to Philadelphia, have performed a journey of at least four hundred and fifty miles, my express finding of her among her friends near Williamsburg, one hundred and fifty miles below my own house.

As you have mentioned nothing in your letters of the cannon, &c., to be had from New York, Ticonderoga, &c., I have, in order to reduce the matter to a certainty, employed Mr. Knox * to go to those places, complete our wants, and to provide such military stores as St. John's can spare.

Flints are greatly wanted here.

With all his military worries, Washington never forgot Mount Vernon. Almost every week his cousin and manager Lund Wash-

---

* Henry Knox, young Boston bookseller who became Major General in command of the American army's artillery.

ington wrote to him detailing minutely all the events that occurred on the plantation, purchases, sales, payments of money, the kinds and quantity of produce, occupations of the laborers, and whatever else would tend to explain the precise condition and progress of the business in his hands. The following letter shows Washington the generous employer and man of means, but there is a note of anxiety underlying his vow of confidence in Lund's integrity and industry.

November 26, 1775.

What follows is part of a Letter wrote to Mr. Lund Washington the 26th. day of November 1775. A copy is taken to remind me of my engagements and the exact purport of them. These paragraphs follow an earnest request to employ good part of my force in cleaning up Swamps, H. Hole Ditching, Hedging, &c.

"I well know where the difficulty of accomplishing these things will lie. Overseers are already engaged (upon shares) to look after my business. Remote advantages to me, however, manifest and beneficial, are nothing to them; and to engage standing Wages, when I do not know that anything I have, or can raise, will command Cash, is attended with hazard; for which reason I hardly know what more to say than to discover my wishes. The same reason, although it may in appearance have the same tendency in respect to you, shall not be the same in its operation. For I will engage for the Year coming, and the year following, that if these troubles, and my absence continues, that your Wages shall be standing and certain, at the highest amount that any one Year's Crop has produced to you yet. I do not offer this as any temptation to induce *you* to go on more chearfully in prosecuting *these* schemes of *mine*. I should do injustice to you, were I not to acknowledge that your conduct has ever appeared to me, above every thing sordid; but I offer it in consideration of the great charge you have upon your hands, and my entire dependance upon your fidelity and industry."

"It is the greatest, indeed it is the only comfortable reflexion I enjoy on this score, to think that my business is in the hands of a person in whose integrity I have not a doubt, and on whose care I can rely. Was it not for this, I should feel very unhappy on Account of the situation of my affairs; but I am persuaded you will do for me as you would for yourself, and more than this I cannot expect."

"Let the Hospitality of the House, with respect to the poor, be kept up; Let no one go hungry away. If any of these kind of People should be in want of Corn, supply their necessities, provided it does not encourage them in idleness; and I have no objection to your giving my Money in Charity, to the Amount of forty or fifty Pounds a year, when you think it well bestowed. What I mean, by having no objection, is, that it is my desire that it should be done. You are to consider that neither myself or Wife are now in the way to do these good Offices. In all other respects, I recommend it to you, and have no doubts, of your observing the greatest Oeconomy and frugality; as I suppose you know that I do not get a farthing for my services here more than my Expenses; It becomes necessary, therefore, for me to be saving at home."

The above is copied, not only to remind myself of my promises, and requests; but others also, if any mischance happens to G. Washington.

At the scene of war, meanwhile, affairs suddenly took a darker turn. Washington poured out his woes to Joseph Reed, still tarrying in Philadelphia. Here appears the first sign of jealousy and conflict within the Continental Congress. Washington also touches on another alarming problem—his struggle to recruit a new army while the one he was commanding slowly dissolved before his eyes as the militiamen who had come for three and six months service picked up their guns and went home.

Cambridge, December 15, 1775.
DEAR SIR: Since my last, I have had the pleasure of receiving your favours of the 28th ultimo, and the 2d instant. I must again express my gratitude for the attention shown Mrs. Washington at

Philadelphia. It cannot but be pleasing, although it did, in some measure, impede the progress of her journey on the road. I am much obliged to you for the hints contained in both of the above letters, respecting the jealousies which you say are gone abroad. I have studiously avoided in all letters intended for the public eye, I mean for that of the Congress, every expression that could give pain or uneasiness; and I shall observe the same rule with respect to private letters, further than appears absolutely necessary for the elucidation of facts. I cannot charge myself with incivility, or, what in my opinion is tantamount, ceremonious civility, to the gentlemen of this colony; but if such my conduct appears, I will endeavor at a reformation, as I can assure you, my dear Reed, that I wish to walk in such a line as will give most general satisfaction. You know, that it was my wish at first to invite a certain number of gentlemen of this colony every day to dinner, but unintentionally I believed by anybody, we somehow or other missed of it. If this has given rise to the jealousy, I can only say that I am sorry for it; at the same time I add, that it was rather owing to inattention, or, more properly, too much attention to other matters, which caused me to neglect it. The extracts of letters from this camp, which so frequently appear in the Pennsylvania papers, are not only written without my knowledge, but without my approbation, as I have always thought they must have a disagreeable tendency; but there is no restraining men's tongues, or pens, when charged with a little vanity, as in the accounts given of, or rather by, the riflemen.

With respect to what you have said of yourself, and your situation, to what I have before said on this subject I can only add, that whilst you leave the door open to my expectation of your return, I shall not think of supplying your place. If ultimately you resolve against coming, I should be glad to know it, as soon as you have determined upon it. The Congress have resolved well in respect to the pay of and advance to the men; but if they cannot get the money-signers to despatch their business, it is of very little avail; for we have not at this time money enough in camp to answer the commissary's and quartermaster's accounts, much less to pay and advance to the troops. Strange conduct this!

The accounts which you have given of the sentiments of the people respecting my conduct, is extremely flattering. Pray God, I may continue to deserve them, in the perplexed and intricate situation I stand in. Our enlistment goes on slow. By the returns last Monday, only five thousand nine hundred and seventeen men are engaged for the ensuing campaign; and yet we are told, that we shall get the number wanted, as they are only playing off to see what advantages are to be made, and whether a bounty cannot be extorted either from the public at large, or individuals, in case of a draft. Time only can discover this. I doubt the measure exceedingly. The fortunate capture of the store-ship * has supplied us with flints, and many other articles we stood in need of; but we still have our wants. We are securing our approach to Letchmore's Point, unable upon any principle whatever to account for their silence, unless it be to lull us into a fatal security to favour some attempt they may have in view about the time of the great change they expect will take place the last of this month. If this be the drift, they deceive themselves, for, if possible, it has increased my vigilance, and induced me to fortify all the avenues to our camps, to guard against any approaches up on the ice.

If the Virginians are wise, that arch-traitor to the rights of humanity, Lord Dunmore, should be instantly crushed, if it takes the force of the whole colony to do it; otherwise, like a snow ball, in rolling, his army will get size, some through fear some through promises, and some from inclination, joining his standard. But that which renders the measure indispensably necessary is the negroes. For if he gets formidable, numbers will be tempted to join, who will be afraid to do it without. I am exceeding happy to find that that villain Connolly is seized; I hope if there is any thing to convict him, that he will meet with the punishment due to his demerit and treachery.

We impatiently wait for accounts from Arnold. Would to God we may hear he is in Quebec, and that all Canada is in our possession.

* The British brig *Nancy*, with supplies for Quebec. Her cargo included two thousand stand of small arms, many flints, tons of musketshot, and a brass mortar.

Washington's worries about the military situation in Virginia soon ended. John Murray, Earl of Dunmore, had been a popular Royal Governor. But on November 7, 1775, he declared Virginia under martial law and offered freedom to all slaves and servants of rebels. These acts, together with his establishing a Negro regiment, alienated almost everyone in the state. On December 11, 1775, Dunmore's small army was defeated by nine hundred Virginians and North Carolinians at Great Bridge. He then withdrew from his base at Norfolk to ships of the British fleet and shelled that town on January 1, 1776. Thereafter, he was no cause for military concern, though he did not retire from his post at Gwynnes Island off the coast until September 1776, when he retreated to New York.

The other man Washington mentions, Lieutenant Colonel John Connolly, was a far larger potential threat than Dunmore. Connolly had been a noted Indian fighter during the frontier troubles that followed the peace of 1763. With his extensive contacts among the Indians and frontiersmen, he was planning to attack Virginia from the west with a Loyalist and Indian army when he was captured in Hagerstown, Maryland. The Continental Congress held him prisoner for five years on rather vague charges, releasing him in 1780, when events made him no longer dangerous.

In the first week of the new year Washington wrote to Joseph Reed again. It is hard for us at this distance to remember that when Washington wrote this letter the Declaration of Independence was still six months away. The harsh sarcasm with which Washington describes the King's speech from the throne is a significant sign that he, like other Americans, was beginning to abandon the idea of an eventual reconciliation.

Cambridge, January 4, 1776.
DEAR SIR: Since my last I have received your obliging favours of the 19th and 23rd ulto., and thank you for the articles of intelligence therein contained, as I also do for the buttons which accompanied the last letter, although I had got a set better, I think, made at Concord. I am exceeding glad to find that things wear a better face in Virginia than they they did some time ago; but I do not

think that anything less than the life or liberty will free the colony from the effects of Lord Dunmore's resentments and villainies.

We are at length favored with a sight of his Majesty's most gracious speech, breathing sentiments of tenderness and compassion for his deluded American subjects; the echo is not yet come to hand; but we know what it must be, and as Lord North said, and we ought to have believed (and acted accordingly,) we now know the ultimatum of British justice. The speech I send you. A volume of them was sent out by the Boston gentry, and, farcical enough, we gave great joy to them, (the red coats I mean,) without knowing or intending it; for on that day, the day which gave being to the new army, (but before the proclamation came to hand,) we had hoisted the union flag in compliment to the United Colonies. But, behold, it was received in Boston as a token of the deep impression the speech had made upon us, and as a signal of submission. So we learned by a person out of Boston last night. By this time I presume they begin to think it strange, that we have not made a formal surrender of our lines. Admiral Shuldham is arrived at Boston. The 55th and the greatest part, if not all, of the 17th regiment, are also got in there. The rest of the 5 regiments from Ireland were intended for Halifax and Quebec; those for the first, have arrived there, the others we know not where they are got to.

It is easier to conceive than to describe the situation of my mind for some time past, and my feelings under our present circumstances. Search the vast volumes of history through, and I much question whether a case similar to ours is to be found; to wit, to maintain a post against the flower of the British troops for six months together, without——, and at the end of them to have one army disbanded and another to raise within the same distance of a reinforced enemy. It is too much to attempt. What may be the final issue of the last manoeuvre, time only can tell. I wish this month was well over our heads. The same desire of retiring into a chimney-corner seized the troops of New Hampshire, Rhode Island, and Massachusetts, (so soon as their time expired,) as had worked upon those of Connecticut, notwithstanding many of them made a tender of their services to continue, till the lines could be sufficiently strengthened. We are now left with a good deal less than half raised regiments, and about five thousand militia, who only stand ingaged to the middle of this month; when, according to custom, they will depart, let the necessity of their stay be never so urgent. Thus it is, that for more than two months past, I have scarcely immerged from one difficulty before I have plunged into another. How it will end, God in his great goodness will direct. I am thankful for his protection to this time. We are told that we shall soon get the army completed, but I have been told so many things which have never come to pass, that I distrust every thing.

I fear your fleet has been so long in fitting, and the destination of it so well known, that the end will be defeated, if the vessels escape. How is the arrival of French troops in the West Indies, and the hostile appearance there, to be reconciled with that part of the King's speech, wherein he assures Parliament, "that as well from the assurances I have received, as from the general appearance of affairs in Europe, I see no probability that the measures, which you may adopt, will be interrupted by disputes with any foreign power"? I hope the Congress will not think of adjourning at so important and critical a juncture as this. I wish they would keep a watchful eye to New York. From Captain Sears' account, (now here,) much is to be apprehended from that quarter.

A fleet is now fitting out at Boston, consisting of five transports and two bomb-vessels, under convoy of the Scarborough and Fowey men-of-war. Three hundred, some say, others more, troops are on board, with flat-bottomed boats. It is whispered, as if designedly, that they are intended for Newport; but it is generally believed that they are bound either to Long Island or Virginia; the other transports are taking in water and a good deal of bisquet is baking, some say for the shipping to lay in Nantasket Road, to be out of the way of ice, whilst others think a more important move is in agitation. All, however, is conjecture.

A few weeks later, Washington wrote to Reed again. This time he replied more directly to Reed's hints that there were criticisms of him in the Continental Congress, particularly among the Massa-

chusetts, and other *New England* men. In a striking phrase, "I know the integrity of my own heart," he summed up how he was to deal with criticism throughout the war. He also revealed in the strongest terms the shift in his attitude toward independence. In the center of this letter a long discussion of the problems of disposing of privateers' captures, and other minor matters, has been omitted.

Cambridge, February 10, 1776.

DEAR SIR: Your obliging favors of the 28th ult. and 1st inst. are now before me and claim my particular thanks for the polite attention you pay to my wishes in an early and regular communication of what is passing in your quarter.

If my dear sir, you conceive that I took any thing wrong or amiss, that was conveyed in any of your former letters, you are really mistaken. I only meant to convince you, that nothing would give more real satisfaction, than to know the sentiments, which are entertained of me by the public, whether they be favorable or otherwise; and I urged as a reason, that the man, who wished to steer clear of shelves and rocks, must know where they lay. I know—but to declare it, unless to a friend, may be an argument of vanity—the integrity of my own heart. I know the unhappy predicament I stand in; I know that much is expected of me; I know, that without men, without arms, without ammunition, without any thing fit for the accommodation of a soldier, little is to be done; and, which is mortifying, I know, that I cannot stand justified to the world without exposing my own weakness, and injuring the cause, by declaring my wants, which I am determined not to do, further than unavoidable necessity brings every man acquainted with them.

If, under these disadvantages, I am able to keep above water, (as it were) in the esteem of mankind, I shall feel myself happy; but if, from the unknown peculiarity of my circumstances, I suffer in the opinion of the world, I shall not think you take the freedom of a friend, if you conceal the reflections that may be cast upon my conduct. My own situation feels so irksome to me at times, that, if

I did not consult the public good, more than my own tranquility, I should long ere this have put every thing to the cast of a Dye. So far from my having an army of twenty thousand men well armed &c., I have been here with less than one half of it, including sick, furloughed, and on command, and those neither armed nor clothed, as they should be. In short, my situation has been such, that I have been obliged to use art to conceal it from my own officers. The Congress, as you observe, expect, I believe, that I should do more than others,—for whilst they compel me to enlist men without a bounty, they give 40 dollars to others, which will, I expect, put a stand to our enlistments; for notwithstanding all the publick virtue which is ascrib'd to these people, there is no nation under the sun, (that I ever came across) pay greater adoration to money than they do—I am pleas'd to find that your Battalions [Pennyslvania troops] are cloathed and look well, and that they are filing off for Canada. I wish I could say that the troops here had altered much in Dress or appearance. Our regiments are little more than half compleat, and recruiting nearly at a stand—In all my letters I fail not the mention of Tents, and now perceive that notice is taken of yr. application. I have been convinced, by General Howe's conduct, that he has either been very ignorant of our situation (which I do not believe) or that he has received positive orders (which, I think, is natural to conclude) not to put anything to the hazard till his reinforcements arrive; otherwise there has [not] been a time since the first of December, that we must have fought like men to have maintained these Lines, so great in their extent.

The party to Bunker's Hill * had some good and some bad men engaged in it. One or two courts have been held on the conduct of part of it. To be plain, these people—among friends—are not to be depended upon if exposed; and any man will fight well if he thinks himself in no danger. I do not apply this to these people only. I suppose it to be the case with all raw and undisciplined troops. You may rely upon it, that transports left Boston six weeks ago with troops; where they are gone, unless driven to the West

* A night raid in which several houses where the British were quartering troops were burned and a handful of prisoners was captured.

Indies, I know not. You may also rely upon General Clinton's sailing from Boston about three weeks ago, with about four or five hundred men; his destination I am also a stranger to. I am sorry to hear of the failures you speak of from France. But why will not Congress forward part of the powder made in your province? They seem to look upon this as the season for action, but will not furnish the means. But I will not blame them. I dare say the demands upon them are greater than they can supply. The cause must be starved till our resources are greater, or more certain within ourselves.

With respect to myself, I have never entertained an idea of an accommodation, since I heard of the measures, which were adopted in consequence of the Bunker's Hill fight. The king's speech has confirmed the sentiments I entertained upon the news of that affair; and if every man was of my mind, the ministers of Great Britain should know, in a few words, upon what issue the cause should be put. I would not be deceived by artful declarations, nor specious pretences; nor would I be amused by unmeaning propositions; but in open, undisguised, and manly terms proclaim our wrongs, and our resolution to be redressed. I would tell them, that we had borne much, that we had long and ardently sought for reconciliation upon honorable terms, that it had been denied us, that all our attempts after peace had proved abortive, and had been grossly misrepresented, that we had done every thing which could be expected from the best of subjects, that the spirit of freedom beat too high in us to submit to slavery, and that, if nothing else could satisfy a tyrant and his diabolical ministry, we are determined to shake off all connexions with a state so unjust and unnatural. This I would tell them, not under covert, but in words as clear as the sun in its meridian brightness.

I observe what you say, in respect to the ardor of the chimney-corner heroes. I am glad their zeal is in some measure abated, because if circumstances will not permit us to make an attempt upon B[oston], or if it should be made and fail, we shall not appear altogether so culpable. I entertain the same opinion of the attempt now, which I have ever done. I believe an assault would be attended with considerable loss, and I believe it would succeed, if the men should behave well. As to an attack upon B[unker's] Hill, (unless it could be carried by surprise,) the loss, I conceive, would be greater in proportion than at Boston; and, if a defeat should follow, it would be discouraging to the men, but highly animating if crowned with success. Great good, or great evil, would consequently result from it. It is quite a different thing to what you left, being by odds the strongest fortress they possess, both in rear and front. . . .

I recollect nothing else worth giving you the trouble of, unless you can be amused by reading a letter and poem addressed to me by Mrs. or Miss Phillis Wheatley. In searching over a parcel of papers the other day, in order to destroy such as were useless, I brought it to light again. At first, with a view of doing justice to her great poetical genius, I had a great mind to publish the poem; but not knowing whether it might not be considered rather as a mark of my own vanity, than as a compliment to her, I laid it aside, till I came across it again in the manner just mentioned. I congratulate you upon your election [to the Pennsylvania Assembly], although I consider it as the *coup de grace* to my expectation of ever seeing you resident in this camp again. I have only to regret the want of you, if that should be the case; and I shall do it the more feelingly, as I have experienced the good effects of your aid.

Washington found time to write a thank you note to poetess Phyllis Wheatley, who was a Negro and former slave. Her poem eulogized Washington in sentiments of which the following are typical.

> *Proceed, Great Chief, with virtue on thy side*
> *By every action let the goddess guide*
> *A crown, a mansion, and a throne that shine*
> *With gold unfading, Washington! be thine.*

Cambridge, February 28, 1776.

MRS PHILLIS: Your favour of the 26th of October did not reach my hands 'till the middle of December. Time enough, you will say, to have given an answer ere this. Granted. But a variety of important occurrences, continually interposing to distract the mind and withdraw the attention, I hope will apologize for the delay, and plead my excuse for the seeming, but not real neglect.

I thank you most sincerely for your polite notice of me, in the elegant Lines you enclosed; and however undeserving I may be of such encomium and panegyrick, the style and manner exhibit a striking proof of your great poetical Talents. In honour of which, and as a tribute justly due to you, I would have published the Poem, had I not been apprehensive, that, while I only meant to give the World this new instance of your genius, I might have incurred the imputation of Vanity. This and nothing else, determined me not to give it place in the public Prints.

If you should ever come to Cambridge, or near Head Quarters, I shall be happy to see a person so favoured by the Muses, and to whom Nature has been so liberal and beneficent in her dispensations. I am, with great Respect, etc.

On the same day Washington wrote a chatty note to Burwell Bassett.

Cambridge, February 28, 1776.
DEAR SIR: It is with great pleasure I received your favor of the 27th. ult. thereby learning that all our friends at Eltham are well.

I thank you heartily for the attention you have kindly paid to my landed affairs on the Ohio, my interest in which I shall be more careful of, as in the worst event they will Serve for an asylum.

Few things of importance have occured here of late, and to trouble you with my own difficulties and the distresses which occur for want of such articles as are necessary in military operations, can answer no good purpose, and therefore I shall decline it.

We are preparing to take possession of a post (which I hope to do in a few days if we can get provided with the means) which will, it is generally thought, bring on a rumpus between us and the enemy; but whether it will or not, time only can show. It is believed by many, that the troops are preparing for a removal from

Boston; it being certain that they are watering and fitting up their vessels, for the reception of the crews and have actually put some of their heavy ordnance on board; but whether this is for deception or to prepare against orders that may arrive, I know not.

Mrs. Washington says that she has wrote all the news she could get (and ladies you know are never at a loss) to Mrs. Bassett, to her letter therefore I refer you, and with sincere regard for her, the children, Mr. and Mrs. Dandridge &c., I remain, etc.

A few weeks later, Washington acted to break the stalemate around Boston and bring on the rumpus he mentioned. Striking by night, he seized the heights of Dorchester to the east of the city, threw up fortifications, and moved heavy cannon into them. He was now in a position to bombard the British mercilessly. But instead of attacking, the Royal Army decided retreat was the wisest alternative, and it hastily abandoned Boston, ending the long siege. Washington tells the whole story in this exultant letter to his brother Jack.

Cambridge, March 31, 1776.

DEAR BROTHER: Your Letter of the 24th. Ulto. was duely forwarded to this Camp by Colo. Lee, and gave me the pleasure of hearing that you, my Sister and family were well. After your Post is established to Fredericksburg the Intercourse by Letter may become regular and certain (and whenever time, little of which God knows I have for friendly corrispondance, will permit, I shall be happy in writing to you). I cannot call to mind the date of my last to you, but this I recollect, that I have written more Letters to than I have received from you.

The Want of Arms, Powder, &ca., is not peculiar to Virginia, this Country of which doubtless, you have heard such large and flattering Accounts, is more defficient of each than you can conceive, I have been here Months together with what will scarcely be believed; not 30 rounds of Musket Cartridges a Man; have been obliged to submit to all the Insults of the Enemy's Cannon for want of Powder, keeping what little we had for Pistol distance. Another thing has been done, which added to the above, will put it in the power of this Army to say what perhaps none other with justice ever could. We have maintain'd our Ground against the Enemy, under the above want of Powder, and we have disbanded one Army and recruited another, within Musket Shot of two and Twenty Regiments, the Flower of the British Army, when our strength have been little if any, superior to theirs; and, at last, have beat them, in a shameful and precipitate manner out of a place the strongest by Nature on this Continent, and strengthened and fortified in the best manner and at an enormous Expence.

As some Acct. of the late Manouvres of both Armies, may not be unacceptable, I shall, hurried as I always am, devote a little time to it.

Having received a small supply of Powder then; very inadequate to our wants, I resolved to take possession of Dorchester Point, laying East of Boston; looking directly into it; and commanding (absolutely) the Enemy's Lines on the Neck (Boston) To effect this, which I knew would force the Enemy to an Ingagement, or subject them to be enphiladed by our Cannon, it was necessary, in the first Instance to possess two heights (those mentioned in Genl. Burgoyne's Letter to Lord Stanley in his Acct. of the Battle of Bunkers Hill), which had the entire command of it. The grd. at this time being froze upwards of two feet deep, and as impenetrable as a Rock, nothing could be attempted with Earth; we were obligd, therefore to provide an amazing quantity of chandeliers and Fascines * for the Work, and on the Night of the 4th, after a previous severe Cannonade and Bombardment for three Nights together to divert the Enemy's attention from our real design, we removed every material to the spot under Cover of Darkness, and took full possession of those heights without the loss of a single Man.

Upon their discovery of the Works next Morning, great preparations were made for attacking them, but not being ready before

---

* For building earthworks. Fascines were long cylindrical bundles of wood that were placed upright and then had dirt piled against them; chandeliers were the wooden frames that held the fascines in position.

the Afternoon and the Weather getting very tempestuous, much blood was Saved, and a very important blow (to one side or the other) prevented. That this remarkable Interposition of Providence is for some wise purpose, I have not a doubt; but as the principal design of the Manouvre was to draw the Enemy to an Ingagement under disadvantages, as a premeditated Plan was laid for this purpose, and seemed to be succeeding to my utmost wish, and as no Men seem'd better disposed to make the appeal than ours did upon that occasion, I can scarce forbear lamenting the disappointments, unless the dispute is drawing to an accommodation, and the Sword going to be Sheathed.

But to return, the Enemy thinking (as we have since learnt) that we had got too securely posted, before the Second Morning to be much hurt by them, and apprehending great annoyance from our new Works resolved upon a retreat, and accordingly Imbark'd in as much hurry, precipitation and confusion as ever Troops did the 17th, not taking time to fit their transports, but leaving King's property in Boston to the amount, as is supposed, of thirty or £40,000 in Provisions, Stores, &ca. Many Pieces of Cannon, some Mortars, and a number of Shot, Shells &ca. are also left; and Baggage-Waggons, Artillery Carts &ca. which they have been Eighteen Months preparing to take the Field with, were found destroyed, thrown into the Docks, and drifted upon every shore. In short, Dunbar's destruction of Stores after Genl. Braddock's defeat, which made so much noise, affords but a faint Idea of what was to be met with here.

The Enemy lay from the 17th. to the 27th. In Nantasket and King's Roads, abt. Nine Miles from Boston, to take Water (from the Islands thereabouts surrounded by their shipping) and to fit themselves for Sea. Whither they are now bound, and where their Tents will be next pitched, I know not; but as New York and the Hudson's River are the most important objects they can have in view, as the latter secures the communication with Canada, at the same time that it seperates the Northern and Southern Colonies; and the former is thought to abound in disaffected Persons, who only wait a favourable oppertunity, and support, to declare themselves openly, it became equally important for us to prevent their gaining Possession of these advantages; and, therefore, as soon as they Imbarked I detachd a Brigade of Six Regiments to that Government, so soon as they Sailed, another Brigade compos'd of the same number, and to morrow another of Five will March. In a day or two more I shall follow myself and be in New York ready to receive all but the first.

The Enemy left all their Works standing in Boston, and on Bunker's hill, and formidable they are, the Town has shared a much better Fate than was expected, the damage done to the Houses being nothing equal to report, but the Inhabitants have suffered a good deal by being plunder'd by the Soldiery at their departure. All those who took upon themselves the Style, and title of Government Men in Boston, in short, all those who have acted an unfriendly part in this great Contest have Shipped themselves off in the same hurry, but under still greater disadvantages than the King's Troops have done; being obliged to Man their own Vessels (for Seamen could not be had for the Transports for the Kings use) and submit to every hardship that can be conceiv'd. One or two have done, what a great many ought to have done long ago, committed Suicide. By all Accts. there never existed a more miserable set of Beings, than these wretched Creatures now are; taught to believe that the Power of Great Britain was superior to all opposition, and that foreign aid (if not) was at hand, they were even higher, and more insulting in their opposition than the Regulars. When the Order Issued therefore for Imbarking the Troops in Boston, no Electric Shock, no sudden Clap of thunder. In a word the last Trump, could not have struck them with greater Consternation. they were at their Wits' end, and conscious of their black ingratitude chose to commit themselves in the manner I have above describ'd to the Mercy of the Waves at a tempestuous Season rather than meet their offended Countrymen. but with this declaration the choice was made that if they thought the most abject submission would procure them Peace they never would have stir'd.

I believe I may, with great truth affirm, that no Man perhaps since the first Institution of Armys ever commanded one under more difficult Circumstances, than I have done, to enumerate the particulars would fill a volume, many of my difficulties and distresses were of so peculiar a cast that in order to concel them from the Enemy, I was obliged to conceal them from my friends, indeed from my own Army, thereby subjecting my Conduct to interpretations unfavourable to my Character, especially by those at a distance, who could not, in the smallest degree be acquainted with the Springs that govern'd it. I am happy however, to find, and to hear from different Quarters, that my reputation stands fair, that my Conduct hitherto has given universal Satisfaction, the Addresses which I have received, and which I suppose will be published, from the General Court of this Colony the same as our Genl. Assembly and from the Selectmen of Boston upon the evacuation of the Town and my approaching departure from the Colony, exhibits a pleasing testimony of their approbation of my conduct, and of their personal regard, which I have found in various other Instances; and wch, in retirement, will afford many comfortable reflections.

The share you have taken in these Publick disputes is commendable and praiseworth; it is a duty we owe our Country; a claim posterity has on us. It is not sufficient for a Man to be a passive friend and well-Wisher to the Cause. This, and every other Cause of such a Nature, must inevitably perish under such an opposition, every person should be active in some department or other, without paying too much attention to private interest. It is a great stake we are playing for, and sure we are of winning if the Cards are well managed. Inactivity in some, disaffection in others, and timidity in many, may hurt the Cause; nothing else can, for Unanimity will carry us through triumphantly, in spite of every exertion of Great Britain, if link'd together in one indissoluble Bond; this they now know, and are practising every stratagem which Human Invention can divise, to divide us, and unite their own People, upon this principle it is, the restraining Bill is past, and [Peace] Commissioners are coming over. The devise to be sure is shallow, the covering thin, But they will hold out to their own People that the Acts (complain'd of) are repealed, and Commissioners sent to each Colony to treat with us, neither of which will we attend to &ca. this upon weak Minds among us will hate its effect, they wish for reconciliation; or in other Words they wish for Peace without attending to the Conditions. . . .

Washington closes the letter with a discussion of the merits and deficiencies of the Virginians lately appointed as general officers in the Continental army.

CHAPTER FOUR

Revolutionary Warrior

*W*ith Boston secured, Washington *now hurried to New York, where he wrote this reply to Joseph Reed's latest report on fresh troubles in Congress.*

New York, April 15, 1776.

MY DEAR SIR: Your favor of the 13th was this instant put into my hands, scarce time enough to acknowledge the receipt of it (by this Post,) and to thank you for your great care and attention in providing my Camp Equipage. Whatever the list you sent may fall short of your intention of providing, can be got here; and may be delayed; as the want or not of them, will depend upon circumstances.

I am exceedingly concerned to hear of the divisions and parties, which prevail with you, and in the southern colonies, on the score of independence. These are the shelves we have to avoid, or our bark will split and tumble to pieces. Here lies our great danger, and I almost tremble when I think of this rock. Nothing but disunion can hurt our cause. This will ruin it, if great prudence, temper, and moderation is not mixed in our counsels, and made the governing principles of the contending parties. When, my good Sir, will you be with me? I fear I shall have a difficult card to play in this Government [New York], and could wish for your assistance and advice to manage it. I have not time to add more, except that with great sincerity and truth I am, dear Sir, your most obedient and affectionate humble servant.

P.S. Mrs. Washington, &c., came the Harford Road, and not yet arrived—detain'd by the illness (on the Road) of poor Mr. Custis, who is now better and coming on.

Toward the end of May, Washington wrote to his brother Jack congratulating him and his fellow Virginians on the resolution of the Virginia Convention instructing their delegates in the Continental Congress to propose "to that respectable body to declare the colonies free and independent states, absolved from allegiance to or dependence upon the Crown or Parliament of Great Britain." Washington's predictions in regard to the British peace commissioners proved to be extremely accurate. Admiral Lord Howe and his brother Sir William Howe, commander in chief of the British navy and army respectively, were designated as commissioners to negotiate a settlement. But their powers were pitifully limited.

Philadelphia, May 31, 1776.

DEAR BROTHER: I am very glad to find that the Virginia Convention have passed so noble a vote, and with so much unanimity, things have come to that pass now, as to convince us, that we have nothing more to expect from the justice of G. Britain; also, that she is capable of the most delusive Arts, for I am satisfied that no Commissioners ever were design'd, except Hessians and other Foreigners; and that the Idea was only to deceive, and throw us off our guard; the first it has too effectually accomplished, as many Members of Congress, in short, the representation of whole Provences, are still feeding themselves upon the dainty food of reconciliation; and tho' they will not allow that the expectation of it has any influence upon their judgments (with respect to their preparations for defence) it is but too obvious that it has an operation upon every part of their conduct and is a clog to their proceedings, it is not in the nature of things to be otherwise, for no Man, that entertains a hope of seeing this dispute speedily, and equitably adjusted by Commissioners, will go to the same expence and run the same hazards to prepare for the worst event as he who believes that he must conquer, or submit to unconditional terms, and its concomitants, such as Confiscation, hanging, &c., &c.

To form a new Government, requires infinite care, and unbounded attention; for if the foundation is badly laid the superstructure must be bad, too much time therefore, cannot be bestowed in weighing and digesting matters well. We have, no doubt, some good parts in our present constitution; many bad ones we know we have, wherefore no time can be misspent that is imployed in seperating the Wheat from the Tares. My fear is, that you will all get tired and homesick, the consequence of which will be, that you will patch up some kind of Constitution as defective as the present; this should be avoided, every Man should consider, that he is lending his aid to frame a Constitution which is to render Million's happy, or Miserable, and that a matter of such moment cannot be the Work of a day.

I am in hopes to hear some good Accts from No. Carolina. If Clinton has only part of his force there, and not strongly Intrenched, I should think Genl. Lee will be able to give a very good acct. of those at Cape Fare. Surely Administration must intend more than 5000 Men for the Southern district, otherwise they must have a very contemptable opinion of those Colonies, or have great expectation of assistance from the Indians, Slaves, and Tories. We expect a very bloody Summer of it at New York and Canada, as it is there I expect the grand efforts of the Enemy will be aim'd; and I am sorry to say that we are not, either in Men, or Arms, prepared for it; however, it is to be hoped, that if our cause is just, as I do most religiously believe it to be, the same Providence which has in many Instances appear'd for us, will still go on to afford its aid.

Your Convention is acting very wisely in removing the disaffected, Stock, &ca., from the Counties of Princess Anne and Norfolk; and are much to be commended for their attention to the Manufacture of Salt, Salt Petre, Powder &ca. No time, nor expense should be spared to accomplish these things.

Mrs. Washington is now under Innoculation in this City; and will, I expect, have the Small pox favourably, this is the 13th day, and she has very few Pustules; she would have wrote to my Sister but thought it prudent not to do so, notwithstanding there could be but little danger in conveying the Infection in this manner. She joins me in love to you, her, and all the little ones. I am, with every Sentiment of regard, etc.

The bloody summer in New York, which Washington had pre-dicted to Jack, became a certainty when William Howe landed an army on Staten Island.

By the middle of August, Howe had been vastly reinforced by troops from Europe arriving under the escort of his brother. Washington confesses his perplexity at the continuing British inactivity in the following letter to Lund.

New York, August 19, 1776

DEAR LUND: Very unexpectedly to me, another revolving Monday is arrived before an Attack upon this City, or a movement of the Enemy; the reason of this is incomprehensible, to me. True it is (from some later informations) they expect another arrival of about 5000 Hessians; but then, they have been stronger than the Army under my Command; which will now, I expect, gain strength faster than theirs, as the Militia are beginning to come in fast, and have already augmented our numbers in this City and the Posts round about, to about 23,000 Men. The Enemy's numbers now on the Island and in the Transports which lay off it, are by the lowest Accts. 20,000 Men by the greatest 27,000 to these the expected (5000) Hessians are to be added.

There is something exceedingly misterious in the conduct of the Enemy. Lord Howe takes pains to throw out, upon every occasion, that he is the Messenger of Peace; that he wants to accomodate matters, nay, has Insinuated, that he thinks himself authorized to do it upon the terms mentioned in the last Petition to the King of G. Britain. But has the Nation got to that, that the King, or his Ministers will openly dispense with Acts of Parliament. And if they durst attempt it, how is it to be accounted for that after running the Nation to some Millions of Pounds Sterlg. to hire and Transport Foreigners, and before a blow is struck, they are willing to give the terms proposed by Congress before they, or we, had encountered the enormous expence that both are now run to. I say, how is this to be accounted for but from their having received some disagreeable advices from Europe; or, by having some Manouvre in view which is to be effected by procrastination. What this can be the Lord knows, we are now passed the Middle of August and they are in possession of an Island only, which it never was in our power, or Intention to dispute their Landing on. this is but a small step towards the Conquest of this Continent.

The two Ships which went up this River about the middle of the past Month, came down yesterday, sadly frightened I believe, the largest of them, the Phoencx (a 44. Gun Ship) having very narrowly escaped burning the Night before by two Fire Ships which I sent up; one of which was grapnal'd to her for Ten Minutes, in a light blaze, before the Phoenex could cut away so as to clear herself, the other Fire ship run on board of the Tender near the Phoenex, and soon reduced her to Ashes. We lost no lives in the Attempt unless the Captn. of the Ship which made the attempt upon the Phoenex perish'd. We have not heard of him since, but it is thought he might have made his escape by Swimming, which was the Plan he had in contemplation. . . .

The remainder of the letter discusses business and farm problems at Mt. Vernon. In New York, the British soon ended Washington's suspense. With final reinforcements from Germany, they now possessed an army of some thirty-two thousand highly trained professionals. Opposing them, Washington could only muster about twenty-five thousand men, two-thirds of them untrained, short-termed militia. The results were almost foredoomed. The British landed on Staten Island and thrashed the Americans at the battle of Brooklyn Heights. Washington fell back to Manhattan. The British followed, landing at Kip's Bay and sending two brigades of Connecticut militia into headlong flight without firing a shot. Not even Washington's presence could stem the panicky rout. The Americans stumbled back to Harlem Heights on the northern end of Manhattan Island. From there Washington wrote a long, gloomy letter to Lund.

Col. Morris's, on the Heights of Harlem,
September 30, 1776.

DEAR LUND: Your letter of the 18th, which is the only one received and unanswered, now lies before me. The amazement which you seem to be in at the unaccountable measures which have been adopted by ———— [the word "Congress" is omitted in the manuscript] would be a good deal increased if I had time to unfold the whole system of their management since this time twelve months. I do not know how to account for the unfortunate steps which have been taken but from that fatal idea of conciliation which prevailed so long—fatal, I call it, because from my soul I wish it may [not] prove so, though my fears lead me to think there is too much danger of it. This time last year I pointed out the evil consequences of short enlistments, the expenses of militia, and the little dependence that was to be placed in them. I assured (Congress) that the longer they delayed raising a standing army, the more difficult and chargeable would they find it to get one, and that, at the same time that the militia would answer no valuable purpose, the frequent calling them in would be attended with an expense, that they could have no conception of. Whether, as I have said before, the unfortunate hope of reconciliation was the cause, or the fear of a standing army prevailed, I will not undertake to say; but the policy was to engage men for twelve months only. The consequences of which, you have had great bodies of militia in pay that never were in camp; you have had immense quantities of provisions drawn by men that never rendered you one hour's service (at least usefully), and this in the most profuse and wasteful way. Your stores have been expended, and every kind of military discipline destroyed by them; your numbers fluctuating, uncertain, and forever far short of report—at no one time, I believe, equal to twenty thousand men fit for duty. At present our numbers fit for duty (by this day's report) amount to 14,759, besides 3,427 on command, and the enemy within stone's throw of us. It is true a body of militia are again ordered out, but they come without any conveniences and soon return. I discharged a regiment the other day that had in it fourteen rank and file fit for duty only, and several that had less than fifty.

In short, such is my situation that if I were to wish the bitterest curse to an enemy on this side of the grave, I should put him in my stead with my feelings; and yet I do not know what plan of conduct to pursue. I see the impossibility of serving with reputation, or doing any essential service to the cause by continuing in command, and yet I am told that if I quit the command inevitable ruin will follow from the distraction that will ensue. In confidence I tell you that I never was in such an unhappy, divided state since I was born. To lose all comfort and happiness on the one hand, whilst I am fully persuaded that under such a system of management as has been adopted, I cannot have the least chance for reputation, nor those allowances made which the nature of the case requires; and to be told, on the other, that if I leave the service all will be lost, is, at the same time that I am bereft of every peaceful moment, distressing to a degree. But I will be done with the subject, with the precaution to you that it is not a fit one to be publicly known or discussed. If I fall, it may not be amiss that these circumstances be known, and declaration made in credit to the justice of my character. And if the men will stand by me (which by the by I despair of), I am resolved not to be forced from this ground while I have life; and a few days will determine the point, if the enemy should not change their plan of operations; for they certainly will not—I am sure they ought not—to waste the season that is now fast advancing, and must be precious to them. I thought to have given you a more explicit account of my situation, expectation, and feelings, but I have not time. I am wearied to death all day with a variety of perplexing circumstances—disturbed at the conduct of the militia, whose behavior and want of discipline has done great injury to the other troops, who never had officers, except in a few instances, worth the bread they eat. My time, in short, is so much engrossed that I have not leisure for corresponding, unless it is on mere matters of public business. . . .

The letter ends with a few brief paragraphs on repairs to Mt. Vernon.

As the war worsened a fierce, warrior tone began to appear in

Washington's letters. It is especially visible in this letter to Lund, written in early October 1776.

Heights of Haerlam, October 6, 1776.
DEAR LUND: Your Letter of the 25th. Ulto. has reached my hands since the date of my last about this day Week. Nothing material has happened since that time. We are strengthning ourselves in this Post, as the Enemy also are in theirs. They have moved some of their ships up the North River opposite to their own Lines, and a little below ours; whether with a view to cover their own Flanks, or at a proper time to aid in their Attack upon our present Post, time only can discover. We have been in daily expectation of having our Quarters beat up, but as yet nothing of the kind has been attempted. On Wednesday last I expected to have had some pretty warm work, but it turned out otherwise. It arose from this. I sent a Party of 1000 Men to cover some Waggons in bringing of grain from a Place where I expected opposition from them. this occasioned them to strike their Tents, and put their whole Line in motion, and of course brought all our Men under Arms; but nothing more came of it, except that we went on, and brought of all the Grain.

Had I been left to the dictates of my own judgment, New York should have been laid in Ashes before I quitted it; to this end I applied to Congress, but was absolutely forbid; that they will have cause to repent the Order, I have not a moments doubt of, nor never had, as it was obvious to me (covered as it may be by their ships) that it will be next to impossible for us to dispossess them of it again as all their Supplies come by Water, whilst ours were derived by Land; besides this, by leaving it standing, the Enemy are furnished with warm and comfortable Barracks, in which their whole Force may be concentred, the place secured by a small garrison (if they chuse it) having their ships round it, and only a narrow Neck of Land to defend, and their principal force left at large to act against us, or to remove to any other place for the purpose of harrassing us. this in my judgment may be set down amg. one of the capitol errors of Congress.

Their Motives for sending Deputies to hear Lord Howes proposals were in my opinion, tolerably well founded; they had no Idea of treating with him otherwise than as Independant States; they declared so, previous to the appointing of their Commissioners. But as Lord Howe, a thorough paced Courtier, had taken uncommon pains to signify at all times, and upon all occasions, that he was vested with full powers to accommodate matters upon better terms than the Americans ever had askd, and became more importunate, as our Indifference Increased, it had the effect intended by him, on three classes of People. Our open and avowed Enemys, together with the Officers and Soldiers of their army, were exasperated at it, from a conviction that our aim, at the beginning, was Independance; the Neutrals had this doctrine so strongly inculcated into them by the Tories, that they began to adopt the same Sentiments and wondered that we would not accept of more than we asked, whilst it remaind necessary to convince the third class who were really friendly, but great sticklers for the powers of, and the advantages to be derived from the long expected Commissioners, that the whole was a falcy, calculated to deceive, as I suppose they now are; since it evidently appears that Lord Howe had nothing more to propose than that, if we would Submit, his Majesty would consider whether we should be hung or not. If this meeting shd. have a bad effect with foreign Powers, who may be unacquainted with the inducements to it, it will be unlucky.

In speaking of New York, I had forgot to mention that Providence, or some good honest Fellow, has done more for us than we were disposed to do for ourselves, as near One fourth of the City is supposed to be consumed. however enough of it remains to answer their purposes. . . .

The letter ends with a brief discussion of what to do with a young Virginian who had escaped from a British warship in the harbor. Meanwhile, the war was going even worse. Washington tells the grim story in another long letter written in two installments to his brother Jack.

White Plains, November 6, 1776.

DEAR BROTHER: I have had the pleasure to receive your Letter of the 6th. Ulto. We have, I think, by one Manouvre and another, and with a parcel of ——— but it is best to say nothing more about them. Mixed, and ungovernable Troops, spun the Campaign out to this time without coming to any decisive Action, or without letting Genl. How obtain any advantage which, in my opinion, can contribute much to the completion of the business he is come upon, or to the Honour and glory of the British Arms, and those of their Auxilaries. Our numbers from the Beginning have been disjointed and confused, and much less than were apprehended; had we ever hazarded a general action with them therefore, unless it had been in our Works at New York, or Harlem heights, we undoubtedly should have risked a good cause upon a very unfavourable Issue.

Whilst we lay at the upper end of York Island (or the heights of Harlem) How suddenly Landed from the best accts. we cd. get, about 16,000 Men above us, on a place called Frogs point on the East River, or Sound, this obliged Us, as his design was evidently to surround us, and cut of our Communication with the Country, thereby stopping all Supplies of Provisions (of which we were very scant) to remove our Camp and out Flank him, which we have done, and by degrees got strongly posted on advantageous Grounds at this place.

It is not in my power to furnish you with so extensive a Draft as you require, as I have none but printed Maps of the Country you want to see deleniated, and have no person about me that has time enough to Copy one, but a rough sketch of the Country in wch. we have been Manourvreing, and which I had taken off to carry in my pocket, I inclose you as it will afford some Idea of the parts adjacent to New York.

Novr. 19, at Hackensac.

I began this Letter at the White plains as you will see by the first part of it; but by the time I had got thus far the Enemy advanced a Second time (for they had done it once before, and after engaging some Troops which I had posted on a Hill, and driving them from it with the loss of abt. 300 killed and Wounded to them, and little more than half the number to us) as if they meant a genel. Attack, but finding us ready to receive them, and upon such ground as they could not approach without loss, they filed of and retreated towards New York.

As it was conceived that this Manoeuvre was done with a design to attack Fort Washington (near Harlem heights) or to throw a body of Troops into the Jerseys, or what might be still worse, aim a stroke at Philadelphia, I hastend over on this side with abt. 5000 Men by a round about March (wch. we were obliged to take on Acct. of the Shipping opposing the passage at all the lower Ferries) of near 65 Miles, but did not get hear time enough to take Measures to save Fort Washington tho I got here myself a day or two before it surrendered, which happened on the 16th. Instt. after making a defence of about 4 or 5 hours only.

We have no particular Acct. of the loss on either side, or of the Circumstances attending this matter, the whole Garrison after being drove from the out lines, and retiring within the Fort surrendered themselves Prisoners of War, and giving me no Acct. of the terms. By a letter, which I have just receivd from Genl. Greene at Fort Lee, (wch. is opposite to Fort Washington) I am informd that "one of the Train of Artillery came across the River last Night on a Raft, by his Acct. the Enemy have suffered greatly on the North side of Fort Washington. Colo. Rawlings's Regiment (late Hugh Stephenson's) was posted there, and behaved with great Spirit. Colo. Magaw could not get the Men to Man the Lines, otherwise he would not have given up the Fort."

This is a most unfortunate affair, and has given me great Mortification as we have lost not only two thousand Men that were there, but a good deal of Artillery, and some of the best Arms we had. And what adds to my Mortification is, that this Post, after the last Ships went past it, was held contrary to my Wishes and opinion; as I conceived it to be a dangerous one: but being determind on by a full Council of General Officers, and recieving a resolution of Congress strongly expressive of their desires, that the Channel of the River (which we had been labouring to stop for a long time at this place) might be obstructed, if possible; and knowing that this could not be done unless there were Batteries to protect the obstruction I did not care to give an absolute order for withdrawing the Garrison till I could get round and see the Situation of things and then it became too late as the Fort was Invested. I had given it, upon the passing of the last Ships, as my opinion to Genl. Greene, under whose care it was, that it would be best to evacuate the place; but, as the order was discretionary, and his opinion differed from mine, it unhappily was delayed too long, to my great grief, as I think Genl. Howe, considering his Army and ours, would have had but a poor tale to have told without it and would have found it difficult, unless some Southern Expedition may prove successful, to have reconciled the People of England to the Conquest of a few pitiful Islands, none of wch. were defensible, considering the great number of their Ships and the power they have by Sea to surround and render them unapproachable.

Your Letter of the 30th. of Octr. was delivered to me a few days ago by Colo. Woodford. It is a matter of great grief and surprize to me, to find the different States so slow, and inattentive to that essential business of levying their quota's of Men. In ten days from this date, there will not be above 2000 Men, if that, on this Side of Hudson's River (of the fixed and establish'd Regiments) to oppose Howe's whole Army, and very little more on the other to secure the Eastern Colonies and the Important Passes leading through the Highlands to Albany and the Country about the Lakes. In short it is impossible for me in the compass of a Letter, to give you any Idea of our Situation, of my difficulties, and the constant perplexities and mortifications I constantly meet with, derived from the unhappy policy of short enlistments, and delaying them too long. Last fall or Winter, before the Army which was then to be raised, was set about, I represented in clear and explicit terms the evils wch. would arise from short Inlistments, the expence that must attend the raising an Army every year, the futility of such an Army when raised; and, in a word, if I had spok with a prophetick Spirit, could not have foretold the evils with more accuracy than I did; all the year since I have been pressing them to delay no time in engaging Men upon such terms as would Insure success, telling them that the longer it was delayed the more difficult it would grow; but the measure was not set about till it was too late to be effected, and then in such a manner as to bid adieu to every hope of getting an Army, from which any Services are to be expected; the different States without regard to the merits or qualifications of an Officer, quarelling about the appointments, and nominating such as are not fit to be Shoe Blacks from the local attachments of this or that Member of Assembly.

I am wearied almost to death with the retrograde Motions of things, and I solemnly protest that a pecuniary reward of 20,000 £ a year would not induce me to undergo what I do; and after all, perhaps, to loose my Character as it is impossible under such a variety of distressing Circumstances to conduct matters agreeably to public expectation, or even of those who employ me, as they will not make proper allowances for the difficulties their own errors have occasioned.

I am glad to find by your last Letter that your family are tolerably well recoverd from the Indisposition they labourd under. God grant you all health and happiness; nothing in this world would contribute so much to mine as to be once more fixed among you in the peaceable enjoyment of my own Vine, and fig Tree.

As Washington reeled across New Jersey with the British in hot pursuit, a letter from Major General Charles Lee, America's second-ranking officer, came into camp addressed to Colonel Joseph Reed, who was serving as Washington's Adjutant General. Thinking it was official business, Washington opened it and found to his shock that it was a reply to a private correspondence between Reed and the conniving Lee in which Reed cruelly criticized Washington behind his back. A lesser man would have found such treachery unforgivable, but Washington simply passed the letter on to Reed with the following note.

Brunswick, November 30, 1776.
DEAR SIR: The inclosed was put into my hands by an Express from

the White Plains. Having no Idea of its being a Private Letter, much less suspecting the tendency of the correspondence, I opened it, as I had done all other Letters to you, from the same place and Peekskill, upon the business of your Office, as I conceived and found them to be.

This, as it is the truth, must be my excuse for seeing the contents of a Letter, which neither inclination or intention would have prompted me to.

I thank you for the trouble and fatigue you have undergone in your Journey to Burlington, and sincerely wish that your labours may be crowned with the desired success.

By December tenth Washington had retreated to the western side of the Delaware, abandoning New Jersey to the triumphant British advance. It was the low point of the American Revolution. Washington tells the grim truth to his brother Jack.

Camp, near the Falls of Trenton,
December 18, 1776.

DEAR BROTHER: In the number of Letters I write, the recollection of any particular one is destroyed, but I think my last to you was by Colo. Woodford of Hackensack. Since that period and a little before, our Affairs have taken an adverse turn but not more than was to be expected from the unfortunate Measures, which had been adopted for the establishment of our Army.

The Retreat of the Enemys Army from the White Plains led me to think that they would turn their thoughts to the Jerseys, if no further, and induced me to cross the North River with some of the Troops, in order if possible to oppose them. I expected to have met at least 5000 Men of the Flying Camp and Militia; instead of which I found less than one half and no disposition in the Inhabitants to afford the least aid. This being perfectly well known to the Enemy, they threw over a large body of Troops, which pushed us from place to place till we were obliged to cross the Delaware with less than 3000 Men fit for duty owning to the dissolution of our force by short Inlistments; the Enemy's numbers, from the best

Accts. exceeding Ten and by some 12,000 Men.

Before I removed to the South Side of the River, I had all the Boats, and other Vessels brought over, or destroyed from Philadelphia upwards for 70 Miles, and, by guarding the Fords have as yet, baffled all their attempts to cross. But, from some late movements of theirs, I am left in doubt whether they are moving off for Winter Quarters or making a feint to throw us off our guard.

Since I came on this side, I have been join'd by about 2000 of the [Philadelphia] City Militia, and understand that some of the Country Militia (from the back Counties,) are on their way; *but we are in a very disaffected part of the Provence, and between you and me, I think our Affairs are in a very bad situation; not so much from the apprehension of Genl. Howe's Army, as from the defection of New York, Jerseys, and Pennsylvania. In short, the Conduct of the Jerseys has been most Infamous. Instead of turning out to defend their Country and affording aid to our Army, they are making their submissions as fast as they can.* If they the Jerseys had given us any support, we might have made a stand at Hackensack and after that at Brunswick, but the few Militia that were in Arms, disbanded themselves (or slunk off in such a manner upon the appearance of danger as to leave us quite unsupported and to make the best shifts we could without them) and left the poor remains of our Army to make the best we could of it.

I have no doubt but that General Howe will still make an attempt upon Philadelphia this Winter. I see nothing to oppose him a fortnight hence, as the time of all the Troops, except those of Virginia (reduced almost to nothing,) and Smallwood's Regiment of Maryland, (equally as bad) will expire in less than that time. In a word my dear Sir, *if every nerve is not strain'd* to recruit the New Army with all possible expedition, *I think the game is pretty near up, owing, in a great measure, to the insidious Arts of the Enemy, and disaffection of the Colonies before mentioned, but* principally to the accursed policy of short Inlistments, and placing too great a dependence on the Militia the Evil consequences of which were foretold 15 Months ago with a spirit almost Prophetick.

Before this reaches you, you will no doubt have heard of the

Captivity of Genl. Lee; this is an additional misfortune, and the more vexatious, as it was by his own folly and Imprudence (and without a view to answer any good) he was taken, going three Miles out of his own Camp (for the sake of a little better lodging) and within 20 of the Enemy to lodge, a rascally Tory rid in the Night to give notice of it to the Enemy who sent a party of light Horse that seized and carried him with every mark of triumph and indignity.

You can form no Idea of the perplexity of my Situation. No Man, I believe, ever had a greater choice of difficulties and less means to extricate himself from them. However under a full persuasion of the justice of our Cause I cannot entertain an Idea that it will finally sink tho' it may remain for some time under a Cloud.

My love, and sincere regards attend my Sister and the Family and Compliments to all enquiring friends. With every Sentiment of friendship, as well as love, I am etc.

With his back to the wall, Washington did the one thing the British never expected him to do: attack. On Christmas night he slashed across the ice-choked Delaware to capture nine hundred bewildered Hessian troops at Trenton. On January first, he crossed the Delaware again, and when the British sent an army hustling across New Jersey to contain him, he produced another midnight march which left the British staring at an empty American camp while Washington was twenty miles in their rear annihilating three regiments at Princeton. The stunned British hastily abandoned two-thirds of New Jersey and allowed Washington to go into winter quarters at Morristown. From there he wrote to his stepson John Parke Custis in a mood that shows he had no illusions about the extent of his minor victories.

Morris Town, January 22, 1777.

DEAR SIR: Your letter of the seventh came to my hands a few days ago, and brought with it the pleasing reflection of your still holding me in remembrance.

The misfortune of short enlistments, and an unhappy dependance upon militia, have shown their baneful influence at every period, and almost upon every occasion, throughout the whole course of this war. At no time, nor upon no occasion, were they ever more exemplified than since Christmas; for if we could but have got in the militia in time, or prevailed upon those troops whose times expired (as they generally did) on the first of this instant, to have continued (not more than a thousand or twelve hundred agreeing to stay), we might, I am persuaded, have cleared the Jerseys entirely of the enemy. Instead of this, all our movements have been made with inferior numbers, and with a mixed, motley crew, who were here to-day, gone to-morrow, without assigning a reason, or even apprizing you of it. In a word, I believe I may with truth add, that I do not think that any officer since the creation ever had such a variety of difficulties and perplexities to encounter as I have. How we shall be able to rub along till the new army is raised, I know not. Providence has heretofore saved us in a remarkable manner, and on this we must principally rely. Every person in every state should exert himself to facilitate the raising and marching the new regiments to the army with all possible expedition.

I have never seen (but heard of) the resolve you mentioned, nor do I get a paper of Purdie's [Alexander Purdie published *The Virginia Gazette*] once a month. Those who want faith to believe the account of the shocking wastes committed by Howe's army—of their ravaging, plundering, and abuse of women—may be convinced to their sorrow, perhaps, if a check can not be put to their progress.

It is painful to me to hear of such illiberal reflections upon the eastern troops as you say prevails in Virginia. I always have, and always shall say, that I do not believe that any of the states produce better men, or persons capable of making better soldiers, but it is to be acknowledged that they are (generally speaking) most wretchedly officered. To this, and this only, is to be attributed their demerits. The policy of those states has been, to level men as much as possible to one standard. The distinction, therefore, between officers and soldiers, ——— [word blotted] and that hunger and thirst after glory which ——— [word blotted] This is the true secret, and we have found, that wherever a regiment is well officered, their men have behaved well—when otherwise, ill—the misconduct or cowardly behavior always originating with the officers who have set the example. Equal injustice is done them, in depriving them of merit in other respects; for no people fly to arms readier than they do, or come better equipped, or with more regularity into the field than they . . .

The letter ends with a discussion of some business problems Jack was having with his estate.

With both armies in winter quarters—Washington in and around Morristown, the British largely in New York—there was a lull in the war. Washington had time to deal with less pressing matters. In the following letter he shows he had decided to remain a passive spectator no longer while other men made all the appointments to the army. He has obviously done some thoughtful politicking for his old friend, Dr. James Craik.

Morristown, April 26, 1777.
DEAR DOCTOR: I am going to address you on a subject which may lay some claim to *your* attention, as I do to your candor in the determination of the proposition. In the Hospital department for the Middle District (which District includes the States between the North or Hudson's River, and Patowmack) there are at present two places vacant, either of which I can obtain for you: The One is Senior Physician, and Surgeon of the Hospital, with the pay of four Dollars and six Rations pr Day, and Forage for one Horse: The other is Assistant Director General, with the pay of three Dollars and six Rations pr Day; and two Horses, and travelling expenses found, according to Doctor Shippen's Director General's Account, who also adds that he thinks this latter the most honorable and desirable of the two. Had I expected that Congress would have proceeded to the Appointments in this department, at the time they did, I have no doubt, but that it might have been in my power to have got you any other place (except that of Director General) but that is now over; and the matter in which I claim your candor, is,

that you will not let my introducing the present proposition to you, have any undue influence.

You know the extent, and profit of your present practice; you know what prospects are before you. You know how far you may be benefitted, or injured, by such an Appointment; and you must know, whether it is advisable, or practicable, for you to quit your Family, and practice, at this time. All these matters I am ignorant of; and request, as a friend, that my proposing this matter to you may have no influence upon your acceptance of it. I have no other end in view than to serve you; consequently, if you are not benefitted by the Appointment, my end is not answered. I have only to add, therefore, a request, that you will let me know the result of your determination by the Return of the Post, or as soon as possible, as the places will be kept vacant 'till I hear from you.

My best Respects to Mrs. Craik and your Family; and believe me to be, etc.

Craik took the job and eventually became chief physician and surgeon of the Continental Army.

While Washington waited in the New Jersey hills for the British to make the first move in the campaign of 1777, what should arrive on his desk but a letter from his ex-friend and confidant Joseph Reed, who had resigned from the army and was now a prominent Pennsylvania politician. Reed was still trying to explain his conniving letter to General Charles Lee. "A hope of introducing honesty and courage, at least among our troops, betrayed me into a warmth of expression which, considering with whom I had to do, was imprudent tho not unjust," Reed wrote in an odd mixture of confession and self-justification. He ended by admitting his regret "that I did not avail myself of your example of patience and silence."

Middlebrook, June 14, 1777.

DEAR SIR: Your favor of the 4th was given me by Jos. Arrowsmith, just as Mr. Peters inform'd me that he was about to set out for Philadelphia. I could not resist the inclination, however, of detaining him long enough to write you a short letter, to thank you as I do most sincerely, for the friendly and affectionate sentiments contain'd in yours of the above date towards me, and to assure you that I am perfectly convinc'd of the sincerity of them.

True it is, I felt myself hurt by a certain letter, which appear'd at that time to be the echo of one from you. I was hurt, not because I thought my judgment wronged by the expressions contain'd in it, but because the same sentiments were not communicated immediately to myself. The favorable manner in which your opinion, upon all occasions, had been received, the impression they made, and the unreserved manner in which I wished and required them to be given, entitled me, I thought to your advice upon any point in which I appeared to be wanting. To meet with any thing, then that carried with it a complexion of withholding that advice from me, and censuring my conduct to another, was such an argument of disingenuity, that I was not a little mortified at it. However, I am perfectly satisfied that matters were not as they appeared from the letter alluded to.

I sincerely wish that you may accept the appointment of Congress, and the post I am desirous of placing you in, and must beg to be favor'd with an answer immediately upon the subject, as the service will not admit of delay. A general officer in that department would not only take off a great deal of trouble from me, but be a means of bringing those regiments into order and service with much more facility than it is in my power, divided as my attention is, can possibly do. Mr. Peter's waiting obliges me to conclude, and I do it with great truth, Dear Sir etc.

The Post Washington offered Reed was the command of the American cavalry.

For the next few weeks Washington and Howe fought a war of maneuver in New Jersey. Howe tried to lure Washington down from the mountains; Washington declined to come. This left the British perplexed and considerably annoyed. In this letter to his brother Jack, Washington tells in vivid detail these opening moves in the campaign of 1777.

Camp at Middlebrook, June 29, 1777.

DEAR BROTHER: Whether it is owing to your not writing to me, or to the miscarriage of Letters, I cannot undertake to say; but certain it is, I have not received a Letter from you for some considerable time.

Finding Genl. Howe was Assembling his whole Force (excepting the necessary Garrisons for New York &ca.) at Brunswick, in this State, I began to collect mine at this place; (a strong piece of ground) ten Miles distant from him, where I have now been (in my Tent) about 5 Weeks. On the Night of the 13th, He March'd out of Brunswick, and advanc'd the head of his Column to Somerset Court House, Nine Miles, whilst the Rear Remaind at Middlebush about 4. In this Situation he lay till the 19th; his left Wing coverd by Brunswick; his Right by the River Millstone, and his Front by the Rariton, perfectly secure from any attempt of ours, if we had been, in other respects, ripe for an Attack.

Our conjectures of this move were two, either that it was designd immediately to Philadelphia, or, which was much the most probable, against this Army; as it was not to be conceived that Genl. Howe would be rash enough to proceed across the Country with one Army in Front, whilst this, under my Commd. was so situated as to fall, at any time upon his Flank and rear, without making an attempt to defeat and disperse it.

Be the real design which it would, certain it is, a disappointment, and much chagreen followed; for on the Night of the 19th: a sudden retreat was made back to Brunswick, burning and destroying Houses &ca. as they went; this Retreat, I am persuaded, was the effect of dispair at finding the Militia of this, and the State of Pennsylvania turning out to oppose them; whilst they would have part of my force (if they had attempted to cross the Delae.) to oppose them in Front, at the passage of the River, whilst I should be laying at them behind; and to attack my Troops, Situated as I am, they found impracticable, without great loss, and a probable defeat.

On Sunday the 22d. they retired from Brunswick to Amboy; but having intimation of the design the Evening before, I detached three Brigades to fall upon their Rear, from whom, I believe, they receivd a pretty good peppering. some Accts. make their loss in killed and Wounded near 500, but the truth of this I do not undertake to vouch for, as they are equal to Indians in concealing their loss, by a removal of their dead, and were they to take up the business of Scalping they would much resemble Savages, in every respects! so much is the boasted generosity, and glory of Britains fallen!

So soon as they got to Amboy they began to Transport their Baggage and Stores as fast as possible to Staten Island, and having divested themselves of all Incumbrance of this kind, they movd out their whole force on thursday last, and advanced rapidly, towards us. What was the design of this New Manoeuvre I know not, whether to attempt our strength on the left as they had before on our Right. Whether to cut off the light Troops which I had advanced towards their lines. Whether, finding themselves a little disgrac'd by their former move, they wanted to flourish off a little at quitting the Jerseys, or, whether by this sudden eruption they meant to possess themselves of as much fresh Provision as they could, plunder the Inhabitants; and spread desolation; as I have said before, I know not; but certain it is they have left nothing which they could carry off, Robbing, Plundering, and burning Houses as they went. We followed them with light Troops to their Works at Amboy, but could not prevent the Desolation they committed.

I expect from appearances and my Intelligence, they will be Imbarked in a few hours for Staten Island, or New York; for what other Expedition time, not I, can discover. By means of their Shipping and the easy transportation that Shipping affords, they have it much in their power to lead us a very disagreeable dance. My best wishes attends my Sister and all the rest of the Family and with every Sentimt. of regd. &c.

Six weeks later, Washington found time to write to Jack once more. The shape of British plans for 1777 was now cruelly clear.

General John Burgoyne was invading New York from the north, in a move designed to split off New England from the rest of the colonies. General William Howe, meanwhile, had embarked his army on troop ships and sailed south for a presumed attack on Philadelphia. But instead of coming up the Delaware River he disappeared into the Atlantic, leaving Washington in a state of suspended animation, not sure whether he should march back into New Jersey or stay in position to defend Philadelphia. Toward the end of this letter Washington adds some interesting observations on his hope (or lack of it) for French aid.

Germantown, near Philada., August 5, 1777.

DEAR BROTHER: . . . Since Genl. Howes remove from the Jerseys, the Troops under my Command have been more harrassed by Marching, and Counter Marching, than by any thing that has happen'd to them in the course of the Campaign.

After Genl. Howe had Imbarkd his Troops, the presumption that he would operate upon the North River, to form a junction with General Burgoyne, was so strong, that I removed from Middle Brook to Morristown, and from Morristown to the Clove (a narrow pass leading through the Highlands) about 18 Miles from the River. Indeed, upon some pretty strong presumptive evidence, I threw two divisions over the North River. In this Situation we lay till about the 24th. ulto., when, Receiving certain Information that the Fleet had actually Saild from Sandy hook (the outer point of New York harbour) and the concurring Sentiment of every one, (tho I acknowledge my doubts of it were strong,) that Philadelphia was the object, we counter Marchd, and got to Coryells Ferry on the Delaware (abt. 33 Miles above the City) on the 27th. where I lay till I receiv'd Information from Congress that the Enemy were actually at the Capes of Delaware. This brought us in great haste to this place for defence of the City, but in less than 24 hours after our arrival we got Accts. of the disappearance of the Fleet on the 31st; since which nothing having been heard of them, we remain here in a very irksome State of Suspense. Some imagining that they are gone to the Southward, whilst a Majority (in whose opinion upon this occasion I concur) are satisfied they are gone to the Eastward. The fatigue however, and Injury, which Men must Sustain by long Marches in such extreme heat as we have felt for the last five days, must keep us quiet till we hear something of the destination of the Enemy.

I congratulate you very sincerely on the happy passage of my Sister and the rest of your Family, through the Small pox. Surely the daily Instances which present themselves of the amazing benefits of Inoculation must make converts of the most rigid opposers, and bring on a repeal of that most impolitic Law which restrains it.

Our Affairs at the Northward have taken a turn not more unfortunate, than unexpected; * the public Papers will convey every information that I can on this Subject, to these therefore I shall refer, with this addition, that a public enquiry is order'd into the conduct of the Genl. Officers in that department; which will give them oppertunity of Justifying their conduct, or the publick one of making examples. this however will not retrieve the misfortune; for certain it is, that this affair has cast a dark shade upon a very bright prospect, our Accts. from that Quarter being very gloomy. But some reinforcements being sent up, and some good Officers, it is to be hoped the cloud will, in time, dispel. One thing absolutely necessary, is, that all the Gentlemen, in every State, should exert themselves to have their quota of Troops compleated; for believe me, the whole are most shamefully deficient.

I have, from the first, been among those few who never built much upon a French war. I ever did, and still do think, they never meant more than to give us a kind of underhand assistance; that is, to supply us with Arms &ca. for our Money, and trade; this may indeed, if G. B. has spirit, and strength to resent it, bring on a War; but the declaration, if on either side, must, I am convinced come from the last mentioned power. . . .

---

* On July 5 the American army, retreating before the superior British force led by General John Burgoyne, had evacuated Fort Ticonderoga, the so-called "key to the continent" at the confluence of Lake Champlain and Lake George.

Two momentous months now passed before Washington found time to write another personal letter. In these nine harrassed weeks he fought two of the war's biggest battles. The first clash was on September 11 at Brandywine Creek. Washington with about 10,500 men had taken up a defensive position barring the British advance on Philadelphia. Howe launched a two-pronged attack, and after some fierce fighting Washington's right flank collapsed and the Americans retreated. On September 26, part of Howe's army occupied Philadelphia, but his main encampment was at Germantown, outside the city. Here, on October 4, Washington came close to destroying the British in a dawn attack that proved to be fatally complicated by a heavy fog.

In the following letter Washington tells Jack the story in mournful detail. Then, at the very end we all but participate in the moment when Washington heard the best news of the war thus far: General John Burgoyne had surrendered to Horatio Gates at Saratoga.

Philadelphia County, October 18, 1777.
DEAR BROTHER: Your kind and Affectionate Letters of the 21st. of Septr. and 2d. Instt. came Safe to hand. When my last to you was dated I know not, for truely I can say, that my whole time is so much engross'd that I have scarce a moment (but sleeping ones) for relaxation, or to endulge myself in writing to a friend. The anxiety you have been under, on Acct. of this Army, I can easily conceive; would to God there had been less Cause for it; or, that our Situation at present, was such, as to promise much from it. The Enemy crossed the Schuylkill, which, by the by, above the Falls (and the Falls you know is only five Miles from the City) is as easily crossed in any place as Potomack Run, Aquia, or any other broad and Shallow Water. rather by stratagem; tho' I do not know that it was in our power to prevent it, as their Manoeuvres made it necessary for us to attend to our Stores which lay at Reading, towards which they seemed bending their course, and the loss of which must have proved our Ruin. After they had crossed, we took the first favourable oppertunity of attacking them; this was at-

tempted by a Nights March of fourteen Miles to Surprize them (which we effectually did) so far as reaching their Guards before they had notice of our coming, and but for a thick Fog rendered so infinitely dark at times, as not to distinguish friend from Foe at the distance of 30 Yards, we should, I believe, have made a decisive and glorious day of it. But Providence or some unaccountable something, designed it otherwise; for after we had driven the Enemy a Mile or two, after they were in the utmost confusion, and flying before us in most places, after we were upon the point, (as it appeard to everybody) of grasping a compleat Victory, our own Troops took fright and fled with precipitation and disorder. how to acct. for this I know not, unless, as I before observed, the Fog represented their own Friends to them for a Reinforcement of the Enemy as we attacked in different Quarters at the same time, and were about closing the Wings of our Army when this happened, one thing indeed contributed not a little to our Misfortune, and that was want of Ammunition on the right wing, which began the Ingagement, and in the course of two hours and 40 Minutes which it lasted, had (many of them) expended the 40 Rounds which they took into the Field.

After the Ingagement we removd to a place about 20 Miles from the Enemy, to collect our Force together, to take care of our Wounded, get furnished with necessaries again, and be in a better posture, either for offensive, or defensive operations. We are now advancing towards the Enemy again, being at this time within 12 Miles.

Our loss in the late action was, in killed, wounded, and Missing, about 1000, but of the missing, many, I dare say took advantage of the times, and deserted. Genl. Nash of No. Carolina was Wounded and died two or three days after. Many valuable Officers of ours was also wounded and some killed. The Enemys loss is variously reported; none make it less than 1500 (killed and wounded) and many estimate it much larger. Genl. Agnew of theirs was certainly killed, many Officers wounded among whom some of distinction; this we certainly know that the Hospital at Philadelphia and several large Meeting Houses are filled with their wounded besides private Houses with the Horses. In a word, it was a bloody day; would to Heaven I could add, that it had been a more fortunate one for us.

Our distress on Acct. of Cloathing is great; and in a little time must be very Sensibly felt, unless some expedient can be hit upon to obtain them. We have since the Battle got in abt. 1200 Militia from Virginia; about the same number have gone off from this state and Jersey but others are promised in lieu of them, with truth however it may be said, that this State [Pennsylvania] acts most infamously, the People of it I mean as we derive little or no assistance from them. In short they are, in a manner, totally, disaffected, or in a kind of Lethargy.

The Enemy are making vigorous efforts to remove the obstructions in the Delaware, and to possess themselves of the Works which have been constructed for the Defence of them. I am doing all I can in my present situation to save them, God only, knows which will succeed.

I very sincerely congratulate you on the change in your Family. tell the young couple, after wishing them joy of their union, that it is my sincere hope, that it will be as happy, and lasting as their present joys are boundless. the Inclosed Letter of thanks to my Sister for her elegant present you will please to deliver; and with sincere Affection for you all, I am, &c.

P.S. I had scarce finish'd this Letter when by express from the State of New York, I received the Important and glorious News which follows. . . .

I most devoutly congratulate you, my Country, and every well wisher to the Cause on this Signal Stroke of Providence. Yrs. as before.

Washington's mood is more exultant in this letter to his brother Samuel. He opens with a discussion of some local matters —purchase of some lots at Warm Springs, even then developing as a resort, and the possibility of getting Samuel's son, Thornton, a commission. Washington then describes in some detail the fight for the forts along the Delaware, a bitter series of battles in which the survival of the British army in Philadelphia was at stake. Unless the British reduced these forts they could get no supplies up the river and could be starved into surrender.

Phila. County, October 27, 1777.

DEAR BROTHER: . . . To recite at this time, the circumstances of the Ingagement of Brandywine, which have been bandied about in all the Newspapers would be totally unnecessary, almost equally so, would it be, to say any thing at this time, of the subsequent Ingagement on the 4th. Instt. wch. had every appearance (after a contest of two hours and 40 Minutes) of deciding in our favour, till something, to this moment unaccounted for, determined it otherwise. The glorious, and fortunate surrender of Genel. Burgoynes whole Army you have doubtless heard of, as an additional piece of good News I can inform you that on the 22d. Instt. a body of 1200 Hessians undertook to storm one of the Forts (called Mercer at red bank) erected for the defence of the Cheveaux de frieze in the Delaware, in which attempt they were repulsed and retreated precipitably, after leaving upwards of 200 Men dead, and badly wounded on the spot, together with Count Donop their chief and several other valuable Officers; their total loss in killed and wounded, on this occasion does, by the best accts. we can get, amount to between four and five hundred Men. the next Morning, the Enemys Ships that has passed the lower Cheveaux de frieze, together with their Batteries on the Pensylvania side (Fort Mercer being on the Jersey shore) began a most furious Canonade on Fort Mifflen which is placed on a small Island in the River nearly opposite to Fort Mercer, and on our little Fleet wch. was posted for the defence of the Cheveaux de frieze, and after an incessant and most tremendous fire of Six hours retreated with the loss of a 64 Gun Ship and a frigate both of which were burnt. Our loss on both these occasions was trifling; at Fort Mercer in killed and wounded between 30 and 40 Men; at Fort Mifflin and on board the Galleis much less, since then the Enemy have been pretty quiet; but using every means to make themselves Masters of the River.

The Situation of the two Armies is shortly this: The Enemy

are in Phila., and we hovering round them, to distress and retard their operations as much as possible; a Letter is too uncertain a conveyance for me to say any thing further of the governing principles of our own. Genl. Sir Henry Clinton's expedition up the North River [to relieve Burgoyne] will, if it has not already done so, end (if not in Smoke) in the burning and destroying of Mills, Gentlemens Seats, and the Villages adjacent to the River; strong evidence of their diabolical designs, and despair.

Remember me kindly to Mr. Warner Washington [a first cousin] and Family, and to other enquiring friends; and be assured that I am with every sentiment of Brotherly love, Yr. etc.

PS. I Inclose you a list of the Prisoners, and artillery taken in the Northern Department this Campaign; where at least 12,000 Militia had assembled in aid of the Continental Troops, and stopd the only Road by which Burgoyne could retreat, whilst this Government [Pennsylvania] which alone could afford that Number, with difficulty could get out any, and left me to struggle on as well as I could with Continental Troops for before a Second set of Militia could be got, the first were always gone by which means we could never collect a respectable body at once. Yrs. etc.

CHAPTER FIVE

New Friends and New Woes

*A*mong his military compatriots only one man stirred Washington's deepest emotions: the Marquis de Layfayette. The young Frenchman had distinguished himself in the battle of Brandywine. His courage, his utter sincerity, his eagerness to serve the cause of liberty, all played a part in winning Washington's friendship. But in this letter we see another, perhaps primary reason: his personal loyalty to Washington. The great victory at Saratoga was not for Washington an unmixed blessing. Connivers in Congress and in the army promptly began scheming to make Saratoga's champion, Major General Horatio Gates, the new American hero. Gates did nothing to discourage the idea that he was a better general, and opened a lively correspondence with his backers in the army and in Congress. Chief among these was Thomas Conway, an Irishman who had served in the French army. He made the mistake of trying to inveigle Layfayette into the plot. The young marquis replied by drinking a toast to Washington and writing a letter telling his commander-in-chief the whole story. Here is Washington's reply.

Head Quarters, December 31, 1777.
MY DEAR MARQUIS: Your favour of Yesterday conveyed to me fresh proof of that friendship and attachment which I have happily experienced since the first of our acquaintance, and for which I entertain sentiments of the purest affection. It will ever constitute part of my happiness to know that I stand well in your opinion, because I am satisfied that you can have no views to answer by throwing out false colours, and that you possess a Mind too exalted to condescend to dirty arts and low intrigues to acquire a reputation. Happy, thrice happy, would it have been for this Army and the

cause we are embarked in, if the same generous spirit had pervaded all the Actors in it. But one Gentleman, whose Name you have mentioned, had, I am confident, far different views. His ambition and great desire of being puffed off as one of the first Officers of the Age, could only be equalled by the means which he used to obtain them; but finding that I was determined not to go beyond the line of my duty to indulge him in the first, nor, to exceed the strictest rules of propriety, to gratify him in the second, he became my inveterate Enemy; and has, I am persuaded, practised every Art to do me an injury, even at the expense of reprobating a measure, which did not succeed, that he himself advised to. How far he may have accomplished his ends, I know not, and, but for considerations of a public Nature, I care not. For it is well known, that neither ambitious, nor lucrative motives led me to accept my present Appointments; in the discharge of which, I have endeavoured to observe one steady and uniform conduct, which I shall invariably pursue, while I have the honour to command, regardless of the Tongue of slander or the powers of detraction.

The fatal tendency of disunion is so obvious, that I have, in earnest terms, exhorted such Officers as have expressed their dissatisfaction at General Conway's promotion [to major general], to be cool and dispassionate in their decision upon the matter; and I have hopes that they will not suffer any hasty determination to injure the service. At the same time, it must be acknowledged that Officers' feelings upon these occasions are not to be restrained, although you may controul their Actions.

The other observations contained in your Letter, have too much truth in them, and it is much to be lamented that things are not now as they formerly were; but we must not, in so great a contest, expect to meet with nothing but Sun shine. I have no doubt but that every thing happens so for the best; that we shall triumph over all our misfortunes, and shall, in the end, be ultimately happy; when, My Dear Marquis, if you will give me your Company in Virginia, we will laugh at our past difficulties and the folly of others; where I will endeavour, by every civility in my power, to shew you how much and how sincerely, I am etc.

A month later, the Conway cabal, as it has come to be known, was in full swing. Among their many tricks was the distribution of anonymous attacks against Washington. One of these was sent to Henry Laurens, president of the Congress and one of Washington's warm friends and admirers. Washington's reply again shows his magnanimity. But there is also evidence that he found this kind of back stabbing difficult to bear. One of the reasons can be glimpsed in the heading of the letter. By now the army had moved to winter quarters outside Philadelphia at a place called Valley Forge.

Valley Forge, January 31, 1778.

SIR: I this morning received your favor of the 27th. Ulto.

I cannot sufficiently express the obligation I feel to you for your friendship and politeness upon an occasion in which I am so deeply interested. I was not unapprized that a malignant faction had been for sometime forming to my prejudice; which, conscious as I am of having ever done all in my power to answer the important purposes of the trust reposed in me, could not but give me some pain on a personal account; but my chief concern arises from an apprehension of the dangerous consequences, which intestine dissentions may produce to the common cause.

As I have no other view than to promote the public good, and am unambitious of honours not founded in the approbation of my Country, I would not desire in the least degree to suppress a free spirit of enquiry into any part of my conduct that even faction itself may deem reprehensible.

The anonymous paper handed you exhibits many serious charges, and it is my wish that it should be submitted to Congress; this I am the more inclined to, as the suppression, or concealment, may possibly involve you in embarrassments hereafter; since it is uncertain how many, or who may be privy to the contents.

My Enemies take an ungenerous advantage of me; they know the delicacy of my situation, and that motives of policy deprive me of the defence I might otherwise make against their insiduous attacks. They know I cannot combat their insinuations, however injurious, without disclosing secrets, it is of the utmost moment to conceal. But why should I expect to be exempt from censure; the unfailing lot of an elevated station? Merits and talents, with which I can have no pretensions of rivalship, have ever been subject to it. My Heart tells me it has been my unremitted aim to do the best circumstances would permit; yet, I may have been very often mistaken in my judgment of the means, and may, in many instances deserve the imputation of error.

I cannot forbear repeating that I have a grateful sense of the favourable disposition you have manifested to me in this affair, and beg you will believe me to be, with sentiments of real Esteem, etc.

With his army starving, indeed on the brink of collapse, and plotters attempting to sabotage his authority, Washington somehow found time to deal with still another worry, a series of vicious British-inspired forgeries which pictured him as a seducer of his servants. Here he writes about them to a politically powerful friend in Virginia, Richard Henry Lee.

Valley Forge, February 15, 1778.
DEAR SIR: Your letter of the 2d ultimo, from Chantilly [Lee's estate], enclosing Lieutenant Colonel Frazer's orders for the management of the grenadiers and light infantry in an action, and upon a march, came to my hands in the course of last month, and merits my thanks, as it may be of use to such corps, one of which (consisting of light infantry) we are now forming. The enemy are governed by no principles that ought to actuate honest men; no wonder then, that forgery should be amongst their other crimes. I have seen a letter published in a handbill at New York, and extracts of it republished in the Philadelphia paper, said to be from me to Mrs. Washington, not one word of which did I ever write; those contained in the pamphlet you speak of, are, I presume, equally genuine, and perhaps written by the same author. I should be glad however to see and examine the texture of them, if a favourable opportunity to send them should present.

Lord Cornwallis has certainly embarked for England, but with what view is not so easy to determine: he was eye witness a few days before his departure, to a scene not a little disgraceful to the pride of British valour, in their manoeuvre to Chestnut hill [on December 4, 1777], and precipitate return, after boasting their intentions of driving us beyond the mountains.

I am very glad to find that the assembly of Virginia, have taken matters up so spiritedly; but wish, instead of attempting to raise so many volunteers, they had resolved at all adventures to complete their regiments by drafting. If all the states would do this, and fall upon ways and means to supply their troops with comfortable clothing upon moderate terms, and Congress would make the commissions of officers of some value to them, every thing would probably go well, making at the same time some reform in the different departments of the army; nothing standing in greater need of it than the quartermasters and commissaries, as no army ever suffered more by their neglect; the consequences of this neglect are much to be dreaded. I am, etc.

Washington let the Conway group plot and correspond, waiting for the moment when they would overreach themselves. It finally came when one of Gates's aides, James Wilkinson, blabbed the whole scheme to one of Washington's generals. Loyally the general wrote to Washington, who blandly forwarded a quote from his letter to Gates. In a panic, Gates denied everything and blusteringly accused Washington of spying on his private correspondence. Conway, meanwhile, in a worse panic, admitted everything. Wilkinson, caught in the middle, challenged Gates to a duel. The plot collapsed into comic opera and ended with Gates writing Washinton a humble apology. Washington swiftly closed the matter with the following conciliatory letter.

Valley Forge, February 24, 1778.
SIR: I yesterday received your favor of the 19th. Instt. I am as averse to controversy, as any Man, and had I not been forced into it, you never would have had occasion to impute to me, even the

shadow of a disposition towards it. Your repeatedly and Solemnly disclaiming any offensive views, in those matters, which have been the subject of our past correspondence, makes me willing to close with the desire, you express, of burying them hereafter in silence, and as far as future events will permit, oblivion. My temper leads me to peace and harmony with all Men; and it is particularly my wish, to avoid any personal feuds or dissentions with those, who are embarked in the same great National interest with myself, as every difference of this kind must in its consequences be very injurious. I am etc.

Meanwhile, there was trouble at home. Lund Washington, the manager of Mount Vernon, was worried about the possibility of being drafted. This filled Washington with alarm, and he wrote home assuring Lund that he was performing an essential service where he was. The original letter has been lost. Only a portion survived, as an extract in Washington's letter book.

February 28, 1778.

. . . If you should happen to draw a *prize* in the *militia*, I must provide a man, either there or here, in your room; as nothing but your having the charge of my business, and the entire confidence I repose in you, could make me tolerable easy from home for such a length of time as I have been, and am likely to be. This therefore leads me to say, that I hope no motive, however powerful, will induce you to leave my business, whilst I, in a manner, am banished from home; because I should be unhappy to see it in common hands. For this reason, altho' from accidents and misfortunes not to be averted by human foresight, I make little or nothing from my Estate, I am still willing to increase your wages, and make it worth your while to continue with me. To go on in the improvement of my Estate in the manner heretofore described to you, fulfilling my plans, and keeping my property together, are the principal objects I have in view during these troubles; and firmly believing that they will be accomplished under your management,

as far as circumstances and acts of providence will allow, I feel
quite easy under disappointments; which I should not do, if my
business was in common hands, liable to suspicions. I am, etc.

*With all Washington's problems at Valley Forge, who should
appear on his doorstep but Bryan Fairfax. Now a professed loyalist,
this idealistic, complex man was horrified by the war and wished to
go to England to see if he could persuade the British leaders to accept a negotiated peace. Washington, at considerable personal risk,
received his old friend with the same hospitality he had always
shown him at Mount Vernon and arranged a safe conduct for him
through the American lines to New York. There Fairfax became so
discouraged by the attitude of British officials that he returned to
Virginia. From his home he wrote a noble letter, perhaps the
best testimony of Washington's genius for friendship. "At
a time your popularity was the highest and mine at the lowest and
when it is so common for men's resentments to run high against
those who differ from them in opinion, you should act with your
wonted kindness towards me hath affected me more than any favor
I have received; it could not be believed by some in New York, it
being above the run of common minds." Washington replies to
this generous tribute and comments wisely on the nature of the
revolutionary conflict.*

Valley forge, March 1, 1778.

DEAR SIR: Your favor of the 8th. of Decr. came safe to my hands
after a considerable delay in its passage. The sentiments you have
expressed of me in this Letter are highly flattering, meriting my
warmest acknowledgements, as I have too good an Opinion of your
sincerity and candour to believe that you are capable of unmeaning
professions and speaking a language foreign from your Heart. The
friendship I ever professed, and felt for you, met with no diminution from the difference in our political Sentiments. I know the
rectitude of my own intentions, and believing in the sincerity of
yours, lamented, though I did not condemn, your renunciation of
the creed I had adopted. Nor do I think any person, or power,

ought to do it, whilst your conduct is not opposed to the general Interest of the people and the measures they are pursuing; the latter, that is our actions, depending upon ourselves, may be controuled, while the powers of thinking originating in higher causes, cannot always be moulded to our wishes.

The determinations of Providence are all ways wise; often inscrutable, and though its decrees appear to bear hard upon us at times is nevertheless means for gracious purposes; in this light I cannot help viewing your late disappointments; for if you had been permitted to have gone to england, unrestrained even by the rigid oaths which are administered on those occns. your feelings as a husband, Parent, &ca. must have been considerably wounded in the prospect of a long, perhaps lasting seperation from your nearest relatives. What then must they have been if the obligation of an oath had left you without a Will? Your hope of being instrumental in restoring Peace would prove as unsubstantial as mist before the Noon days Sun and would as soon dispel: for believe me Sir great Britain understood herself perfectly well in this dispute but did not comprehend America. She meant as Lord Campden in his late speech in Parlt. clearly, and explicitly declared, to drive America into rebellion that her own purposes might be more fully answered by it but take this along with it, that this Plan originating in a firm belief, founded on misinformation, that no effectual opposition would or could be made, they little dreamt of what has happened and are disappd. in their views; does not every act of administration from the Tea Act to the present Session of Parliament declare this in plain and self evidt. Characters? Had the Comrs. any powers to treat with America? If they meant Peace, would Lord Howe have been detain in England 5 Months after passing the Act? Would the powers of these Comrs. have been confined to mere acts of grace, upon condition of absolute submission? No, surely, No! they meant to drive us into what they termed rebellion, that they might be furnished with a pretext to disarm and then strip us of the rights and privileges of Englishmen and Citizens. If they were actuated by principles of justice, why did they refuse indignantly to accede to the terms which were humbly supplicated before hostilities commenced and this Country deluged in Blood; and now make their principal Officers and even the Comrs. themselves say, that these terms are just and reasonable; Nay that more will be granted than we have yet asked, if we will relinquish our Claim to Independency. What Name does such conduct as this deserve? and what punishment is there in store for the Men who have distressed Millions, involved thousands in ruin, and plunged numberless families in inextricable woe? Could that wch. is just and reasonable now, have been unjust four Years ago? If not upon what principles, I say does Administration act? they must either be wantonly wicked and cruel, or (which is only anr. mode of describing the same thing) under false colours are now endeavouring to deceive the great body of the people, by industriously propagating a belief that G.B. is willing to offer any, and that we will accept of no terms; thereby hoping to poison and disaffect the Minds of those who wish for peace, and create feuds and dissentions among ourselves. In a word, having less dependance now, in their Arms than their Arts, they are practising such low and dirty tricks, that Men of Sentiment and honr. must blush at their Villainy, among other manoeuvres, in this way they are counterfeiting Letters, and publishing them, as intercepted ones of mine to prove that I am an enemy to the present measures, and have been led into them step by step still hoping that Congress would recede from their present claims. I am, etc.

Correspondence with one Fairfax apparently reminded Washington of the rest of the family. Here, in the midst of his continuing woes at Valley Forge, we see him writing a chatty letter to George William Fairfax, in England. For a mailman Washington used the captured British general John Burgoyne.

Head Quarters, Pennsa., March 11, 1778.
DEAR SIR: Immediately on my appointment to the command of the American Army and arrival at Cambridge (near Boston) in the year 1775, I informed you of the impracticability of my longer continuing to perform the duties of a friend by having an eye to the

conduct of your Collector and Steward, as my absence from Virginia would not only withdraw every little attention I otherwise might have given to your business; but involve my own in the same neglected predicament. What use you may have made of the information I know not, having heard nothing from you these four years, nor been in Virga. these last three.

I have heard, and fear it is true, that your Seat [Belvoir] is verging fast to destruction. In what condition, and under what management your estate in Berkeley is, I know not; and equally ignorant am I respecting the conduct of Peyton, but earnestly advise you to impower some person to attend to these matters, or the consequence is obvious.

Lord Fairfax (as I have been told) after having bowed down to the grave, and in a manner shaken hands with death, is perfectly restored, and enjoys his usual good health, and as much vigour as falls to the lot of Ninety. Your Sister Washington goes on teeming, but cannot produce a boy. Miss Fairfax was upon the point of Marriage in decemr. last with a relation of mine, a Mr. Whiting, but her ill health delayed it at that time, and what hath happend since I know not. Your Nieces in Alexandria are both Married, the elder to Mr. Herbert, the younger to Mr. Harry Whiting, Son of Frank in Berkeley. Mrs. Cary, her Son Colo. Cary, Mr. Nicholas, Mrs. Ambler, and their respective families were all well about two Months ago. Miss Cary is married to Tom Nelson, second Son to the Secretary.

Mrs. Washington who is now in Qrs. with me joins in most Affecte Complimts to Mrs. Fairfax and yourself, with, Dear Sir, etc.

The complicated family tree along which Washington so smoothly moves needs some explanation. The "Sister" Washington was Hannah Fairfax, wife of Warner Washington. The nieces in Alexandria were daughters of Major John Carlyle, who has appeared earlier. Mrs. Cary was Sally Cary's mother, and her son, Wilson Miles Cary, was Sally's brother. It was his daughter, another Sally, who was married to Tom Nelson, son of the much-

*revered elder statesman of Virginia, Thomas Nelson, Sr., known as
"the Secretary" for his long service to the House of Burgesses.*

*The next letter—to Jack Washington—is far removed from
this sunny domestic tone. The appearance of new British peace
commissioners, who made a last desperate attempt to lure the colonies back to allegiance before they signed an alliance with France,
greatly alarmed Washington.*

Valley-forge, May   , 1778.

DEAR BROTHER: Your letter of the 27th. of Mar. from Bushfield
came safe to hand, and gave me the pleasure of hearing, or rather
inferring (for you are not explicit) that my Sister and the rest of
your family were well. I thank you for your intelligence respecting
the pamphlet of forged Letters which Colo. Lee has, and said to be
written by me; not one sentence of which you may rely on it, did I
ever write; although so many little family circumstances are inter-
spersed through the whole performance to give it the air of authenticity. The Arts of the enemy, and the low dirty tricks which they
are daily practising is an evincing proof that they are lost to all
Sense of virtue and honor, and that they will stick at nothing however incompatible with truth and manliness to carry their points.
They have lately forged, and industriously circulated, a resolve for
Congress, purporting (after reciting with great propriety, and
plausibility, the inconveniences of short enlistments) that all Soldiers who have been drafted for periods short of the War, shall
nevertheless continue in Service during it; and by their emissaries
have endeavoured, and effected the injury of the Service by this
means, alarming the fears of the Soldiery and Country.

I am mistaken if we are not verging fast to one of the most
important periods that ever America saw; doubtless before this
reaches you, you will have seen the Draughts of two Bills intended
to be enacted into Laws, and Lord North's Speech upon the occasion; these our accts. from Phila. say, will be immediately followed
by the Commissioners; and Lord Amherst, Adml. Keppel, and
General Murray are said to be the Commissioners. These Gentlemen I presume, are to move in a civil and Military Line, as Genl.

Howe is certainly recalled, and report adds, Lord Howe also. Be this as it may, it will require all the skill, the wisdom, and policy, of the first abilities of these States, to manage the helm, and steer with judgment to the haven of our wishes through so many Shelves and Rocks, as will be thrown in our way. This, more than ever, is the time for Congress to be replete with the first characters in every State, instead of having a thin Assembly, and many States totally unrepresented, as is the case at present. I have often regretted the pernicious (and what appears to me, fatal) policy of having our able Men engaged in the formation of the more local Governments, and filling Offices in their respective States, leaving the great national concern, on wch. the superstructure of all, and every of them does absolutely depend, and without which none can exist, to be managed by Men of more contracted abilities, indeed those at a distance from the Seat of War live in such perfect tranquility that they conceive the dispute to be at an end in a manner, and those near hand it, are so disaffected that they only serve as embarrassments; between the two, therefore, time Slips away without the necessary means for opening the Campaign in time, or with propriety.

Your accts. of the high prices of fresh Provisions in Philadelphia are true, but it affects the Inhabitants more than the Soldiery, who have plenty of Salt Meat, Pease &ca.

Since I began this Letter, authentic accts. have come to my hands of France having declared the United States free and Independant, and guaranteeing to them all the Territory formerly ceeded by them to Great Britain. My acct. (from the Gentleman who was going on to Congress with the Treaty) adds, that France have done this in the most generous manner, and to our utmost wish. This is great, 'tis glorious News. and must put the Independency of America out of all manner of dispute. and accts. for the gentle gales which have succeeded rude Boreas, of late. A publication of this important intelligence will no doubt be directed by Congress and diffused through the Continent as speedily as possible, I shall add nothing further therefore on the Subject.

It would have been a happy circumstance if the several States had been industrious in pushing their recruits into the field, early; but I see little prospect of it at present, if ever. My love and best wishes, in which Mrs. Washington joins me attend My Sister and the rest of your family and with great truth I subscribe myself Yr., etc.

The news of the French alliance with the Americans forced the British to abandon Philadelphia and retreat to New York. Washington followed them across New Jersey, and at Monmouth Court House, fought one of the war's fiercest battles. The Americans considered it a victory. Even the British conceded it was a draw. Here Washington tells the story to Jack.

Brunswick in New Jersey, July 4, 1778.
DEAR BROTHER: Your Letter of the 20th. Ulto. came to my hands last Night; before this will have reached you, the Acct. of the Battle of Monmouth probably will get to Virginia; which, from an unfortunate, and bad beginning, turned out a glorious and happy day.

The Enemy evacuated Philadelphia on the 18th. Instt.; at ten oclock that day I got intelligence of it, and by two oclock, or soon after, had Six Brigades on their March for the Jerseys, and followed with the whole Army next Morning. On the 21st. we compleated our passage over the Delaware at Coryells ferry (abt. 33 Miles above Philadelphia) distant from Valley forge near 40 Miles. From this Ferry we moved down towards the Enemy, and on the 27th. got within Six Miles of them.

General Lee having the command of the Van of the Army, consisting of fully 5000 chosen Men, was ordered to begin the Attack next Morning so soon as the enemy began their March, to be supported by me. But, strange to tell! when he came up with the enemy, a retreat commenced; whether by his order, or from other causes, is now the subject of inquiry, and consequently improper to be descanted on, as he is in arrest, and a Court Martial sitting for tryal of him. A Retreat however was the fact, be the causes as they may; and the disorder arising from it would have proved fatal to the Army had not that bountiful Providence which has never failed us in the hour of distress, enabled me to form a Regiment or two (of those that were retreating) in the face of the Enemy, and under their fire, by which means a stand was made long enough (the place through which the enemy were pursuing being narrow) to form the Troops that were advancing, upon an advantageous piece of Ground in the rear; hence our affairs took a favourable turn, and from being pursued, we drove the Enemy back, over the ground they had followed us, recovered the field of Battle, and possessed ourselves of their dead. but, as they retreated behind a Morass very difficult to pass, and had both Flanks secured with thick Woods, it was found impracticable with our Men fainting with fatigue, heat, and want of Water, to do any thing more that Night. In the Morning we expected to renew the Action, when behold the enemy had stole of as Silent as the Grave in the Night after having sent away their wounded. Getting a Nights March of us, and having but ten Miles to a strong post, it was judged inexpedient to follow them any further, but move towards the North River least they should have any design upon our posts there.

We buried 245 of their dead on the field of Action; they buried several themselves, and many have been since found in the Woods, where, during the action they had drawn them to, and hid them. We have taken five Officers and upwards of One Hundred Prisoners, but the amount of their wounded we have not learnt with any certainty; according to the common proportion of four or five to one, there should be at least a thousand or 1200. Without exagerating, their trip through the Jerseys in killed, Wounded, Prisoners, and deserters, has cost them at least 2000 Men and of their best Troops. We had 60 Men killed, 132 Wounded, and abt. 130 Missing, some of whom I suppose may yet come in. Among our Slain Officers is Majr. Dickenson, and Captn. Fauntleroy, two very valuable ones.

I observe what you say concerning voluntary enlistments, or rather your Scheme for raising 2000 Volunteers; and candidly own to you I have no opinion of it; these measures only tend to burthen the public with a number of Officers without adding one jot to your strength, but greatly to confusion, and disorder. If the several

States would but fall upon some vigorous measures to fill up their respective Regiments nothing more need be asked of them, but while these are neglected, or in other words ineffectually and feebly attended to, and these succedaniums tried, you never can have an army to be depended upon.

The Enemy's whole force Marched through the Jerseys (that were able) except the Regiment of Anspach, which, it is said, they were affraid to trust, and therefore sent them round to New York by Water, along with the Commissioners; I do not learn that they have received much of a reinforcement as yet; nor do I think they have much prospect of any, worth Speaking of, as I believe they Stand very critically with respect to France.

As the Post waits I shall only add my love to my Sister and the family, and Strong assurances of being with the Sincerest regard and Love, Yr. most Affectt. Brother.

Licking their wounds, the British retreated into their New York bastion, and Washington began a long semi-siege outside the city. The summer slipped away with no real fighting. The only major operation was an attempt to bag the British garrison in Rhode Island, with the aid of a French fleet. The arrival of a relieving British fleet, an unfortunate storm, and indecision in the attacking American army turned the expedition into a near disaster. Lafayette, who was involved in it, returned to Philadelphia in a very bad mood and challenged one of the British commissioners, Lord Carlyle, to a duel because of certain remarks he had passed which struck the marquis as disrespectful to France. Here Washington advises his "adopted son" against such derring-do.

Fish-kill, October 4, 1778.

MY DEAR MARQUIS: I have had the pleasure of receiving, by the hands of Monsr. de la Colombe, your favour of the 28th. Ulto.; accompanied by one of the 24th., which he overtook somewhere on the Road. The leave requested in the former, I am as much interested to grant, as to refuse my approbation of the Cartel, proposed in the latter.

The generous Spirit of Chivalry, exploded by the rest of the World, finds a refuge, My dear friend, in the sensibility of your Nation *only*. But it is in vain to cherish it, unless you can find Antagonists to support it; and however well adapted it might have been to the times in which it existed, in our days it is to be feared that your opponent, sheltering himself behind Modern opinion, and under his present public Character of Commissioner, would turn a virtue of such ancient date, into ridicule. Besides, supposing his Lordship accepted your terms, experience has proved, that chance is as often, as much concerned in deciding these matters as bravery, and always more than the justice of the Cause; I would not therefore have your life, by the remotest possibility, exposed, when it may be reserved for so many greater occasions. His Excellency the Admiral I flatter myself, will be in Sentimt. with me; and, as soon as he can spare you, send you to head Quarters, where I anticipate the pleasure of seeing you.

Having wrote very fully to you a few days ago, and put the Letter under cover to Genl. Sullivan, I have naught to add at this time, but to assure you, that with the most perfect regard, I am etc.

Another correspondent who slowly achieved the status of friend during these trying months was Gouverneur Morris. Eccentric scion of a prominent landed New York family, he served in the Continental Congress during the years 1778 and 1779 and put his keen mind to work on the nation's tangled financial and diplomatic problems. He inspected the army in Valley Forge and there came to know Washington to whom he remained devoted for life. One of Morris' letters on finance brought forth the following reply from Washington.

Fish-kill, October 4, 1778.

DEAR SIR: My public Letters to the President of Congress will inform you of the Wind that wafted me to this place; nothing more therefore need be said on that head.

Your Letter of the 8th. Ulto. contains three questions and answers, to wit: Can the Enemy prosecute the War? Do they mean to stay on the Continent? And is it our interest to put impediments in the way of their departure? To the first you answer in the Negative; to the second you are decided in opinion that they do not; And to the third, say, clearly No.

Much, my good Sir, may be said in favor of these answers; and some things against the two first of them. By way therefore of dissertation on the first, I will also beg leave to put a question, and give it an answer. Can *we* carry on the War much longer? certainly NO, unless some measures can be devised, and speedily executed, to restore the credit of our Currency, restrain extortion, and punish forestallers.

Without these can be effected, what funds can stand the present expences of the Army? And what Officer can bear the weight of prices, that every necessary Article is now got to? A Rat, in the shape of a Horse, is not to be bought at this time for less than £200; a Saddle under thirty or Forty; Boots twenty, and Shoes and other articles in like proportion. How is it possible therefore for Officers to stand this, without an increase of pay? And how is it possible to advance their Pay when Flour is selling (at different places) from five to fifteen pounds pr. Ct. [per hundred weight], Hay from ten to thirty pounds pr. Tunn, and Beef and other essentials, in this proportion.

The true point of light then to place, and consider this matter in, is not simply whether G. Britain can carry on the War, but whose Finances (theirs or ours) is most likely to fail: which leads me to doubt *very much* the infalibility of the answer given to your Second question, respecting the Enemy's leaving the Continent; for I believe, that they will not do it, while ever *hope* and the chapter of *accidents* can give them a *chance* of bringing us to terms short of *Independance*. But this *you* perhaps will say, they are now bereft of. *I* shall acknowledge that many things favor the idea; but add, that upon a comparative view of circumstances there is abundant matter to puzzle and confound the judgment. To your third answer, I subscribe with hand and heart. the opening is now fair, and God grant they may embrace the oppertunity of bidding an eternal adieu to our, once quit of them, happy Land. If the

Spaniards would but join their Fleets to those of France, and commence hostilities, my doubts would all subside. Without it, I fear the British Navy has it too much in its power to counteract the Schemes of France.

The high prices of every necessary. The little, indeed no benefit, which Officers have derived from the intended bounty of Congress in the article of Cloathing, The change in the establishment, by which so many of them are discontinued. The unfortunate delay of this business, which kept them too long in suspence, and set a number of evil spirits to work. The unsettled Rank, and contradictory modes of adjusting it, with other causes which might be enumerated, have conspired to sour the temper of the Army exceedingly; and has, I am told, been productive of a Memorial, or representation of some kind, to Congress, which neither directly, nor indirectly did I know, or ever hear was in agitation, till some days after it was dispatched; owing, as I apprehend, to the secrecy with which it was conducted to keep it from my knowledge, as I had in a similar instance last Spring, discountenanced and stifled a child of the same illigitimacy in its birth. If you have any News worth communicating, do not put it under a bushel, but transmit it to Dr. Sir, Yrs. sincerely.

Washington had little inclination for personal correspondence during these dreary months. Even the letters he wrote home were largely concerned with business affairs. Lafayette, the man who had the strongest hold on Washington's emotions, was in France. This letter brings the adopted son up to date on affairs in America. From the personal side, it is one of the richest letters Washington ever wrote, revealing his sense of inferiority about his poor education, his rough masculine humor, the warmth with which he returned Lafayette's friendship.

West-point, September 30, 1779.
MY DEAR MARQS: A few days ago I wrote you a letter in much haste. the cause a sudden notification of Monsr. Gerards [outgoing French ambassador] having changed the place of his embarkation

from Boston (as was expected) to Philadelphia, and the hurry Monsir. de la Colombe [a Lafayette aide] was in to reach the latter before the Minister should have left it. Since that, I have been honourd with the company of the Chevr. de la Luzerne [new French ambassador], and by him was favour'd with your obliging letter of the 12th. of June which filled me with equal pleasure and surprise; the latter at hearing that you had not received one of the many letters I had written to you, since you left the American Shore. I cannot at this time charge my memory with the precise dates of these letters but the first, which ought and I expected would have reached you at Boston and I much wished it to do so because it contained a Letter from me to Doctr Franklin [Benjamin Franklin, American Ambassador to France] expressive of the Sentiments I entertained of your Services and merit was put into the hands of a Captn. McQueen of Charles Town, who was to Sail from Phila. soon after. In March I wrote you once or twice, and in June or the first of July following, (when it was reported that Monsr. Gerard was about to leave us I took the liberty of committing to his care another of my lettrs. to you,) which sevl. efforts though they may have been unsuccessful will exhibit no bad specimen of my having kept you constantly in remembrance and a desire of giving you proofs of it.

It gave me infinite pleasure to hear from yourself of the favourable reception you met with from your Sovereign, and of the joy which your safe arrival in France had diffused among your friends. I had no doubt but that this wou'd be the case; to hear it from yourself adds pleasure to the acct. and here My dear friend let me congratulate you on your new, honourable and pleasing appointment in the Army commanded by the Count de Vaux which I shall accompy. with an assurance that none can do it with more warmth of Affection, or sincere joy than myself. Your forward zeal in the cause of liberty; Your singular attachment to this infant World; Your ardent and persevering efforts, not only in America but since your return to France to serve the United States; Your polite attention to Americans, and your strict and uniform friend-

ship for *me*, has ripened the first impressions of esteem and attachment which I imbibed for you into such perfect love and gratitude
that neither time nor absence can impair which will warrant my
assuring you, that whether in the character of an Officer at the
head of a Corps of gallant French (if circumstances should require
this) whether as a Major Genl. commanding a division of the
American Army; Or whether, after our Swords and Spears have
given place to the plough share and pruning hook, I see you as a
private Gentleman, a friend and Companion, I shall welcome you
in all the warmth of friendship to Columbia's shore; and in the latter case, to my rural Cottage, where homely fare and a cordial reception shall be substituted for delicacies and costly living. this
from past experience I know *you* can submit to; and if the lovely
partner of your happiness will consent to participate with *us* in
such rural entertainment and amusemts. I can undertake in behalf
of Mrs. Washington that she will do every thing in her power to
make Virginia agreeable to the Marchioness. My inclination and
endeavours to do this cannot be doubted when I assure you that I
love everybody that is dear to you. consequently participate in the
pleasure you feel in the prospt. of again becoming a parent and do
most Sincerely congratulate you and your Lady on this fresh pledge
she is about to give you of her love.

I thank you for the trouble you have taken, and your polite attention in favouring me with a Copy of your letter to Congress;
and feel as I am perswaded they must do, the force of such ardent
zeal as you there express for the interest of this Country. The
propriety of the hint you have given them must carry conviction
and I trust will have a salutary effect; tho' there is not, I believe,
the same occasion for the admonition now, there was some months
ago; many late changes have taken place in that honourable body
which has removed in a very great degree, if not wholly, the dis-
cordant spirit which it is said prevailed in the Winter, and I hope
measures will also be taken to remove those unhappy and improper
differences which have extended themselves elsewhere to the prejudice of our affairs in Europe.

You enquire after Monsr. de la Colombe, and Colo. Neville [Presley Neville of Virginia, another Lafayette aide]; the first (who has been with Baron de Kalb *) left this a few days ago, as I have already observed, for Phila., in expectation of a passage with Monsr. Gerard. Colo. Neville called upon me about a Month since and was to have dined with us the next day but did not come, since which I have not seen him, nor do I know at this time where he is; he had then but just returned from his own home; and it was the first time I had seen him since he parted with you at Boston. It is probable he may be with the Virginia Troops which lye at the mouth of Smiths clove abt. 30 Miles from hence.

I have had great pleasure in the visit which the Chevalier de la Luzerne and Monsr. Marbois did me the honor to make at this Camp; for both of whom I have imbibed the most favourable impressions, and thank you for the honourable mention you made of me to them. The Chevr. till he had announced himself at Congress, did not choose to be received in his public character. If he had, except paying him Military honors, It was not my intention to depart from that plain and simple manner of living which accords with the real Interest and policy of Men struggling under every difficulty for the attainment of the most inestimable blessing of life, Liberty; the Chevalier was polite enough to approve my principle, and condescended to appear pleased with our Spartan living. In a word he made us all exceeding happy by his affability and good humour, while he remained in Camp.

You are pleased my dear Marquis to express an earnest desire of seeing me in France (after the establishment of our Independancy) and do me the honour to add, that you are not singular in your request. let me entreat you to be perswaded, that to meet you anywhere after the final accomplishment of so glorious an event would contribute to my happiness; and that, to visit a country to whose generous aid we stand so much indebted, would be an additional pleasure; but remember my good friend, that I am unacquainted with your language. that I am too far advanced in years

* A French-trained volunteer who had been given command of an American division; he was killed eleven months later at the battle of Camden, South Carolina.

to acquire a knowledge of it. and that to converse through the medium of an interpreter upon common occasions, especially with the *Ladies* must appr. so extremely aukward, insipid, and uncouth, that I can scarce bear it in idea. I will therefore hold myself disengaged for the *present* and when I see you in Virginia, we will talk of this matter and fix our plans.

The declaration of Spain in favour of France has given universal joy to every Whig, while the poor Tory droops like a withering flower under a declining Sun.

We are anxiously expecting to hear of great and important events on your side of the Atlantic. At prest. the imagination is left in the wide field of conjecture. Our eyes one moment are turned to an Invasion of England. then of Ireland. Minorca, Gibralter, &ca. In a word we hope every thing, but know not what to expect or where to fix.

The glorious successes of Count D'Estaing * in the West Indies at the same time that it adds dominion to France and fresh lustre to her Arms is a source of *new* and unexpected misfortune to our *tender* and *generous parent* and must serve to convince her of the folly of quitting the substance in pursuit of a shadow; and as there is no experience equal to that which is bought I trust she will have a superabundance of this kind of knowledge and be convinced as I hope all the World, and every tyrant in it will that the best and only safe road to honour, glory, and true dignity, is *justice*.

We have such repeated advices of Count D'Estaings being in these Seas that (though I have no official information of the event) I cannot help giving entire credit to the report and looking for his arrival every moment and am preparing accordingly. The enemy at New York also expect it, and to guard agt. the consequences as much as it is in their power to do, are reparing and strengthening all the old fortifications and adding New ones in the vicinity of the City; their fear however does not retard an embarkation which was making (and generally believed) to be for the

---

* The commander of the French fleet that had failed so miserably in the Rhode Island operation. In the West Indies he captured the islands of St. Vincent and Grenada, and fought a drawn battle with the British fleet under Admiral John Byron.

West Indies or Charles Town. It still goes forward, and by my intelligence will consist of a pretty large detachment. About 14 days ago one british Regiment (the 44th, compleated) and 3 Hessign Regiments were embarked and are gone, as is supposed, to Hallifax. Under convoy of Admiral Arbuthnot about the 20th. of last month the Enemy recd. a reinforcement consisting of two new raised Scotch Regts. some drafts and a few Recruits amounting altogether to about 3000 Men and a few days ago Sir Andw. Hammond arrived with (as it is said) abt. 2000 more; many of these new Troops died on their passage and since landing, the rest are very sickly as indeed their whole Army is while ours keeps remarkably healthy.

The Operations of the enemy this campaign have been confined to the establishment of works of defence. taking a post at Kings ferry, and burning the defenceless towns of New haven, Fairfield, Norwalk, &ca. on the sound within reach of their Shipping where little else was, or could be opposed to them than the cries of distressed Women and helpless children; but these were offered in vain; since these notable exploits they have never stepped out of their Works or beyond their lines. How a conduct of this kind is to effect the conquest of America the wisdom of a North, a Germaine, or Sandwich [leading British cabinet ministers] best can tell. It is too deep and refined for the comprehension of common understandings and general run of politicians.

Colo. Fleury [French volunteer, an engineer of great ability] who I expect will have the honour of presenting this letter to you, and who acted an important and honourable part in the event, will give you the particulars of the assault and reduction of Stony point the capture of the G. consg. of 600 men with their Colours, Arms, Baggage, Stores, 15 pieces of valuable ordnance, &ca. He led one of the columns; struck the colours of the garrison with his own hands; and in all respects behaved with that intrepidity and intelligence which marks his conduct upon all occasions.

Since that event we surprized and took Paulus hook a very strong fortified post of the enemys, opposite to the city of New York and within reach of the batteries of that place. The garrison consisting of about 160 Men with the colors were brought off, but none of the stores could be removed on acct. of its insular situation and the difficulty of removing them; the first of these enterprizes was made under the command of General Wayne; the other was conducted by Majr. Lee of the light Horse both of whom have acquired much honor by their gallant behaviour in the respective attacks.

By my last advices from Genl. Sullivan * of the 9th. Instt. I am led to conclude that ere this he has completed the entire destruction of the whole Country of the Six nations, excepting so much of it as is inhabited by the Oneidas who have always lived in amity with us; and a few towns belonging to the Cayugas and Onondago's who were disposed to be friendly. At the time these advices came away he had penetrated to the heart of their settlements after having defeated in a general engagement the united force of Indians, Tories, and regulars from Niagara. Burnt between 15 and 20 Towns, destroyed their Crops and every thing that was to be found. He was then advancing to the exterior Towns with a view to complete the desolation of the whole Country, and Remove the cruel inhabitants of it to a greater distance, who were then fleeing in the utmost confusion, consternation and distress towards Niagara, distant 100 Miles through an uninhabited wilderness; experiencing a little of that distress, but nothing of those cruelties which they have exercised on our unhappy frontier Settlers, who (Men, Women and Children) have been deliberately murdered, in a manner shocking to humanity.

But to conclude, you requested from me a long letter, I have given you one; but methinks my dear Marquis, I hear you say, there is reason in all things; that this is too long. I am clearly in sentiment with you, and will have mercy on you in my next. But at present must pray your patience a while longer, till I can make a tender of my most respectful compliments to the Marchioness. Tell her (if you have not made a mistake, and offered your *own*

* Maj. Gen. John Sullivan defeated fifteen hundred Indians, loyalists, and British at Newton, New York, on May 29. This, and the destruction of forty villages by his forces, all but ended the threat of the Iroquois—or, as Washington calls them, the six nations.

love instead of *hers* to me) that I have a heart susceptable of the tenderest passion, and that it is already so strongly impressed with the most favourable ideas of her, that she must be cautious of putting loves torch to it; as you must be in fanning the flame. But here again methinks I hear you say, I am not apprehensive of danger. My wife is young, you are growing old and the atlantic is between you. All this is true, but know my good friend that no distance can keep *anxious* lovers long asunder, and that the Wonders of former ages may be revived in this. But alas! will you not remark that amidst all the wonders recorded in holy writ no instance can be produced where a young Woman from *real inclination* has prefered an old man. This is so much against me that I shall not be able I *fear* to contest the prize with you, yet, under the encouragement you have given me I shall enter the list for so inestimable a Jewell.

I will now reverse the scene, and inform you, that Mrs. Washington (who set out for Virginia when we took the field in June) often has in, her letters to me, enquired if I had heard from you, and will be much pleased at hearing that you are well, and happy. In her name (as she is not here) I thank you for your polite attention to her; and shall speak her sense of the honor confered on her by the Marchioness.

When I look back to the length of this letter I am so much astonished and frightened at it myself, that I have not the courage to give it a careful reading for the purpose of correction. You must therefore receive it with all its imperfections, accompanied with this assurance that though there may be many incorrections in the letter, there is not a single defect in the friendship of my dear Marquis Yr., etc.

The year 1779 dribbled to a close with nothing but worry and disappointment as Washington's reward for his perseverance. The French fleet failed to support him in a hoped-for attack on New York. Instead, the French admiral chose Savannah, Georgia, as his target, landed troops, made an impatient assault, and was beaten off with heavy losses. An attack on Staten Island over the ice fizzled. The Continental currency continued to collapse and supplies for the army were almost nonexistent. *The first months of 1780 were even gloomier. The British campaign in the south reached a climax with the capture of Charleston, South Carolina, and its defending army of 5,400 men. During these months Washington wrote few personal letters. Those few reflected the listless, all but lifeless state of the American war effort.*

Frustration and more frustration is the theme of the following letter to his brother Samuel.

Camp near Fort Lee, August 31, 1780.

DEAR BROTHER: Your letter of the 31st. Ulto. came to my hands by the last Post, from Philadelphia. It gave me much concern to find by it, that you were in such bad health. I hope this, if it should arrive safe, will find you much amended.

It is a considerable time since I wrote to you. in truth it is rare for me to put pen to paper for private corrispondencies, so much is my time and attention engrossed by public business. I wish I could add, as profitably as it might be, but the fatal system of policy whh. we have adopted, and for ought I see to the contrary, are determined to persist in, prevents this.

We are always without an Army, or have a raw and undisciplined one, engaged for so short a time that we are not fit either for the purposes of offence or defence, much less is it in our power to project schemes and execute plans which depend upon well disciplined and permanent Troops. One half the year is spent in getting Troops into the Field, the other half is lost in discharging them, from their limited Service, and the manner and time in which they come and go, the public in the meanwhile incurring an immense expence in paying two setts, that is, the comers and goers, at the same instant. In a waste of Provisions, Stores, Arms, and a thousand things which can scarce be enumerated. In a word short enlistments has been the primary cause of the continuance of the War, and every evil which has been experienced in the course of it. It has been the source from whence the depreciation of our money has flowed, and though it is the cause of our present embarrassments, I much question whether our eyes are yet opened; and whether the fatal policy which heretofore has governed all our measures will not direct Us to another short enlistment when the present force leaves us. It is impossible for any person at a distance to have an idea of my embarrassments, or to conceive how an Army can be kept together under such circumstances as ours is; half its time without Provision, Cloathing or pay.

The flattering prospect which seemed to be opening to our view in the Month of May is vanishing like the Morning Dew. The States, instead of sending the full number of men required of them by the first of July, the consequent supplies, have not furnished one half of them yet. and the second division of French Troops and Ships not being arrived, nor any certainty when they will, I despair of doing anything in this quarter this Campaign, and what may be the consequence, if the combined Arms of France and Spain are not more prosperous in Europe or the West Indies, I shall leave to others to predict. At best, the Troops we have, are only fed from hand to Mouth. and for the last four or five days have been without Meat. In short the limits of a letter would convey very inadequate ideas of our disagreeable situation; and the wretched manner in which our business is conducted. I shall not attempt it therefore, but leave it to some future Pen, and a more favourable period for truths to shine.

The first division of French Troops (as no doubt you have heard) are at Rhode Island, where their Squadron is blocked up by the British fleet under Arbuthnot of superior force. The Army under my command is incamped on the West bank of the North or Hudsons River, about fifteen Miles from the City of New York and within full view of the Enemy, the River only between us. We lately made a Forage opposite to the City and expected to be opposed in it but were not.

I sincerely wish you a perfect restoration of health, and the enjoyment of every blessing of life. My best regards attend my Sister (with whom I should be happy in a better acquaintance) * and all your family, and with the greatest truth I remain Yrs. etc.

* Samuel's fourth wife had died, and he had remarried.

P.S. Have you ever taken the necessary steps to save my Lotts at the Warm Springs?

Now came two blows in swift succession. An army sent south under the command of Horatio Gates, Washington's old enemy, was totally defeated at Camden, South Carolina. A few weeks later came the discovery of Arnold's conspiracy to betray West Point to the enemy. Washington discusses Arnold's treason, which shook the army to its foundations, in a letter to his former aide, Lt. Col. John Laurens, who was on parole after his capture at Charleston.

Hd. Qrs., *Passaic Falls,* October 13, 1780.

MY DEAR LAURENS: Your friendly and Affectione. letter of the 4th. came to my hands on the 10th. and would have been acknowledged yesterday by the Baron de Steuben but for some important business I was preparing for Congress.

In no instance since the commencement of the War has the interposition of Providence appeared more conspicuous than in the rescue of the Post and Garrison of West point from Arnolds villainous perfidy. How far he meant to involve me in the catastrophe of this place does not appear by any indubitable evidence, and I am rather inclined to think he did not wish to hazard the more important object of his treachery by attempting to combine two events the lesser of which might have marred the greater. A combination of extraordinary circumstances. An unaccountable deprivation of presence of Mind in a man of the first abilities, and the virtuous conduct of three Militia men, threw the Adjutant General of the British forces in America (with full proofs of Arnolds treachery) into our hands; and but for the egregious folly, or the bewildered conception of Lieutt. Colo. Jamieson who seemed lost in astonishment and not to have known what he was doing I should as certainly have got Arnold. Andre has met his fate, and with that fortitude which was to be expected from an accomplished man, and gallant Officer. But I am mistaken if at *this time,* Arnold is undergoing the torments of a mental Hell. He wants feeling! From some traits of his character which have lately come to my knowledge, he seems to have been so hackneyed in villainy, and so lost to all sense of honor and shame that while his faculties will enable him to continue his sordid pursuits there will be no time for remorse.

Believe me sincere when I assure you, that my warmest wishes accompany Captn. Wallops endeavours and your expectations of exchange; and that nothing but the principle of Justice and policy wch. I have religiously adhered to of exchanging Officers in the order of their Captivity (where rank would apply) has prevented my every exertion to obtain your release and restoration to a family [Washington's staff] where you will be receiv'd with open arms by every individual of it; but from none with more cordiality and true affection than Your Sincere friend etc.

Meanwhile the defeat at Camden brought on Gates's complete downfall. Congress gave Washington his choice of a successor and he swiftly decided that Nathanael Greene, his second in command, was the man for the job. In a letter to George Mason, his Virginia neighbor and a power among southern politicians, Washington attempts to smooth the path for Greene.

Head Quarters, Passaic Falls,
October 22, 1780.

DEAR SIR: In consequence of a resolve of Congress directing an enquiry into the conduct of Genl. Gates, and authorising me to appoint some other Officer in his place during this enquiry, I have made choice of Majr. Genl. Greene who will, I expect, have the honor of presenting you with this Letter.

I can venture to introduce this Gentn. to you as a man of abilities bravery and coolness. He has a comprehensive knowledge of our affairs, and is a man of fortitude and resources. I have not the smallest doubt therefore, of his employing all the means which may be put into his hands to the best advantage; nor of his assisting in pointing out the most likely ones to answer the purposes of his command. With this character, I take the liberty of recommending him to your civilities and support; for I have no doubt, from the embarrassed situation of Southern affairs; of his standing much in need of the latter from every Gentn. of Influence in the Assemblies of those States.

As General Greene can give you the most perfect information, in detail of our present distresses, and future prospects, I shall content myself with giving the agregate acct. of them; and with respect to the first, they are so great and complicated, that it is scarcely within the powers of description to give an adequate idea of them; with regard to the second, unless there is a material change both in our military, and civil policy, it will be in vain to contend much longer.

We are without money, and have been so for a great length of time, without provision and forage except what is taken by Impress; without Cloathing; and shortly shall be (in a manner) without Men. In a word, we have lived upon expedients till we can live no longer, and it may truly be said that, the history of this War is a history of false hopes, and temporary devices, instead of System, and oeconomy which results from it.

If we mean to continue our struggles (and it is to be hoped we shall not relinquish our claim) we must do it upon an entire new plan. We must have a permanent force; not a force that is constantly fluctuating and sliding from under us as a pedestal of Ice would do from a Statue in a Summers day. Involving us in expence that baffles all calculation, an expence which no funds are equal to. We must at the same time contrive ways and means to aid our Taxes by Loans, and put our finance upon a more certain and stable footing than they are at prest. Our Civil government must likewise undergo a reform, ample powers must be lodged in Congress as the head of the Federal Union, adequate to all the purposes of War. Unless these things are done, our efforts will be in vain, and only serve to accumulate expence, add to our perplexities, and dissatisfy the people without a prospect of obtaining the prize in view. but these Sentimts. do not appear well in a hasty letter, without digestion or order. I have not time to give them otherwise;

and shall only assure you that they are well meant, however crude they may appear. With sincere Affectn. and esteem etc.

Lafayette had returned to America, bringing with him a four thousand-man French expeditionary force, but Washington's depleted army was too weak to enable the allies to take the offensive, and the French decided to stay put in Newport, Rhode Island, where they landed. This inaction mortified Lafayette, and his emotion-charged letters caused Washington and the French commander, Rochambeau, much embarrassment. Here Washington attempts to cool off his agitated warrior "son."

October 30, 1780.

It is impossible my Dear Marquis to desire more ardently than I do to terminate the campaign by some happy stroke; but we must consult our means rather than our wishes; and not endeavour to better our affairs by attempting things, which for want of success may make them worse. We are to lament that there has been a misapprehension of our circumstances in Europe; but to endeavour to recover our reputation, we should take care that we do not injure it more.

Ever since it became evident that the allied arms could not co-operate with this campaign, I have had an eye to the point you mention, determined if a favourable opening should offer to embrace it; but so far as my information goes, the enterprise would not be warranted. It would in my opinion be imprudent to throw an Army of ten thousand men upon an Island against Nine thousand, exclusive of seamen and militia. This from the accounts we have appears to be the enemy's force. All we can therefore do at present is to endeavour to gain a more certain knowledge of their situation and act accordingly. This I have been some time employed in doing but hitherto with little success. I shall thank you for any aids you can afford. Arnold's flight seems to have frightened all my intelligencers out of their senses. I am etc.

CHAPTER SIX

The "Luckiest" Victory

*A*s the war moved to its climax, Washington's personal correspondence dwindled almost to the vanishing point. In the following letter to Lund Washington he is at first disgusted by the failure of a French attempt to capture Benedict Arnold and his raiding battalions in Virginia. Then in a sudden change of subject, he shows that Mount Vernon is still very much on his mind, though he has not seen it in six years.

New Windsor, March 28, 1781.

DEAR LUND: . . . We have heard nothing certain of the two Fleets since they left their respective ports. We wait with impatient anxiety for advices from Chesapeake, and the Southern Army. God send they may be favourable to us; a detachment from New York has made two or three attempts to put to Sea (for the purpose, it is said, of reinforcing either Arnold or Cornwallis *) and as often returned. My last accts. from New York mention another attempt on the 25th; but whether with truth, or not, it is not in my power to say. It was unfortunate; but this I mention in confidence, that the French Fleet and detachment did not undertake the enterprize they are now upon, when I first proposed it to them; the destruction of Arnolds Corps would then have been inevitable before the British fleet could have been in a condition to put to Sea. instead of this the small squadron, which took the Romulus and other Vessels was sent, and could not, as I foretold, do any thing without a Land force at Portsmouth.

How many Lambs have you had this Spring? How many Colts are you like to have? Is your covered ways done? What are you going about next? Have you any prospect of getting paint and Oyl?

* Cornwallis was heading another British army in the Carolinas.

Are you going to repair the Pavement of the Piazza? is anything doing, or like to be done with respect to the Wall at the edge of the Hill in front of the House? Have you made good the decayed Trees at the ends of the House, in the Hedges, &ca. Have you made any attempts to reclaim more Land for meadow? &ca. &ca. An acct. of these things would be satisfactory to me, and infinitely amusing in the recital, as I have these kind of improvements very much at heart. As soon as you can conveniently do it after receipt of this letter, give me a list of the number and kind of Mares I possess. the number of Colts from 4 years old (inclusive) to those of this spring with the ages, colour, kind, and Sexes. Mrs. Washington (from report only, I believe) has taken a fancy to a Horse belonging to Mr. James Cleveland, brother to the one had from him before (and wch. I think a fine horse), if you can get him in the way of barter, provided he is as handsome, and as fine a horse as represented, and the colour of the set she drives, I shall be very well pleased with your doing it.

Washington's letter to Lund criticizing the French operation to relieve Virginia was captured by the British and published in Rivington's Gazette, the Loyalist newspaper in New York. It upset the French considerably, and Lafayette, in Virginia attempting to repel the British raiders, wrote to Washington asking if it was true. Toward the end of his reply, Washington remarks on another unhappy minor episode, the resignation of Alexander Hamilton as his aide. Hamilton resigned in a pique when Washington reprimanded him for letting his chief wait at the head of the stairs for ten minutes while Hamilton chatted with Lafayette. Washington now explains why he never mentioned the affair to Lafayette.

New Windsor, April 22, 1781.

MY DEAR MARQS: Since writing the inclosed your several letters (acknowledged in my public one of this date) are come to hand; all of them except that of the 12th arrived at Hd. Quarters within the course of one hour.

The reasons assigned in some of your letters, and others which have occurred to me, chiefly of a political nature, assure me that great advantages will be derived from your being wherever the French Army and the American head Quarters are. I therefore not only repeat the offer contained in the inclosed letter, but accompany it with a wish that you may return, if you can, consistently with your own inclination, relinquish your present command for the prospects I have mentioned; not else; as it always has been, and ever will be my wish to make things as agreeable to you as the nature of the service will admit. To recall the detachment I cannot, for reasons which in my judgment are conclusive.

The accidents to which letters are liable, forbid me, unless I could write to you in cypher, to go into a full explanation of some matters wch. you seem not to be well informd of and wch. I wish to set you write in; but I dare not attempt it in a common letter; nor will there be any necessity for it if you return.

I am very sorry that any letter of mine should be the subject of public discussion, or give the smallest uneasiness to any person living. The letter, to which I presume you allude, was a confidential one from me to Mr. Lund Washington (with whom I have lived in perfect intimacy for near 20 Years). I can neither avow the letter as it is published by Mr. Rivington, nor declare that it is spurious, because my letter to this Gentn. was wrote in great haste, and no copy of it was taken; all I remember of the matter is, that at the time of writing it, I was a good deal chagreened to find by your letter of the 15th. of March (from York Town in Virginia) that the French fleet had not, at that time, appeared within the Capes of Chesapeak; and meant (in strict confidence) to express my apprehensions and concern for the delay; but as we know that the alteration of a single word does, oftentimes; pervert the Sense, or give force to expression unintended by the letter writer, I should not be surprized at Mr. Rivington's or the Inspector of his Gazette having taken this liberty with the letter in question; especially as he, or they have I am told, published a letter from me to Govr. Hancock and his answer, which never had an existence but in the Gazette. That the enemy fabricated a number of Letters for me formerly, is a fact well known; that they are not less capable of doing it now few will deny, as to his asserting, that this is a genuine copy of the original, he well knows that their friends do not want to convict him of a falsehood and that ours have not the oppertunity of doing it though both sides are knowing to his talents for lying.

The event, which you seem to speak of with regret, my friendship for you would most assuredly have induced me to impart to you in the moment it happened had it not been for the request of H——— who desired that no mention should be made of it: Why this injunction on me, while he was communicating it himself, is a little extraordinary! but I complied, and religiously fulfilled it. With every sentiment of Affecte. regard etc.

P.S. The letter wch. you say has made much noise, I enclose you, lest you may not have had it from any other Quarter.

A few weeks later, Washington was forced to write his cousin Lund a letter of remonstrance because of his tactics in dealing with British raiders operating along the Potomac.

New Windsor,. April 30, 1781.
DEAR LUND: Your letter of the 18th. came to me by the last Post. I am very sorry to hear of your loss; I am a little sorry to hear of my own; but that which gives me most concern, is, that you should go on board the enemys Vessels, and furnish them with refreshments. It would have been a less painful circumstance to me, to have heard, that in consequence of your non-compliance with their request, they have burnt my House, and laid the Plantation in ruins. You ought to have considered yourself as my representative, and should have reflected on the bad example of communicating with the enemy, and making a voluntary offer of refreshments to them with a view to prevent a conflagration.

It was not in your power, I acknowledge, to prevent them from sending a flag on shore, and you did right to meet it; but you should, in the same instant that the business of it was unfolded, have declared, explicitly, that it was improper for you to yield to the request; after which, if they had proceeded to help themselves, *by force,* you could but have submitted (and being unprovided for defence) this was to be prefered to a feeble opposition which only serves as a pretext to burn and destroy.

I am thoroughly perswaded that you acted from your best judgment; and believe, that your desire to preserve my property, and rescue the buildings from impending danger, were your governing motives. But to go on board their Vessels; carry them refreshments; commune with a parcel of plundering Scoundrels, and request a favor by asking the surrender of my Negroes, was exceedingly ill-judged, and 'tis to be feared, will be unhappy in its consequences, as it will be a precedent for others, and may become a subject of animadversion.

I have no doubt of the enemys intention to prosecute the plundering plan they have begun. And, unless a stop can be put to it by the arrival of a superior naval force, I have as little doubt of its ending in the loss of all my Negroes, and in the destruction of my Houses; but I am prepared for the event, under the prospect of which, if you could deposit, in safety, at some convenient distance from the Water, the most valuable and least bulky articles, it might be consistent with policy and prudence, and a mean of preserving them for use hereafter. such, and so many things as are necessary for common, and present use must be retained and run their chance through the firy trial of this summer.

Mrs. Washington joins me in best and affectionate regard for you, Mrs. Washington and Milly Posey; and does most sincerely regret your loss. I do not know what Negroes they may have left you; and as I have observed before, I do not know what number they will have left me by the time they have done; but this I am sure of, that you shall never want assistance, while it is in my power to afford it. I am etc.

Two months later Washington wrote a frank letter to his brother-in-law, Fielding Lewis, expressing his mortification at Virginia's inability to resist Cornwallis, who had marched from North Carolina to combine his army with the British force already in the state.

Peaks-kill, June 28, 1781.

MY DEAR SIR: Nothing but the hurry of business, and a mind always on the stretch on acct. of the variety of matter that is constantly presented to it, could have induced me to let your letter of the 24th. of April remain so long unacknowledged. I shall not be able to write to you so fully at this time as I could wish, but this reason shall no longer prevent me from writing at all.

I lament most sincerely, the System of policy which has been but too generally adopted in all the States, to wit, that of temporary expedients; which like quack medicines are so far from removing the causes of complaint that they only serve to increase the disorder; this has, in a most remarkable manner, been the case with respect to short enlistmts; which has been the primary cause of all our misfortunes. all our expences (which may, through a thousand different channels, be traced up to this source), and of the calamities which Virginia, the two Carolinas and Georgia now groan under. That there should be such wretched management in our State as you describe, is much to be regretted. that your representation of this matter is not exagerated I have every reason to believe, because my Estate bears evidence of the truth of it, as I shall be obliged to sell one part to pay taxes on the other, but this I should do with chearfulness if the taxes were equally laid, and judiciously applied. but flagrant partiality is enough to sower the minds of any people, and bring curses on the authors of it. A Man may err once, and he may err twice but when those who posess more than a common share of abilities persevere in a regular course of destructive policy, one is more apt to suspect their hearts than their heads; this from what I have heard may not be misapplied to a person whose name you have mentioned [Patrick Henry].

I feel much for the present distress of Virginia; and for the many worthy persons on whom the calamities of War have been most severe; and wish my ability to serve them was equal to my wishes, but it is not, I want the means, and yet it is miserable even in contemplation to think, that such a State as Virginia should be overrun by a handful of Men. The spirit of the people is certainly departed from them, for nothing but exertion can be wanting to drive Lord Cornwallis into the Mountains, or to his Ships. Why then does it go undone? I am doing all I can to counteract the enemys plan to the Southward, but how far I shall succeed time only can discover, the same languor, and the same policy prevails here as elsewhere; how far therefore I shall be able to collect men (and they are yet to be collected) is more than I can say; fatal experience has convinced us that to carry Troops from this quarter to the Southward is to encounter (upon the March only) the loss of one third if not half, in a land March by sickness and desertion, arising from a disinclination to serve in that part of the Continent.

We have nothing verry interesting at this time, in this quarter except the Marching of the French Army from Rhode Island to form a junction with ours on this River which event will, probably, take place in about six days. I wish the girls who have lately taken Husbands all the happiness this life affords and very sincerely wish you a perfect recovery of your health. Mrs. Washington left me on Monday last in a very low and weak state having been sick for more than a Month with a kind of Jaundice. It was uncertain whether she would proceed further than Philadelphia till our affairs in Virginia should take a more favourable turn. Remember me in the most Affectionate manner to my Sister and the rest of the family and be assured that I am with much truth Dr. Sir Yr. etc.

The strategy that resulted in the triumph at Yorktown was now beginning to take shape. Lafayette, with a small army, fought a war of maneuver against Cornwallis in Virginia. Nathanael Greene conducted a highly successful campaign against exposed British outposts in the Carolinas. Washington remained in New York, hoping to strike a knockout blow there.

Finally comes the letter that commits the allied army to Yorktown. The decision of the French admiral, the Comte de Grasse, to sail his fleet directly to the Chesapeake, rather than first rendezvousing at New York, forced Washington to abandon his disinclination to march south. It is fitting that this letter was written to

Lafayette, the man who had done more than anyone else to bring Washington the French troops and ships that made victory possible.

Head Quarters, Dobbs's Ferry, August 15, 1781.
MY DEAR MARQUIS: I have recd. your letters of the 26th. and 30th. ulto. and 1st. Inst. I cannot learn that any troops have yet arrived at New York from Virginia. A fleet of 20 sail came in last Saturday with troops, but they are said to be Hessian Recruits from Europe.

The Concorde Frigate is arrived at Newport from Counte de Grasse. He was to leave St. Domingo the 3d. of this month with a Fleet of between 25 and 29 sail of the line and a considerable Body of land forces. His destination is immediately for the Chesapeak. So that he will either be there by the time this reaches you, or you look for him every moment. Under these circumstances, whether the enemy remain in full force, or whether they have only a detachment left, you will immediately take such a position as will best enable you to prevent their sudden retreat thro' North Carolina, which I presume they will attempt the instant they perceive so formidable an Armament. Should General Wayne with the troops destined for South Carolina still remain in the neighborhood of James River and the enemy should have made no detachment to the Southward, you will detain those troops untill you hear from me again, and inform Genl. Greene of the cause of their delay. If Wayne should have marched, and should have gained any considerable distance, I would not have him halted.

You shall hear further from me as soon as I have concerted plans and formed dispositions for sending a reinforcement from hence. In the mean time I have only to recommend a continuation of that prudence and good conduct which you have manifested thro' the whole of your Campaign. You will be particularly careful to conceal the expected arrival of the Count, because if the enemy are not apprised of it, they will stay on board their transports in the Bay, which will be the luckiest Circumstance in the World.

You will take measures for opening a communication with

Count de Grasse the moment he arrives, and will concert measures with him for making the best uses of your joint forces untill you receive aid from this quarter. I am &c.

P.S. I would not wish you to call out a large body of Militia upon this occasion, but rather keep those you have compact and ready for service.

Dozens of brisk letters flowed from Washington's headquarters as the plan for the Yorktown campaign went into operation. There was time now only for the business of victory. Bamboozling the British in New York with a rash of false rumors and planted intelligence reports, Washington left only a skeleton force to guard the Hudson highlands, while he and the French battalions marched south to trap Cornwallis at Yorktown. In the midst of the siege however, he did find time to write a letter to his brilliant lieutenant, Nathanael Greene, in which there is more friendship than business. The splendid victory to which Washington refers was the bloody four-hour battle Greene fought at Eutaw Springs, South Carolina, on September 8, 1781. Though the British remained in possession of the battlefield, their casualties were so heavy that the next day they were forced to retreat.

Camp before York, October 6, 1781.

How happy am I, my dear Sir, in at length having it in my power to congratulate you upon a victory as splendid as I hope it will prove important. Fortune must have been coy indeed had she not yielded at last to so persevering a pursuer as you have been; I hope now she is yours, she will change her appellation of fickle to that of constant.

I can say with sincerity that I feel with the highest degree of pleasure the good effects which you mention as resulting from the perfect good understanding between you the Marquis and myself. I hope it will never be interrupted, and I am sure it never can while we are all influenced by the same pure motive, that of love to our

Country and interest in the cause in which we are embarked. I have happily had but few differences with those with whom I have the honor of being connected in the Service; with whom, and of what nature these have been, you know. I bore much for the sake of peace and the public good. My conscience tells me I acted rightly in these transactions, and should they ever come to the knowledge of the world I trust I shall stand acquitted by it.

The Baron [Friedrich Von Stauben, Prussian-born "drillmaster" of the American Army], from the warmth of his temper, had got disagreeably involved with the State, and an enquiry into part of his conduct must one day take place, both for his own honor and their satisfaction. I have for the present given him a command in this Army which makes him happy.

I shall always take pleasure in giving Mrs. Greene's letters a conveyance and shd. she persist in the resolution of undertaking so long a journey as that from New England to Carolina I hope she will make Mount Vernon, (where Mrs. Knox now is) a stage of more than a day or two. With much truth and sincere affection etc.

On October 17 Lord Cornwallis despaired of receiving reinforcements from New York and asked for terms. By October 19 Britain's finest army had laid down its arms. Washington was, of course, by no means convinced that the fighting was over, and he was to spend the next two years anxiously struggling to keep some semblance of an army together so that America could negotiate a peace from strength. There are few letters of friendship in Washington's correspondence during this time. Even to Lafayette he wrote businesslike letters discussing the needs of the army and the nation. The war trickled on with no fighting. But to Washington's distress he could persuade neither France nor his fellow Americans to muster enough men and ships to strike the weakened enemy a final blow.

During this trying period Washington also had to cope with a vexing family problem. His stepson Jack Custis had died three weeks after the victory at Yorktown. Only then did his family discover that his estate, over which Washington had presided with

scrupulous care when Jack was a boy, had been plundered by a
thieving manager. To make matters even worse, the manager was
the son of a neighbor. Washington had helped to pay for the education of him and his brothers out of his own pocket, and had lent
his father money several times. All these factors explain Washington's wrath in the following letter. At the same time it is interesting to compare the letter with the other angry note he wrote as a
much younger man to the coward George Muse. There is a different voice here, the voice of a man who speaks with maturity and
power.

Head Qrs. Newburgh, August 7, 1782.

SIR: With a mixture of surprize, concern, and even horror; have I
heard of your treatment of the deceased Mr. Custis; in the abuse,
and misapplication of the Estate which he had committed, with
much confidence I am sure, and I believe personal regard, to your
management.

If what I have heard, or the half of it be true, you must not
only be lost to the feelings of virtue, honor and common honesty;
but you must have suffered an unwarrantable thirst of gain to lead
you into errors which are so pregnant with folly and indiscretion, as
to render you a mark for every mans arrow to level at. Can you suppose Sir, that a Manager, can dissipate his Employers Estate with
impunity? That there are not Laws in every free Country by which
justice is to be otained? or, that the Heirs of Mr. Custis will not
find friends who will pursue you to the end of the Earth in order to
come at it? If you do, you are proceeding upon exceedingly mistaken principles. but, for a moment only let us suppose that you
have taken the advantage of an unsuspecting friend; for such I am
sure Mr. Custis was to you. and, that you have acted so covertly, as
to elude the Law; do you believe that in the hours of cool reflection, in the moment perhaps, when you shall find that ill-gotten
pelf can no longer avail you; that your conscience will not smite
you severely for such complicated inequity as arises not only from
acts of injustice, but the horrors of ingratitude; in abusing the confidence of a man who supposed you incapable of deceiving him,

and who was willing, and I believe did, in a great degree, commit his whole property to your care?

But this by the by, I do not mean to put this matter upon the footing of Conscience. Conscience, must have been kicked out of doors before you could have proceeded to the length of selling another Mans Negros for your own emolument and this too after having applyed the greatest part, or the whole of the profits of his Estate to your own benefit. Conscience again seldom comes to a Mans aid while he is in the zenith of health, and revelling in pomp and luxury upon ill gotten spoils; it is generally the *last* act of his life and comes too late to be of much service to others here, or to himself hereafter. But Sir, the footing I expect to see you put this matter upon, is, to settle without delay, such Accts. with the Administrator of Mr. Custis's Estate, whose duty it is to have it done, as you can support by authentic vouchers. That you will show by what authority you have sold any of his Negros, and to what purposes the money has been applied. and lastly, what Crops you have made, what Stocks you have raisd and how they have been disposed of. A settlement of this kind, altho' it should appear by it, that you have applied the greatest part, or even the whole of the money arising fm. the sales of them to your own purposes, will be the next best thing to never having committed the wrong.

How far Mr. Dandridge [Martha Washington's brother, Bartholemew], as an Administrator, may chuse to push matters, I cannot undertake (never having heard from him on the subject) to say. but this you may *rely on*, that this affair shall be most critically investigated, and probed to the bottom; let the trouble and cost of doing it be what it may; as a Man therefore who wishes for your own sake as well as that of an injurd family to see you act properly, I advise, and warn you of the consequences of a contrary conduct, being Sir Yr. etc.

A few weeks later Joseph Reed wrote to Washington asking him for a testament of his loyalty during the gloomy months of 1776. Reed had become engaged in a political controversy with General John Cadwallader, who had charged him with meditating the possibility of switching sides at that time.

Head Quarters, September 15, 1782.

DEAR SIR: The Appeal contained in your Letter of the 11th instant, is equally unexpected and surprising.

Not knowing the particular Charges which are alledged against you, it is impossible for me to make a specific Reply, I can therefore only say in general Terms, that the Employments you sustained in the Year 1776, and in that period of the Year, when we experienced our greatest Distress, are a proof that you was not suspected by me of Infidelity or Want of Integrity, for had the least Suspicion of the kind reached my mind, either from Observation or Report, I should most assuredly have marked you out as a fit Object of Resentment.

While on Our retreat thro' Jersey, I remember your being sent from Newark, to the Assembly of N. Jersey then sitting, to rouse and animate them to spirited Measures for our Support; And at the same time Genl Mifflin was sent to Pennsylvania for the same purpose. This Employ was certainly a Mark of my Confidence in you at that Time.

Your Conduct, so far as it came to my immediate notice during the short period we lay on the West [bank] of the Delaware, appeared sollicitous for the public Good; And your Conduct at Princetown evidenced a Spirit and Zeal, which to me appeared laudable and becomg a Man well affected to the cause we were engaged in.

It is rather a disagreeable circumstance, to have private and confidential Letters, hastily written as all mine of that Class are, upon a Supposition that they would remain between the parties only, produced as Evidence in a Matter of public Discussion; but conscious that my public and private Sentiments, are at all times alike; I shall not withhold the Letters, should you think them absolutely necessary to your Justification.

If I have in my possession any such Letter as you particularly allude to, it is not at present with me; being in the field, perfectly light, I have divested myself of all Papers public and private, but such, of late Date, as I tho't might have occasion, in my present Situation, to refer to; the others remain at a considerable Distance from me. I am &c.

Now comes a long newsy letter to Lafayette, who had re-turned to France, bringing him up to date on the war and the death of old friends and acquaintances such as John Laurens and Charles Lee.

Verplanks point, October 20, 1782.

MY DEAR MARQS: Whilst I thought there was a probability of my letters finding you in France, I continued to write to you at Paris; after that, I ceased to do so, expecting the more agreeable pleasure of embracing you in America. Your favor of the 29th. of June, placing the time of your departure from thence on a contingency, and our latest advices from Europe, reporting that Negotiations for Peace were nearly in the same state as at the commencement of it, I shall renew my correspondence.

I approve, very highly, the motives which induced you to remain at your Court, and I am convinced Congress will do the same.

The campaign, as you supposed has been very inactive. We formed the junction with the French Corps (whch. is now Encamped on our left, ten miles distant) the Middle of September; and have remained in perfect unison with them ever since their arrival. It may I believe with much truth be said, that a greater harmony between two Armies never subsisted than that which has prevailed between the French and American since the first junction of them last year. I had prepared a beautiful Corps for you to command, that would not, I am convinced either in their appearance or action, have discredited any Officer, or Army what ever. It consisted of all the light Infantry of the Northern Army, to which Sheldon's Legion would have been added. But we have done nothing more than to keep a watch upon the enemy this Campaign except restraining them from detaching; which I believe has been the consequence of our junction, and lying here. A few German Troops, and Refugees have been sent to Hallifax; from thence it was supposed they were to proceed to Canada; this took place before I came into the Field, which was on the last day of August.

The Cold weather puts us in mind of warm firesides; and the two Armies will seperate for this or some other purpose, in the course of a few Days. The French Army will go Easterly, we Northerly, and shall fix our Cantonments in the Vicinity of West point.

The Enemy in New York make no scruple of declaring their intention of evacuating Charles town; many Transports went from the former about a Month ago; with design, it was said, to take off the Garrison; but whether it is to be brought to the last mentioned place or carried to the West Indies is mere matter of conjecture; very probably the British Troops may go to the Latter, and the foreigners to the former. time only will shew this, as indeed it may another thing, viz: that the late changes in the British Councils may prevent the evacuation of it at all. With respect to New York, various opinions have prevailed; some thought the speedy evacuation of it inevitable, others, that it would be delayed till the spring, while a third set, less sanguine than either of the other two, believed that nothing short of a Military force would ever free the City of them; their whole design being, to amuse the Belligerent Powers, and deceive America till they could put their Marine and other matters in a more prosperous train for prosecuting the War; the first, it is certain were in an error, because the Troops are still at New York, but wch. of the other two may be right your knowledge from what is transacting in the European theatre enables you to judge better of than I. certain it is, the loyalists and Refugees in New York are very much alarmed, and know not what to expect; as certain it is Sir Guy Carleton [the new British commander in chief] holds himself in readiness to evacuate, or perform any other movement with his Army, while he endeavors assiduously in the mean while to propagate the favourable disposition of Great Britain to grant every thing American can require. Their Transports have Wooded and watered, and lay ready for any Service, so have the Ships of War, under Admiral Pigot; but I believe they are designed for the West Indies, with *part* of the Troops at New York, more than for any other purpose.

You will have heard before this Letter can reach you, of the loss of the L'Eagle; * it will be unpleasant therefore to repeat it, everybody laments the misfortune, and pities poor L'Touche. Duke Lauzun has been very sick but is now recovering fast, tho' very thin, and pale.

Poor Laurens is no more. He fell in a trifling skirmish in South Carolina, attempting to prevent the Enemy from plundering the Country of rice. Genl. Lee is also dead, he breathed his last at Philadelphia about a fortnight ago. Your Aid GW— [George Augustine Washington, son of Washington's brother Charles] has had an intermittant fever ever since April and by the last Accts. of him from Mount Vernon where he is, he was very low and weak.

As I despair of seeing my home this Winter I have just sent for Mrs. Washington who will think herself honored by your and Madm. La Fayettes notice. Make a tender of my best respects to her, and offer a blessing in my name to your Son, and my Godson. present me also to Counte Charlux and others with whom I have the honor of an Acquaintance. the Count de Noialles [Lafayette's brother-in-law] will have the trouble of reading a letter from me.

Adieu my dear Marqs; believe me to be, what I really am, your etc.

The several Frenchmen mentioned were officers in the French expeditionary force.

A few weeks later Washington wrote, full of concern, to his nephew George Augustine Washington. He is obviously suffering from the family affliction, tuberculosis.

Newburgh, November 14, 1782.

DEAR GEORGE: I have received your Letter of the 23d. Ulto, from Berkeley; and am sorry to find that your fever and pain in the Breast still continues. If they should not have left you 'ere this gets to hand, you had, in my opinion best take a trip to the Southward. Doctr. Craik advises one to the West Indies, if there is the least

---

* A French frigate commanded by Vicomte de la Touche-Treville, which surrendered to a British squadron after an unequal combat in September 1782.

appearance of the disorder falling upon your Lungs. the only objection I see to this is, that the Vessel may be captured, and a disagreeable captivity, perhaps imprisonment, may add to your Compalints; when possibly a Southern climate, during the Winter Season, may be equally effecatious.

If you should make choice of the latter experiment to recover your health, and should go as far as the Southern Army, this letter, shewn to General Green, will, I am perswaded, procure your every aid, assistance, and advice that may be in his power to afford you; and I request you to make use of it accordingly.

The Army has retired into Winter Quarters; the principal part of it is in this vicinity, where I have taken, and shall remain in the same confined Quarters I had last Spring.

There is no duty for you to return to at present, consequently there can be no cause for your anxicty to rejoin the Army, but if there was, ill health is a sufficient plea for absence; and an attempt to recover it, a consideration to which every other should yield.

We have no certainty of what the British Cabinet design; various are the reports, and all equally vague. My own opinion of the matter is, that the unwillingness of the King, and his present Prime Minister Lord Shelburn to acknowledge the Independency, of this Country, is such, as to induce them to trust to the Chapter of accidents (altho by so doing they hazard all) rather than swallow this bitter pill. The Negociations are going on, but very limpingly, this Winter will, no doubt, bring them to a conclusion; but whether they will terminate in a peace or protraction of the War, is beyond my ken.

Remember me in the most Affectionate manner to your Father, Mother, and all friends; and be assured that I am with great truth, and Affection, and best wishes for your recovery. Yrs.,

As the year 1782 came to a close, Rochambeau, leader of the French expeditionary force, prepared to sail home. Washington sent him on his way with the following letter of friendship and thanks.

Newburgh, December 14, 1782.

I cannot, My dear Genl., permit you to depart from this Country without repeating to you the high sense I entertain of the Services you have rendered America, by the constant attention which you have paid to the Interests of it.

By the exact order and discipline of the Corps under your Command, and by your readiness, at all times, to give facility to every measure which the force of the Combined Armies was competent to.

To this testimony of your Public character I should be wanting to the feelings of my heart, was I not to add expressions of the happiness I have enjoyed in your private friendship. The remembrance of which, will be one of the most pleasing Circumstances of my life.

My best wishes will accompany you to France, where I have no doubt of your meeting the Smiles and rewards of a generous Prince; and the warmest embraces of Affectionate friends. I have the honor etc.

The great drama of the Revolutionary War was coming to a close and Washington's mind was turning more and more to Mount Vernon. He wrote long, detailed letters to Lund about replanting and preparing fields for crops. He was also taking more interest in the Washington family, particularly the nephews of his favorite brother, Jack. Bushrod, his oldest son, had decided to study law and Washington warmly approved of his choice. As the young man left for Philadelphia he received the following advice on the conduct of his personal life.

Newburgh, January 15, 1783.

DEAR BUSHROD: You will be surprized perhaps at receiving a letter from me; but if the end is answered for which it is written, I shall not think my time miss-spent.

Your Father, who seems to entertain a very favorable opinion of your prudence, and I hope you merit it: in one or two of his letters to me, speaks of the difficulty he is under to make you remittances. Whether this arises from the scantiness of his funds, or the extensiveness of your demands, is matter of conjecture, with me. I hope it is not the latter, because common prudence, and every other consideration which ought to have weight in a reflecting mind is opposed to your requiring more than his conveniency and a regard to his other Children will enable him to pay; and because he holds up no idea in his Letter, which would support me in the conclusion. yet when I take a view of the inexperience of Youth, the temptations in, and vices of Cities; and the distresses to which our Virginia Gentlemen are driven by an accumulation of Taxes and the want of a market; I am almost inclined to ascribe it, in part to both. Therefore, as a friend, I give you the following advice.

Let the object, which carried you to Philadelphia, be always before your Eyes; remember, that it is not the mere study of the Law, but to become eminent in the Profession of it which is to yield honor and profit; the first was your choice, let the second be your ambition. and that dissipation is incompatible with both.

That the Company in which you will improve most, will be least expensive to you; and yet I am not such a Stoic as to suppose you will, or to think it right that you ought, always to be in Company with Senators and Philosophers; but, of the young and juvenile kind let me advise you to be choice. It is easy to make acquaintances, but very difficult to shake them off, however irksome and unprofitable they are found after we have once committed ourselves to them; the indiscretions, and scrapes which very often they involuntarily lead one into, proves equally distressing and disgraceful.

Be courteous to all, but intimate with few, and let those few be well tried before you give them your confidence; true friendship is a plant of slow growth, and must undergo and withstand the shocks of adversity before it is entitled to the appellation.

Let your *heart* feel for the affliction, and distresses of everyone, and let your *hand* give in proportion to your purse; remembering always, the estimation of the Widows mite. But, that it is not every one who asketh, that deserveth charity; all however are worthy of the enquiry, or the deserving may suffer.

Do not conceive that fine Clothes make fine Men, any more than fine feathers make fine Birds. A plain genteel dress is more admired and obtains more credit than lace and embroidery in the Eyes of the judicious and sensible.

The last thing I shall mention, is first of importance. and that is, to avoid Gaming. This is a vice which is productive of every possible evil. equally injurious to the morals and health of its votaries. It is the child of Avarice, the brother of inequity, and father of Mischief. It has been the ruin of many worthy familys; the loss of many a man's honor; and the cause of Suicide. To all those who enter the list, it is equally fascinating; the Successful gamester pushes his good fortune till it is over taken by a reverse; the loosing gamester, in hopes of retrieving past misfortunes, goes on from bad to worse; till grown desperate, he pushes at every thing; and looses his all. In a word, few gain by this abominable practice (the profit, if any, being diffused) while thousands are injured.

Perhaps you will say my conduct has anticipated the advice, and that "not one of these cases apply to me." I shall be heartily glad of it. It will add not a little to my happiness, to find those, to whom I am so nearly connected, pursuing the right walk of life; it will be the sure road to my favor, and to those honors, and places of profit, which their Country can bestow, as merit rarely goes unrewarded. I am, etc.

Bushrod put this advice to good use. He became a distinguished attorney and was appointed Associate Justice of the Supreme Court by President John Adams.

The next day Washington wrote another letter home, this time to Jack. Their brother Samuel had died, leaving his affairs in a frightful tangle. Their mother was at her favorite sport of troubling her famous son.

Newburgh, January 16, 1783.
MY DEAR BROTHER: Since the letter which Bushrod delivered me in Philadelphia, I have received your favors of the 24th. of July from

Westmoreland, and 12th. of Novr. from Berkley.

The latter gave me extreme pain. In Gods name how did my Brothr. Saml. contrive to get himself so enormously in debt? Was it by purchases? By misfortunes? or shear indolence and inattention to business? From whatever cause it proceeded, the matter is now the same, and curiosity only prompts the enquiry, as it does to know what will be saved, and how it is disposed of. In the list of his debts did it appear that I had a claim upon him for the purchase of money of the Land I sold Pendleton on Bullskin? I have never received a farthing for it yet, and think I have been informed by him that he was to pay it.

I have heard a favourable acct. of Bushrod, and doubt not but his prudence will direct him to a proper line of Conduct. I have given him my sentiments on this head; and perswade myself that, with the advice of Mr. Wilson [James Wilson, later a Supreme Court justice, at the time an outstanding Philadelphia lawyer], to whose friendship as well as instruction in his profession I recommended him and the admontion of others, he will stand as good a chance as most youth of his age to avoid the Vices of large Cities, which have their advantages and disadvantages in fitting a man for the great theatre of public Life.

I have lately received a letter from my Mother in which she complains much *of the Knavery of the Overseer at the little Falls Quarter.* that She says she can get nothing from him. it is pretty evident I believe, that I get nothing from thence, which I have the annual rent of between Eighty and an hundred pounds to pay. *The whole profit of the Plantation according to her Acct. is applied to his own use,* which is rather hard upon me as I had no earthly inducement to meddle with it but to comply with her wish, and to free her from care, this like every other matter of private concern, with me, has been totally neglected; but it is too much while I am suffering in every other way (and hardly able to keep my own Estate from Sale), to be saddled with all the expence of hers and not be able to derive the smallest return from it. She has requested that I would get somebody to attend to it. I must therefore desire the favor of you to take it under your care. I know of none in whose hands it can be better placed, to none to whom it can be less inconvenient, and who is more interested in the good managemt. of the Land. For as it lyes directly in your Route to Berkley, and in the Neighbourhood of our friends where you must always make a halt, it will give you very little additional trouble to provide an Overseer. Call upon him as you pass and repass, and set the annual Accts. with him, so as that I may have some knowledge of his transactions and a certainty that whatever is made goes towards payment of the Rent. I shall by this Post inform my Mother of this application to you, hoping you will find no difficulty in the undertaking.

While I am talking of my Mother and her concerns, I am impelled to mention somethings which has given, and still continues to give me pain. About two years ago a Gentleman of my acquaintance informed me that it was in contemplation to move for a pension for her in the Virginia Assembly. That he did not suppose I knew of the measure, or that it would be agreeable to me to have it done; but wished to know my sentiments on it. I instantly wrote him that it was new and astonishing to me and begged that he would prevent the motion if possible, or oppose it if made; for I was sure she had not a Child that would not share the last farthing with her, and that would not be hurt at the idea of her becoming a Pensioner, or in other words receiving charity. Since *then* I have heard nothing of *that* matter; but I learn from very good authority that she is upon all occasions, and in all Companies complaining of the hardness of the times, of her wants and distresses; and if not in direct terms, at least by strong innuendos inviting favors which not only makes *her* appear in an unfavourable point of view but *those* also who are connected with her. That she can have no *real* wants that may not be supplied I am sure of; *imaginary* wants are indefinite and oftentimes insatiable, because they are boundless and always changing. the reason of my mentioning these matters to you is, that you may enquire into her real wants and see what is necessary to make her comfortable. If the Rent is insufficient to do this, while I have anything I will part with it to make her so; and wish you to take measures in my behalf accordingly; at the sametime I wish you to represent to her in delicate terms the impropriety of her complaints and acceptance of favors even where they are voluntarily offered, from any but relations. It will not do to touch upon this subject in a letter to her, and therefore I have avoided it.

I do not believe that Sir Guy Carleton gives any countenance to those dirty piccaroons that infest your Rivers. If they are encouraged at all, it must be by the Admiral in whose Element they are; but I am rather inclined to think that they are Navigated by a Lawless Banditti who would rob both sides with equal facility, if they could do it with equal impunity.

With respect to Peace, we are held in a very disagreeable state of suspence; and shall I expect remain in it till sometime in February. My opinion of it however, has been uniformly the same since the death of the Marquis of Rockingham and appointment of the present Premier. It is thought nothing would be concluded till the meeting of the British Parliament in November, and if the influence of the Crown could prevent it, that it would not take place even then, if the Independence of this Country is to be the consequence of it. . . .

The remainder of this letter is too mutilated to read.

A few weeks later, Washington received a letter from Bryan Fairfax, to which he replied with all his customary warmth.

Newburgh, February 5, 1783.

DEAR SIR: Your letter begun on the 26th. of Decr. and finished the 8th. of Jany. came to my hands by the last Post. The Inclosures for Lord Fairfax and your Brother I have put under cover to Sir Guy Carleton who will I am perswaded send them in the Packet for England. I have only to add on this subject that you need not at any time hesitate at, or apologize for sending Letters of friendship or on business through my hands into New York; as I shall always have pleasure in being the medium of conveyance. and if Lord Fairfax and your Brother would adopt the same mode, nothing but the danger of the Seas, and risque of capture, would impede their passage to, and from you. . . .

At present, we are fast locked in Frost and Snow; without a title of News. We look wisfully to the East, and to the South for an Arrival; supposing the first European Vessel will bring the Speech of the British King, the Addresses, and debates thereupon; the last of which I expect, will discover the Ultimatum of the National determination respecting the continuance of the War, or acceptance of Peace upon such terms as the Negociations for it have been able to strike out. If happily for all parties, the last should be the choice, it would give me much pleasure to assure you personally, of the unimpaired friendship of Dr. Sir, etc.

Washington wrote the following warm letter to Nathanael Greene when his second in command was on his way home from the southern states. The "day" to which Washington refers is the anniversary of the signing of the Treaty of Alliance with France...

Newburgh, February 6, 1783.

MY DEAR SIR: I have the pleasure to inform you that your Packet for Govr. Greene [of Rhode Island—no relation] which came inclosed to me (in your private Letter of the 12th. of December) was forwarded in an hour after it came to my hands by a Gentleman returning to Rhode Island (Welcome Arnold Esquire); there can be no doubt therefore of its having got safe to the Governor.

It is with a pleasure which friendship only is susceptible of, I congratulate you on the glorious end you have put to hostilities in the Southern States; the honor and advantage of it, I hope, and trust, you will live long to enjoy. when this hemisphere will be equally free is yet in the womb of time to discover; a little whole, however 'tis presumed, will disclose the determinations of the British Senate with respect to Peace or War as it seems to be agreed on all hands, that the present Premier (especially if he should find the opposition powerful) intends to submit the decision of these matters to Parliament. The Speech, the Addresses, and Debates for which we are looking in every direction, will give a data from which the bright rays of the one, or the gloomy prospect of the other, may be discovered.

If Historiographers should be hardy enough to fill the page of History with the advantages that have been gained with unequal numbers (on the part of America) in the course of this contest, and attempt to relate the distressing circumstances under which they have been obtained, it is more than probable that Posterity will bestow on their labors the epithet and marks of fiction; for it will not be believed that such a force as Great Britain has employed for eight years in this Country could be baffled in their plan of Subjugating it by numbers infinitely less, composed of Men oftentimes half starved; always in Rags, without pay, and experiencing, at times, every species of distress which human nature is capable of undergoing.

I intended to have wrote you a long letter on sundry matters but Majr. Burnett popped in unexpectedly, at a time when I was preparing for the Celebration of the day; and was just going to a review of the Troops, previous to the Fue de joy. As he is impatient, from an apprehension of the Sleighing failing. and as he can give you the occurrences of this quarter more in detail than I have time to do, I will refer you to him. I cannot omit informing you however, that I let no oppertunity slip to enquire after your Son George at Princeton, and that it is with pleasure I hear he enjoys good health, and is a fine promising boy.

Mrs. Washington joins me in most Affectionate regards, and best wishes for Mrs Greene and yourself. With great truth and sincerity and every sentiment of friendship, I am etc.

It was a time for exchanging sentimental letters with many men to whom Washington had written often in official capacities. Thomas Jefferson, en route to France as a peace negotiator, wrote Washington a fulsome letter, which Washington answered with equal warmth.

Newburgh, February 10, 1783.

DEAR SIR: I have been honored with your favor of the 22d. of Jany. from Philadelphia. I feel myself much flattered by your kind re-

membrance of me in the hour of your departure from this Continent. and for the favourable Sentiments you are pleased to entertain of my Services for this our common Country. To merit the
approbation of good and virtuous Men is the height of my ambition, and will be a full compensation for all my toils and Sufferings
in the long and painful Contest we have been engaged.

It gave me great pleasure to hear that the call upon you from
Congress to pass the Atlantic in the Character of one of their Ministers for Negotiating Peace, had been repeated. But I hope you
will have found the business already done.

The Speech of his Britainic Majesty is strongly indicative of
the Olive branch; and yet, as he observes, unforeseen events may
place it out of reach. At present, the prospect of Peace absorbs, or
seems to do so, every other consideration among us; and would, it
is to be feared, leave us in a very unprepared state to continue the
War if the Negociations at Paris should terminate otherwise than
in a general pacification. but I will hope that it is the dearth of
other News that fills the Mouths of every person with Peace while
their Minds are employed in contemplating on the means for
prosecuting the War, if necessity should drive us to it.

You will please to accept my grateful thanks for your obliging
offer of Services during your stay in France. To hear frequently
from you, will be an honor and very great satisfaction to Dr. Sir etc.

*More and more Washington's thoughts turned to Mount
Vernon. This pressing letter to Lund reveals his eagerness to take
up the reins of his own estate once more...*

Newburgh, February 12, 1783.
DEAR LUND: Your letter of the 29th. of Jany. came by the last Post.
You do not seem to have considered the force and tendency of the
words of yr. letter when you talk of the probability *only* of sending
me "the long promised account" "the irregularity of them"; not,
you add, "for want of knowledge in keeping them but neglect; your
aversion to writing" &ca. &ca. These are but other words for saying,
"as I am not fond of writing, and it is *quite* immaterial whether

you have any knowledge or information of your private concerns or whether the accts. are kept properly or not, I have delayed, and do not know how much longer I may continue to delay bringing you acquainted with these accts. irregular as they are."

Delicacy hitherto, and a hope that you long ago would have seen into the propriety of the measure, without a hint of it from me, has restrained me from telling you that annual Accts. of my Crops, together with the receipts and expenditure of my money, state of my stocks, &ca. ought to have been sent to me as regularly as the year came about. It is not to be supposed, that all the avocations of my public duties, great and laborious as they have been, could render me totally insensible to the *only means* by which myself and family; and the character I am to maintain in life hereafter, is to be supported, or that a precise acct. of these matters would not have been exceedingly satisfactory to me. Instead of this, except the Acct. rendered at Valley forge in the year 1778 I have received none since I left home; and not till after two or 3 applications in the course of last year could I get any acct. of the Crop of the preceeding one; and then only of the Corn by the Post on Sunday last.

I have often told you, and I repeat it with much truth; that the entire confidence which I placed in your integrity made me easy, and I was always happy at thinking that my Affairs were in your hands, which I could not have been, if they had been under the care of a common Manager; but this did not excempt me from the desires which all men have, of knowing the exact state of them. I have now to beg that you will not only send me the Account of your receipts, and expenditures of Specie; but of every kind of money subsequent to the Acct. exhibited at Valley Forge, which ended sometime in April 1778.

I want to know before I come home (as I shall come home with empty pockets whenever Peace shall take place) how Affairs stand with me, and what my dependence is.

I wish to know also, what I have to expect from the Wheat of 1781 and 82, as you say the two Crops are so blended that they cannot be rendered seperately? How are settlements to be made with and justice done to the several Parties Interested under these circumstances?

Alexander Hamilton had left the army to become New York's delegate to the Congress. In this letter to him Washington sounds the alarm against a danger that threatened to destroy the revolution. The army, embittered by Congress' refusal to make good on back pay, was threatening to win justice with its bayonets.

Newburgh, March 4, 1783.

DEAR SIR: I have received your favor of February, and thank you for the information and observations it has conveyed to me. I shall always think myself obliged by a free communication of Sentiments, and have often thought (but suppose I thought wrong as it did not accord with the practice of Congress) that the public interest might be benefitted, if the Commander in Chief of the Army was let more into the political and pecuniary state of our Affairs than he is. Enterprises, and the adoption of Military and other arrangements that might be exceedingly proper in some circumstances would be altogether improper in others. It follows then by fair deduction, that where there is a want of information there must be chance medley; and a man may be upon the brink of a precipice before he is aware of his danger. when a little foreknowledge might enable him to avoid it. But this by the by.

The hint contained in your letter, and the knowledge I have derived from the public Gazettes respecting the nonpayment of Taxes, contain all the information I have received of the danger that stares us in the face on Acct. of our funds, and so far was I from conceiving that our Finances was in so deplorable a state *at this time* that I had imbibed ideas from some source or another, that with the prospect of a loan from Holland, we should be able to rub along.

To you, who have seen the danger, to which the Army has been exposed, to a political dissolution for want of subsistence, and the unhappy spirit of licentiousness which it imbided by becoming in one or two instances its own proveditors,* no observations are necessary to evince the fatal tendency of such a measure; but I shall give it as my opinion, that it would at this day be productive of Civil commotions and end in blood. Unhappy situation this! God forbid we should be involved in it.

The predicament in which I stand as Citizen and Soldier, is as critical and delicate as can well be conceived. It has been the Subject of many contemplative hours. The sufferings of a complaining Army on one hand, and the inability of Congress and tardiness of the States on the other, are the forebodings of evil, and may be productive of events which are more to be deprecated than prevented; but I am not without hope, if there is such a disposition shewn as prudence and policy will dictate, to do justice, that your apprehensions, in case of Peace, are greater than there is cause for. In this however I may be mistaken, if those ideas, which you have been informed are propagated in the Army should be extensive; the source † of which may be easily traced as the old leven, *it is said*, for I have no proof of it, is again, beginning to work, under a mask of the most perfect dissimulation, and apparent cordiallity.

Be these things as they may, I shall pursue the same steady line of conduct which has governed me hitherto; fully convinced that the sensible, and discerning part of the Army, cannot be unacquainted (altho' I never took pains to inform them) of the Services I have rendered it on more occasions than one. This, and pursuing the suggestions of your Letter, which I am happy to find coincides with my practice for several Months past and which was the means of directing the business of the Army into the Channel it now is, leaves me under no *great* apprehension of its exceeding the bounds of reason and moderation, notwithstanding the prevailing sentiment in the Army is, that the prospect of compensation for past Services will terminate with the War.

The just claims of the Army ought, and it is to be hoped will,

---

* Early in 1781 there were two serious mutinies in the American army.

† This may be a reference to Horatio Gates, who had been acquitted by a court martial for his defeat at Camden, and rejoined the army.

have their weight with every sensible Legislature in the Union, if Congress point to their demands; shew (if the case is so) the reasonableness of them, and the impracticability of complying with them without their Aid. In any other point of view it would, in my opinion, be impolitic to introduce the Army on the Tapis; lest it should excite jealousy, and bring on its concomitants. the States cannot, surely, be so devoid of common aid on a full, clear, and candid representation of facts from Congress; more especially if these should be enforced by members of their own Body; who might demonstrate what the inevitable consequences of failure will lead to.

In my opinion it is a matter worthy of consideration how far an Adjournment of Congress for a few Months is advisable. The Delegates in that case, if they are in Unison themselves, respecting the great defects of their Constitution, may represent them fully and boldly to their Constituents. to me, who know nothing of the business which is before Congress, nor of the Arcanum, it appears that such a measure would tend to promote the public weal; for it is clearly my opinion, unless Congress have powers competent to all *general* purposes, that the distresses we have encountered, the expence we have incurred, and the blood we have spilt in the course of an Eight years war, will avail us nothing.

The contents of your letter is known only to myself, and your prudence will direct what should be done with this. With great esteem etc.

The crisis was averted by a dramatic confrontation between Washington and the officers in the army. He urged them to rely on the promises of Congress and restrain their just indignation. As he began to read a letter from Congress, Washington paused and took out a new set of spectacles. "You will pardon me, gentlemen," he said. "I have grown gray in your service, and now am growing blind." The impact of this simple remark was immense. Many men wept openly. After Washington left the meeting, they voted overwhelmingly to follow his advice.

CHAPTER SEVEN

Home for Christmas

A few weeks later peace became a fact. Washington hailed it with a letter to the man who, after him, did more than anyone else to achieve the victory, Nathanael Greene.

Head Quarters, March 31, 1783.

DEAR SIR: I have the pleasure to inclose to you a letter from the Marquis de la fayette, which came under cover to me, by the Packet Triumph, dispatched by the Marquis and the Count de Estaing from Cadiz to Phila.

All the Accounts which this Vessel has bro't, of a Conclusion of a General Peace, you will receive before this can reach you.

You will give the highest Credit to my Sincerity, when I beg you to accept my warmest Congratulations on this glorious and happy Event, an Event which crowns all our Labors and will sweeten the Toils which we have experienced in the Course of Eight Years distressing War. The Army here, universally participate in the general Joy which this Event has diffused, and, from this Consideration, together with the late Resolutions of Congress, for the Commutation of the Half pay, and for a Liquidation of all their Accounts, their Minds are filled with the highest Satisfaction. I am sure you will join with me in this additional occasion of joy.

It remains only for the States to be Wise, and to establish their Independence on that Basis of inviolable efficacious Union, and firm Confederation, which may prevent their being made the Sport of European Policy; may Heaven give them Wisdom to adopt the Measures still necessary for this important Purpose. I have the honor etc.

A few days later he wrote in a similar vein to Lafayette.

Head Qrs., Newburgh, April 5, 1783.

MY DEAR MARQS.: It is easier for you to conceive than for me to express the sensibility of my Heart at the communications in your letter of the 5th. of Feby. from Cadiz. It is to these communications we are indebted for the only acct. yet recd of a general Pacification. My mind upon the receipt of this news was instantly assailed by a thousand ideas, all of them contending for preeminence, but believe me my dear friend none could supplant, or ever will eradicate that gratitude, which has arisen from a lively sense of the conduct of your Nation: from my obligations to many illustrious characters of it, among whom (I do not mean to flatter, when) I place you at the head of them; And from my admiration of the Virtues of your August Sovereign; who at the same time that he stands confessed the Father of his own people, and defender of American rights has given the most exalted example of moderation in treating with his Enemies.

We now stand an Independent People, and have yet to learn political Tactics. We are placed among the Nations of the Earth, and have a character to establish; but how we shall acquit ourselves time must discover; the probability, at least I fear it is, that local, or state Politics will interfere too much with that more liberal and extensive plan of government which wisdom and foresight, freed from the mist of prejudice, would dictate; and that we shall be guilty of many blunders in treading this boundless theatre before we shall have arrived at any perfection in this Art. In a word that the experience which is purchased at the price of difficulties and distress, will alone convince us that the honor, power, and true Interest of this Country must be measured by a Continental scale; and that every departure therefrom weakens the Union, and may ultimately break the band, which holds us together. To avert these evils, to form a Constitution that will give consistency, stability and dignity to the Union; and sufficient powers to the great Council of the Nation for general purposes is a duty which is incumbent upon every Man who wishes well to his Country, and will meet with my aid as far as it can be rendered in the private walks of life; for henceforward my Mind shall be unbent; and I will endeavor to glide down the stream of life 'till I come to that abyss, from whence no traveller is permitted to return.

The Armament wch. was preparing at Cadiz,* and in which you were to have acted a distinguished part would have carried such conviction with it, that it is not to be wondered at, that Great Britain should have been impressed with the force of such reasoning. To this cause I am perswaded, the Peace is to be ascribed. Your going to Madrid from thence, instead of coming immediately to this Country, is another instance My Dear Marquis of your Zeal for the American Cause; and lays a fresh claim to the gratitude of her Sons, who will, at all times, receive you with open Arms; but as no Official dispatches are yet received, either at Phila. or New York of the completion of the treaty, nor any measures taken for the reduction of the Army, my detention therewith is quite uncertain; to say then (at this time) where I may be at the epoch for your intended visit to this Continent is too vague even for conjecture; but nothing can be more true than that the pleasure with which I shall receive you, will be equal to your wishes. I shall be better able to determine *then* than now, on the practicability of accompanying you to France. A Country to which I shall ever feel a Warm Affection; and if I do not pay it that tribute of respect which is to be derived from a visit it may be ascribed with more justice to any other cause, than a want of inclination; or the pleasure of going there under the auspices of your friendship.

I have already observed, that the determinations of Congress, if they have come to any, respecting the Army, is yet unknown to me; but as you wish to be informed of *every thing* that concerns it, I do, for your satisfaction, transmit authentic documents of some very interesting occurrences, which have happened within the last Six Months. but I ought first to have premised, that from accumulated sufferings, and little or no prospect of relief, the discontents of the Officers last Fall put on the threatning appearance of a total

* A combined French-Spanish fleet of forty-nine ships and twenty thousand men, of which Lafayette was chief of staff.

resignation, till the business was diverted into the channel which produced the Address and Petition to Congress which stands first on the file herewith inclosed. I shall make no comment on these proceedings; to one as well acquainted with the sufferings of the American Army as you are, it is unnecessary, it will be sufficient to observe, that the more Virtue and forbearence of it is tried, the more resplendent it appears. My hopes, that the military exit of this valuable class of the community will exhibit such a proof of Amor patriae as will do them honor in the page of history.

These papers with my last letter (which was intended to go by Colo. Gouvion, containing extensive details of Military Plans) will convey to you every information I can give, in the present uncertainty, worthy of attention. If you should get sleepy, and tired of reading them, recollect, for my exculpation, that it is in compliance with your request, I have run into such prolixity.

The scheme, my dear Marqs. which you propose as a precedent, to encourage the emancipation of the black people of this Country from that state of Bondage in wch. they are held, is a striking evidence of the benevolence of your Heart. I shall be happy to join you in so laudable a work; but will defer going into a detail of the business, 'till I have the pleasure of seeing you.

Lord Stirling [William Alexander, American major general] is no more; he died at Albany in Jany. last, very much regretted. Colo. Barber [Francis Barber of New Jersey] was snatched from us about the same time; in a way equally unexpected, sudden and distressing; leaving many friends to bemoan his fate.

Tilghman [Colonel Tench Tilghman of Maryland, a Washington aide] is on the point of Matrimony with a namesake and Couzin; Sister to Mrs. Carroll of Baltimore. It only remains for me now, My dear Marqs., to make a tender of my respectful Compliments in which Mrs. Washington unites, to Madame La Fayette; and to wish you, her, and your little offspring, all the happiness this life can afford. I will extend my Compliments to the Gentlemen, with whom I have the honor of an Acquaintance, in your circle. I need not add how happy I shall be to see you in America, and more particularly at Mount Vernon; or with what truth and warmth of Affection I am etc.

Lafayette's "scheme" for emancipating the Negroes involved purchasing, with Washington, a small estate on which they would establish free Negroes, making them tenants of the land. If the experiment were successful, Lafayette proposed to expand it to the West Indies.

Meanwhile, there were more letters of farewell to write. Throughout the war Major General Israel Putnam, the hero of Bunker Hill, had been more of a liability than an asset. But Washington managed to shift Putnam to relatively unimportant duties while enabling him to preserve his dignity and sense of honor. In this letter Washington completes his considerate treatment with a graceful goodbye.

Head Quarters, June 2, 1783.

DEAR SIR: Your favor of the 20 of May I received with much pleasure. For I can assure you, that, among the many worthy and meritorious Officers, with whom I have had the happiness to be connected in Service, through the Course of this War, and from whose cheerful Assistance and Advise, I have received much support and Confidence in the various and trying Vicissitudes of a Complicated Contest, the Name of a Putnam is not forgotten; nor will it be, but with that Stroke of Time which shall obliterate from my Mind, the remembrance of all those Toils and Fatigues, through which we have struggled for the preservation and Establishment of the Rights, Liberties and Independence of our Country.

Your Congratulations on the happy prospects of Peace and Independent Security, with their attendant Blessings to the United States, I receive with great Satisfaction; and beg that you will accept a Return of my Gratulations to you, on this auspicious Event; an Event, in which, great as it is in itself, and glorious as it will probably be in its Consequences, you have a right to participate largely, from the distinguished part you have contributed towards its attainment.

But while I contemplate the greatness of the Object for which we have contended, and felicitate you on the happy Issue of our Toils and Labors, while have terminated with such general Satisfaction, I lament that you should feel the ungrateful Returns of a Country in whose Service you have exhausted your Bodily Health and expended the Vigor of a youthful Constitution. I wish however that your Expectations of returng Sentiments of Liberality may be verified. I have a hope they may. But should they not, your case will not be a singular One. Ingratitude has been experienced in all Ages, and Republics in particular have ever been famed for the exercise of that unnatural and Sordid Vice.

The Secretary at War, who is now here, informs me that you have ever been considered as entitled to full pay, since your Absence from the field, and that you will be still considered in that Light 'till the Close of the War, at which period, you will be equally entitled to the same emoluments of half pay or Commutation, as other Officers of your Rank. The same Opinion is also given by the P M Genl, who is now with the Army, empowered by Mr. Morris for the Settlement of all their Accounts, and who will attend to yours whenever you shall think proper to send on for the purpose; which it will probably be best for you to in a short Time.

I anticipate with pleasure the Day, and that I trust not far off, when I shall quit the busy Scenes of a military Employment, and retire to the more tranquil Walks of Domestic Life. In that, or whatever other Situation, Providence may dispose of my future Days, the Remembrance of the many friendships and Connections I have had the happiness to contract with the Gentlemen of the Army, will be one of my most grateful Reflections. Under this Contemplation and Impressed with the Sentiments of Benevolence and Regard, I commend you, my Dear Sir, my other Friends, and with them, the Interests and Happiness of our Dear Country, to the keeping and Protection of Almighty God. With great Truth etc.

July of 1783 found Washington still waiting outside New York for a British evacuation. With peace looming on the horizon, his thoughts naturally turned toward home, which in turn undoubtedly made it doubly pleasing to answer a letter from George William Fairfax, still in England.

State of New York, July 10, 1783.

MY DEAR SIR: With very sincere pleasure I receiv'd your favor of the 26th. of March. It came to hand a few days ago only; and gave me the satisfaction of learning that you enjoyed good health, and that Mrs. Fairfax had improved in hers. there was nothing wanting in this Letter to give compleat satisfaction to Mrs. Washington and myself, but some expression to induce us to believe you would once more become our Neighbours. Your House at Belvoir I am sorry to add is no more, but mine (which is enlarged since you saw it) is most sincerely and heartily at your Service till you could rebuild it.

As the path, after being closed by a long, arduous, and painful contest, is to use an Indian Methaphor, now opened and made smooth, I shall please myself with the hope of hearing from you frequently; and till you forbid me to endulge the wish I shall not *despair* of seeing you and Mrs. Fairfax once more the Inhabitants of Belvoir, and greeting you both there, the intimate companions of our old Age, as you have been of our younger years.

I cannot sufficiently express my sensibility for your kind congratulations on the favourable termination of the War, and for the flattering manner in wch. you are pleased to speak of my instrumentality in effecting a revolution, which I can truely aver was not in the Beginning, premeditated; but the result of dire necessity brought about by the persecuting spirit of the British Government. This no man can speak to with more certainty, or assert upon better ground than myself, as I was a member of Congress and in the Councils of America till the Affair at Bunker hill and was an attentive observer and witness to those interesting and painful struggles for accommodation, and redress of grievances in a Constitutional way which all the world saw and must have approved, except the ignorant, deluded, and designing.

I unite my prayers most fervently with yours, for Wisdom to these U States and have no doubt, after a little while all errors in the present form of their Government will be corrected and a happy temper be diffused through the whole; but like young heirs come a little prematurely perhaps to a large Inheritance it is more than probable they will riot for a while; but, in this, if it should happen, tho' it is a circumste wch is to be lamented (as I would have the National character of America be pure and immaculate) will work its own cure, as there is virtue at the bottom.

You speak of having written many Letters to me during the War; but few, very few indeed have ever reached me. Early, and repeatedly, did I advise you of the impracticability, while I continued to direct the Military operations of this Country, of my paying the smallest attention to your Interest in Virginia, and pressed you to name some other friend to superintend your business. Upon your suggestion of Mr. Nicholas I wrote to him on the subject without obtaining an answer; and wrote, and wrote again to him Months after he was dead, so little acquainted was I with the private occurrences of our own State; nor to this moment have I got an answer from any one on the Subject, and know as little, perhaps less than you do, of the situation of your Affairs in Virginia. I have been in the State but once since the 4th. of May 1775 and that was at the Siege of York; in going thither I spent one day at my own House, and in returning I took 3 or 4 without attempting to transact a particle of private business, even for myself. I do not conceive that it would be any consolation to you to hear that your Neighbours were equal Sufferers with yourself or you might thank God as an Overseer in the Serive of your Father in Law did when he was rendering an Acct. to his Employer in the time of a calamatous drth. of the miserable prospect before him and the probability of their starving, that his Neighbours were as bad off as himself.

The amiable Mr. Custis was taken Sick at the Siege of York, and died at Colo. Bassetts the — of Novr. he has left four lovely Children; three girls and a boy (the latter is the youngest) who were all very well and promising when we heard last from them. His widow is yet single, and lives where he did, at the place formerly Robt. Alexanders (above Alexandria) which he bought and handsomely approved before his death.

Mrs. Washington enjoys an incompetent share of health; Billious Fevers and Cholic's attack her very often, and reduce her low; at this moment she is but barely recovering from one of them; at the same time that she thanks Mrs. Fairfax and you for your kind suggestion of Doctr. James's Annaliptic Pills, she begs you both to accept her most Affectionate regards; she would have conveyed these in a letter of her own, with grateful acknowledgments of Mrs. Fairfax's kind remembrance by Mr. Lee [Arthur Lee, American representative in France], if her health would have allowed it.

I wait with great impatience the arrival of the Definitive Treaty, that I may quit my Military employments, and bid adieu to public life, and in the shades of retirement seek that repose and tranquillity to which I have been an entire stranger for more than Eight years. I wish for it too because it will afford me some leizure to attend to an impaired fortune and recover, as it were from a state of torpidity or suspension; except in the instances of having money paid to me at a depreciated value.

My warmest and best Affections attend Mrs. Fairfax and yourself; and I am etc.

Widows did not stay single long in eighteenth century Virginia, especially when they had inherited a fortune. Jack Custis' Nelly began to think fondly of Dr. David Stuart, and asked Lund's advice. He promptly passed the buck to Washington, who proceeded to engage in the following evasive maneuvers.

Rocky Hill, September 20, 1783.

DEAR LUND: Mrs. Custis has never suggested in any of her Letters to Mrs. Washington (unless ardent wishes for her return, that she might then disclose it to her, can be so construed) the most distant attachment to D.S.; but if this should be the case, and she wants advice upon it; a Father and Mother, who are at hand, and competent to give it, are at the same time most proper to be consulted on so interesting an event. For my own part, I never did, nor do I believe I ever shall give advice to a woman who is setting out on a matrimonial voyage; first, because I never could advise one to marry without her own consent; and secondly, because I know it is to no purpose to advise her to refrain, when she has obtained it. A woman very rarely asks an opinion or requires advice on such an occasion, 'till her resolution is formed; and then it is with the hope and expectation of obtaining a sanction, nor that she means to be governed by your disapprobation, that she applies. In a word, the plain english of the application may be summed up in these words: "I wish you to think as I do; but if unhappily you differ from me in opinion, my heart, I must confess is fixed, and I have gone too far *now* to retract."

If Mrs. Custis should ever suggest any thing of this kind to me, I will give her my opinion of the *measure*, not of the *man*, with candour, and to the following effect. I never expected you would spend the residue of your days in widowhood; but in a matter so important, and so interesting to yourself, children and connexions; I wish you would make a prudent choice; to do which, many considerations are necessary; such as the family and connexions of the man, his fortune (which is not the *most* essential in my eye), the line of conduct he has observed, and disposition and frame of his mind. You should consider, what prospect there is of his proving kind and affectionate to you; just, generous and attentive to your children; and, how far his connexions will be agreeable to you; for when they are once formed, agreeable or not, the die being cast, your fate is fixed. Thus far, and no farther I shall go in my opinions. I am etc.

The treaty of peace at last arrived. The British evacuated New York, and Washington occupied it on November 25. On December 4 the last British troops left Staten Island and Long Island, and their fleet put to sea. On that same day Washington said farewell to his officers in a tearful scene at Fraunces Tavern. He then rode to Annapolis, where Congress was meeting, and surrendered his commission as *Commander in Chief.* On *Christmas Eve, hard riding brought him home at last to Mount Vernon. His sense of release can be glimpsed in this cheerful letter to Charles Thomson, secretary of Congress.*

Mount Vernon, January 22, 1784.

DEAR SIR: . . . If my Commission is not necessary for the files of Congress I should be glad to have it deposited amongst my own Papers. It may serve *my Grand Children* some fifty or a hundd. years hence for a theme to ruminate upon, *if they should* be contemplatively disposed.

We have been so fast locked in Snow and Ice since Christmas, that all kinds of intercourse have been suspended; and a duty which I owed my Mother, and intended 'ere this to have performed, has been forced to yield to the intemperence of the Weather: but, as this again must submit to the approaching Sun, I shall soon be enabled, I expect, to discharge that duty on which Nature and inclination have a call; and shall be ready afterwards to welcome my friends to the shadow of this Vine and Fig tree; where I hope it unnecessary to add, I should be exceedingly happy to see you, and any of *my late Masters,* now representatives. Mrs. Washington, if she knew I was writing to you in the stile of Invitation would, I am certain, adduce arguments to prove that I ought to include Mrs. Thompson; but before she should have half spun the thread of her discourse, it is more than probable I should have nonplused her, by yielding readily to the force of her reasoning.

Next comes a letter to Lafayette in which Washington parries another invitation to visit Paris.

Mount Vernon, February 1, 1784.

At length my Dear Marquis I am become a private citizen on the banks of the Potomac, and under the shadow of my own Vine and my own Fig-tree, free from the bustle of a camp and the busy scenes of public life, I am solacing myself with those tranquil enjoyments, of which the Soldier who is ever in pursuit of fame, the

Statesman whose watchful days and sleepless nights are spent in devising schemes to promote the welfare of his own, perhaps the ruin of other countries, as if this globe was insufficient for us all, and the Courtier who is always watching the countenance of his Prince, in hopes of catching a gracious smile, can have very little conception. I am not only retired from all public employments, but I am retiring within myself; and shall be able to view the solitary walk, and tread the paths of private life with heartfelt satisfaction. Envious of none, I am determined to be pleased with all; and this my dear friend, being the order for my march, I will move gently down the stream of life, until I sleep with my Fathers.

Except an introductory letter or two, and one countermanding my request respecting plate, I have not written to you since the middle of October by Genl. Duportail.* To inform you at this late hour, that the city of New York was evacuated by the British forces on the 25th. of November; that the American Troops took possession of it the same day, and delivered it over to the civil authority of the State; that good order, contrary to the expectation and predictions of Gl. Carleton, his Officers and all the loyalists, was immediately established; and that the harbour of New York was finally cleared of the British flag about the 5th. or 6th. of Decemr., would be an insult to your intelligence. And to tell you that I remained eight days in New York after we took possession of the city; that I was very much hurried during that time, which was the reason I did not write to you from thence; that taking Phila. in my way, I was obliged to remain there a week; that at Annapolis, where Congress were then, and are now sitting, I did, on the 23d. of December present them my commission, and made them my last bow, and on the Eve of Christmas entered these doors an older man by near nine years, than when I left them, is very uninteresting to any but myself. Since that period, we have been fast locked up in frost and snow, and excluded in a manner from all kinds of intercourse, the winter having been, and still continues to be, extremely severe.

* Major General Louis Duportail, Chief Engineer of the American Army.

I have now to acknowledge, and thank you for your favors of the 22d of July and 8th of September, both of which, altho' the first is of old date, have come to hand since my letter to you of October. The accounts contained therein of the political and commercial state of affairs as they respect America, are interesting, and I wish I could add that they were altogether satisfactory; and the agency you have had in both, particularly with regard to the free ports in France, is a fresh evidence of your unwearied endeavours to serve this country; but there is no part of your Letters to Congress My Dear Marquis, which bespeaks the excellence of your heart more plainly than that, which contains those noble and generous sentiments on the justice which is due to the faithful friends and Servants of the public; but I must do Congress the justice to declare, that as a body, I believe there is every disposition in them, not only to acknowledge the merits, but to reward the services of the army: There is a contractedness, I am sorry to add, in some of the States, from whence all our difficulties on this head, proceed; but it is to be hoped, the good sense and perseverance of the rest, will ultimately prevail, as the spirit of *meanness* is beginning to subside.

From a letter which I have just received from the Governor of this State I expect him here in a few days, when I shall not be unmindful of what you have written about the bust, and will endeavour to have matters respecting it, placed on their proper basis. I thank you most sincerely My Dear Marqs. for your kind invitation to your house, if I should come to Paris. At present I see but little prospect of such a voyage, the deranged situation of my private concerns, occasioned by an absence of almost nine years, and an entire disregard of all private business during that period, will not only suspend, but may put it for ever out of my power to gratify this wish. This not being the case with you, come with Madame la Fayette and view me in my domestic walks. I have often told you, and repeat it again, that no man could receive you in them with more friendship and affection than I should do; in which I am sure Mrs. Washington would cordially join me. We unite in respectful compliments to your Lady, and best wishes for your little flock. With every sentiment of esteem, Admiration and Love, I am etc.

Washington's close companion during the eight-year struggle for independence, Major General Henry Knox, was now acting Secretary of War. In the following letter Washington discusses such matters as Knox's pay and the organization of the Society of the Cincinnati, whose membership was limited to Revolutionary officers and their descendants. Named after the famed Roman general who returned from his military triumphs and took up the life of a simple farmer once more, it is still flourishing today. But the dominant note of this letter is the joy Washington feels at escaping the burdens of power.

Mount Vernon, February 20th, 1784.
MY DEAR SIR: The bad weather and the great care which the post riders take of themselves prevented your letters of the 3rd and the 9th of last month from getting to my hands 'till the 10th of this. Setting off next morning for Fredericksburg to pay my duty to an aged mother and not returning 'till yesterday will be admitted, I hope, as sufficient apology for my silence 'till now.

I am much obliged by the trouble you have taken to report the state of the Garrison and Stores, together with the disposition of the Troops at West-Point, to me, and think the allowance of Rations, or subsistence money to such Officers as could not retire at that inclement season, was not only perfectly humane, but perfectly just. and that it must appear so to Congress.

It would seem to me, without having recourse to calculation, that the allowance of a Majr. General in a seperate department, to the person who shall discharge the duties of Secretary at War, Master of Ordnance, and Commanding Officer of the Forces which may be retained, or Raised for a Peace Establishment is as low as it well can be. I expect the President and some Members of Congress here in a day or two, and will tell them so.

It was amongst my first Acts after I got home, to write to the

President of each State Society, appointing Philadelphia (and the first Monday in May) for the general meeting of the Cincinnati. Colo. Walker [Benjamin Walker, as staff officer] took with him all the Letters for those Eastward of this, before New Years day; the others for the Southward, I dispatched by the Post about the same-time; I have even sent duplicates for fear of miscarriage; yet 'though it is the most eligable method, it is to be feared it will not prove so effectual a communication, as a general notification in the public Gazettes would have been. And, in case of failure, I shall be exceedingly concerned for not having adopted the most certain; as it would give me pleasure to have the first general meeting, a very full one. I have named Philadelphia (contrary to my own judgment, as it is not Central) to comply with the wishes of South Carolina, who, being the most Southern State, have desired it. North Carolina I have not heard a tittle from, nor any thing Official from New Hampshire. all the other States have acceded very unanimously to the propositions which were sent from the Army.

I am just beginning to experience that ease, and freedom from public cares which, however desirable, takes some time to realize; for strange as it may tell, it is nevertheless true, that it was not 'till lately I could get the better of my usual custom of ruminating as soon as I waked in the Morning, on the business of the ensuing day; and of my surprize, after having revolved many things in my mind, to find that I was no longer a public Man, or had any thing to do with public transactions.

I feel now, however, as I conceive a wearied Traveller must do, who, after treading many a painful step, with a heavy burden on his shoulders, is eased of the latter, having reached the Goal to which all the former were directed; and from his House top is looking back, and tracing with a grateful eye the Meanders by which he escaped the quicksands and Mires which lay in his way; and into which none but the All-powerful guide, and great disposer of human Events could have prevented his falling.

I shall be very happy, and I hope I shall not be disappointed, in seeing you at the proposed meeting in Philadelphia. The friendship I have conceived for you will not be impaired by absence, but it may be no unpleasing circumstance to brighten the Chain, by a renewal of the Covenant. My best wishes attend Mrs. Knox and the little folks, in which Mrs. Washington most heartily joins me. With every sentiment of the purest esteem &c.

P.S. I hope Genl Greene will be in the Delegation from Rhode Island, and that we shall see him at the Genl meeting of the Cincinnati; will you intimate this to him?

Lafayette having failed, Madame Lafayette attempted to lure Washington to Paris. He replies with a masterful counter invitation.

Mount Vernon, April 4, 1784.

MADAM: It is now, more than ever, I want words to express the sensibility and gratitude with which the honor of your felcitations of the 26th. of Decr. has inspired me. If my expression was equal to the feelings of my heart the homage I am about to render you, would appear in a more favourable point of view, than my most sanguine expectations will encourage me to hope for. I am more inclined therefore to rely upon the continuance of your indulgent sentiments of me, and that innate goodness for which you are remarked, than upon any merit I possess, or any assurances I could give of my sense of the obligation I am under for the honor you have conferred upon me by your corrispondence.

Great as your claim is, as a French or American woman; or as the wife of my amiable friend, to my affectionate regards; you have others to which the palm must be yielded. The charms of your person, and the beauties of your mind, have a more powerful operation. These Madam, have endeared you to me, and every thing which partakes of your nature will have a claim to my affections. George and Virginia (the offspring of your love), whose names do honor to my Country, and to myself, have a double claim and will be the objects of my vows.

From the clangor of arms and the bustle of a camp, freed from the cares of public employment, and the responsibility of office, I am now enjoying domestic ease under the shadow of my own Vine, and my own Fig tree; and in a small Villa, with the implements of Husbandry, and Lambkins around me, I expect to glide gently down the stream of life, 'till I am entombed in the dreary mansions of my Fathers.

Mrs. Washington is highly honored by your participations, and feels very sensibly the force of your polite invitation to Paris; but she is too far advanced in life, and is too much immersed in the care of her little progeny, to cross the Atlantic. This My Dr. Marchioness (indulge me with this freedom) is not the case with you. You have youth (and if you should not incline to bring your children, can leave them with all the advantages to Education), and *must* have a curiosity to see the Country, young, rude and uncultivated as it is; for the liberties of which your husband has fought, bled, and acquired much glory. Where every body admires, every body loves him. Come then, let me entreat it, and call my Cottage your home; for your own doors do not open to you with more readiness, than mine wou'd. You will see the plain manner in which we live; and meet the rustic civility, and you shall taste the simplicity of rural life. It will diversify the Scene and may give you a higher relish for the gaieties of the Court, when you return to Versailles. In these wishes, and in most respectful compliments Mrs. Washington joins me. With sentiments of strong attachment, and very great regard, I have the honor etc.

Few men ever persuaded Washington to write a letter for them, to help them land a political job. In an era when it was almost impossible for writers to support themselves, he obviously felt Thomas Paine deserved to be an exception, and wrote this plea to James Madison, at that time a leader in the Virginia legislature.

Mount Vernon, June 12, 1784.
DEAR SIR: Can nothing be done in our Assembly for poor Paine? Must the merits, and Services of *Common Sense* continue to glide down the stream of time, unrewarded by this Country? His writings certainly have had a powerful effect on the public mind; ought they not then to meet an adequate return? He is poor! he is

chagreened! and almost, if not altogether, in despair of relief. New York it is true, not the least distressed, nor best able State in the Union, has done something for him. This kind of provision he prefers to an allowance from Congress; he has reasons for it, which to him are conclusive, and such I think as would have weight with others. His views are moderate; a decent independency is, I believe, all he aims at. Should he not obtain this? If you think so, I am sure you will not only move the matter, but give it your support. For me, it only remains to feel for his Situation, and to assure you of the sincere esteem and regard with which I have the honor &c.

To Washington's great joy, Lafayette returned for a postwar visit, which included a lengthy sojourn at Mount Vernon. He did not bring his wife with him. He did, however, bring letters from her and his daughter that Washington was quick to answer. In much the same terms of his earlier letter, he urged the Marchioness to come along on Lafayette's next visit. Then he added the following little note to Mademoiselle de Lafayette.

November 25, 1784.

Permit me to thank you my dear little correspondent for the favor of her letter of the 18th. of June last, and to impress her with the idea of the pleasure I shall derive in a continuation of them. Her papa is restored to her with all the good health, paternal affection and honors her tender heart could wish.

He will carry a kiss to her from me, (which might be more agreeable from a pretty boy) and give her assurances of the affectionate regard with which I have the pleasure of being her well wisher.

Lafayette's departure brought forth these mournful intimations of Mortality from Washington.

Mount Vernon, December 8, 1784.

MY DEAR MARQS: The peregrination of the day in which I parted with you, ended at Marlbro': the next day, bad as it was, I got home before dinner.

In the moment of our separation upon the road as I travelled, and every hour since, I felt all that love, respect and attachment for you, with which length of years, close connexion and your merits have inspired me. I often asked myself, as our carriages distended, whether that was the last sight, I ever should have of you? And tho' I wished to say no, my fears answered yes. I called to mind the days of my youth, and found they had long since fled to return no more; that I was now descending the hill, I had been 52 years climbing, and that tho' I was blessed with a good constitution, I was of a short lived family, and might soon expect to be entombed in the dreary mansions of my father's. These things darkened the shades and gave a gloom to the picture, consequently to my prospects of seeing you again: but I will not repine, I have had my day.

Nothing of importance has occurred since I parted with you; I found my family well, and am now immersed in company; notwithstanding which, I have in haste, produced a few more letters to give you the trouble of, rather inclining to commit them to your care, than to pass them thro' many and unknown hands.

It is unnecessary, I persuade myself to repeat to you my Dr. Marqs. the sincerity of my regards and friendship, nor have I words which could express my affection for you, were I to attempt it. My fervent prayers are offered for your safe and pleasant passage, happy meeting with Madame la Fayette and family, and the completion of every wish of your heart, in all which Mrs. Washington joins me, as she does in complimts. to Capt. Grandchean and the Chevr. of whom little Wash:n often speaks. With every sentimt. wch. is propitious and endearing, I am, etc.

The two Frenchmen "Grandchean and the Chevr." accompanied Lafayette on his visit. Captain Guillaume Granchain had represented the French navy at Cornwallis' surrender. The Chevalier Caraman, Maurice Riquet, was an officer of the Touraine Regiment. "Little Washington" is George Washington Parke Custis, Martha's grandson. Much as he enjoyed these foreign friendships, Washington remained deeply attached to the friends of his youth.

Particularly was this true of George William Fairfax, still in England.

Mount Vernon, February 27, 1785.

MY DEAR SIR: In a letter of old date, but lately received, from the Countess of Huntington, she refers me to a letter which her Ladyship says you obligingly undertook to forward to me: never having received one from her to the purport she mentions, there can be no doubt but that this letter with your cover to it, have met the fate of some of mine to you; as I have wrote several within the last twelve or eighteen months, without any acknowledgement of them from you. . . .

I cannot at this moment recur to the contents of those letters of mine to you which I suspect have miscarried; further than that they were all expressive of an earnest wish to see you and Mrs. Fairfax once more fixed in this country; and to beg that you would consider Mt. Vernon as your home until you could build with convenience, in which request Mrs. Washington joins very sincerely. I never look towards Belvoir, without having this uppermost in my mind. But alas! Belvoir is no more! I took a ride there the other day to visit the ruins, and ruins indeed they are. The dwelling house and the two brick buildings in front, underwent the ravages of the fire; the walls of which are very much injured: the other Houses are sinking under the depredation of time and inattention, and I believe are now scarcely worth repairing. In a word, the whole are, or very soon will be a heap of ruin. When I viewed them, when I considered that the happiest moments of my life had been spent there, when I could not trace a room in the house (now all rubbish) that did not bring to my mind the recollection of pleasing scenes, I was obliged to fly from them; and came home with painful sensations, and sorrowing for the contrast. Mrs. Morton still lives at your Barn quarter. The management of your business is entrusted to one Muse (son to a Colonel of that name, whom you cannot have forgotten), he is, I am told, a very active and industrious man; but in what sort of order he has your Estate, I am unable to inform you, never having seen him since my return to Virginia.

It may be and I dare say is presumed that if I am not returned to my former habits of life, the change is to be ascribed to a preference of ease and indolence to exercise and my wonted activity: But be assured my dear Sir, that at no period of the War have I been obliged myself to go thro' more drudgery in writing, or have suffered so much confinement to effect it, as since what is called my retirement to domestic ease and tranquility. Strange as it may seem, it is nevertheless true, that I have been able since I came home, to give very little attention to my own concerns, or to those of others, with which I was entrusted. My Accounts stand as I left them near ten years ago; those who owed me money, a very few instances excepted, availed themselves of what are called the tender Laws, and paid me off with a shilling and sixpence in the pound. Those to whom I owed, I have now to pay under heavy taxes with specie, or its equivalent value. I do not mention these matters by way of complaint, but as an apology for not having rendered you a full and perfect statement of the Acct. as it may stand between us, 'ere this. I allotted this Winter, supposing the drearyness of the season would afford me leisure to overhaul and adjust all my papers (which are in sad disorder, from the frequent hasty removals of them, from the reach of our trans-atlantic foes, when their Ships appeared): but I reckoned without my host; Company, and a continual reference of old military matters, with which I ought to have no concern; applications for Certificates of service &c., copies of orders and the Lord knows what besides, to which whether they are complied with or not, some response must be made, engross nearly my whole time. I am now endeavoring to get some person as a Secretary or Clerk to take the fatigueing part of this business off my hands. I have not yet succeeded, but shall continue my enquiries 'till one shall offer, properly recommended.

Nothing has occurred of late worth noticing, except the renewed attempts of the Assemblies of Virginia and Maryland to improve and extend the navigation of the river Potomac as far as it is practicable, and communicating it by good roads (at the joint and equal expence of the two States) with the waters of the amazing territory behind us. A copy of this Act (exactly similar in both states) I do myself the honor to enclose you. One similar to it passed the Legislature of this State for improving and extending the navigation of James river, and opening a good road between it and Green-briar. These acts were accompanied by another of the Virginia Assembly, very flattering and honorable for me, not more so for the magnitude of the gift, than the avowed gratitude, and delicacy of its expression, in the recital to it. The purport of it is, to vest 100 shares (50 in each navigation) in me and my heirs forever. But it is not my intention to accept of it; altho', were I otherwise disposed, I should consider it as the foundation of the *greatest* and most *certain* income that the like sum can produce in any speculation whatever. So certain is the accomplishment of the work, if the sum proposed should be raised to carry it on, and so inconceivably will the tolls increase by the accumulating produce which will be water borne on the navigation of these two rivers, which penetrate so far and communicate so nearly, with the navigable waters to the Westward.

At the same time that I determine not to accept this generous and gratuitous offer of my Country, I am at a loss in what manner to decline it, without an apparent slight or disrespect to the Assembly on the one hand, or exposing myself to the imputation of pride, or an ostentatious display of disinterestedness on the other, neither have an existence in my breast, and neither would I wish to have ascribed to me. I shall have time however to think of the matter, before the next session; for as if it was meant that I should have no opportunity to decline the offer at the *last*, it was the closing act thereof, without any previous intimation, or suspicion in my mind, of the intention. Admitting that Companies should be incorporated for the purposes mentioned in the Act, do you conceive my good Sir, that a person perfectly skilled in works of this sort, could be readily obtained from England? And upon what terms?

It is unnecessary I persuade myself, to use arguments to convince Mrs. Fairfax and yourself, to the sincere regard and attachment and affection Mrs. Washington and I have for you both, or to assure you how much, I am, etc.

P.S. Do you think it would be in your power, with ease and convenience, to procure for me, a male and female Deer or two, the cost of transportation I would gladly be at. If I should ever get relieved from the drudgery of the pen, it would be my wish to engage in these kind of rural amusements, raising of shrubberies &c. After what I have said in the body of this letter, I will not trouble you with an apology for such a scrawl as it now exhibits, you must receive it, my good Sir, as we have done better things, better for worse.

As he grew older, Washington's letters on family matters became more pungent and interesting. This one, to Burwell Bassett, dealing with the prospect of a marriage between his nephew George Augustine Washington and Fanny Bassett, niece of Martha, has him holding forth once more on one of his favorite subjects, matrimony.

Mount Vernon, May 23, 1785.

DEAR SIR: It would have given me much pleasure to have seen you at Richmond; and it was part of my original plan to have spent a few days with you at Eltham, whilst I was in the lower parts of the country; but an intervention of circumstances not only put it out of my power to do the latter, but would have stopped my journey to Richmond altogether, had not the meeting (the time and the place) been of my own appointing. I left company at home when I went away, who proposed to wait my return, among whom a Mr. Pine, an artist of eminence, came all the way from Philadelphia for some materials for an historical painting which he is about, and for which he was obliged to stay 'till I got back, which I did after an absence of eight days only.

My Nephew G. Aug: Washington is just returned from his peregrination; apparently much amended in his health, but not quite free from the disorder in his breast. I have understood that his addresses to your Daughter were made with your consent; and I now learn that he is desirous, and she is willing to fulfill the engagement they have entered into; and that they are applying to you for permission therefor.

It has ever been a maxim with me thro' life, neither to promote, nor to prevent a matrimonial connection, unless there should be something indispensably requiring interference in the latter: I have always considered marriage as the most interesting event of one's life, the foundation of happiness or misery; to be instrumental therefore in bringing two people together who are indifferent to each other, and may soon become objects of hatred; or to prevent a union which is prompted by mutual esteem and affection, is what I never could reconcile to my feelings; and therefore, neither directly nor indirectly have I ever said a syllable to Fanny or George upon the subject of their intended connexion; but as their attachment to each other seems to have been early formed, warm and lasting, it bids fair to be happy: if therefore you have no objection, I think the sooner it is consummated the better.

I have just now informed them (the former thro' Mrs. Washington) that it is my wish they should live here.

It is unnecessary I hope to say how happy we should be to see you, her brothers, and any of her friends here upon this occasion (who can make it convenient and are disposed to come); all here join in best wishes for you, and with very sincere esteem etc.

Second only to Lafayette among the friendships Washington contracted during the war was David Humphreys. A writer of considerable talent, he frequently sent Washington copies of his poems. Washington replies here to a letter from Europe, where Humphreys was serving as secretary to the American mission in Paris. Among many topics, he discussed European affairs and urged Washington to write his own history of the war. Humphreys later took advantage of Washington's counteroffer—that he write the history—and came to Mount Vernon and spent several weeks with Washington taking notes and discussing the proposed book. Unfortunately, Humphreys was more poet than historian and never finished it.

Mount Vernon, July 25, 1785.

MY DR. HUMPHREYS: Since my last to you, I have received your letter of the 15th. of January, and I believe that of the 11th. of November, and thank you for them. It always gives me pleasure to hear from you; and I should think if *amusements* would spare you, business could not so much absorb your time as to prevent your writing more frequently, especially as there is a regular conveyance once a month by the Packet.

As the complexion of European politics seems now (from letters I have received from the Marqs. de la Fayette, Chevrs. Chastellux, Dc la Luzerne, &c.,) to have a tendency to Peace, I will say nothing of war, nor make any animadversions upon the contending powers; otherwise, I might possibly have said that the retreat from it seemed impossible after the explicit declaration of the parties: My first wish is to see this plague to mankind banished from off the Earth, and the sons and Daughters of this world employed in more pleasing and innocent amusements, than in preparing implements and exercising them for the destruction of mankind: rather than quarrel about territory let the poor, the needy and oppressed of the Earth, and those who want Land, resort to the fertile plains of our western country, the *second Promise*, and there dwell in peace, fulfilling the first and great commandment.

In a former letter, I informed you my Dr. Humphreys, that if I had *talents* for it, I have not *leisure* to turn my thoughts to commentaries: a consciousness of a defective education, and a certainty of the want of time, unfit me for such an undertaking; what with company, letters and other matters, many of them quite extraneous, I have not been able to arrange my own private concerns so as to rescue them from that disorder'd state into which they have been thrown by the war, and to do which is become absolutely necessary for my support, whilst I remain on this stage of human action. The sentiments of your last letter on this subject gave me great pleasure; I should be pleased indeed to see you undertake this business: your abilities as a writer; your discernment respecting the principles which lead to the decision by arms; your personal knowledge of many facts as they occurred in the progress of the War; your disposition to justice, candour and impartiality, and your diligence in investigating truth, combining fit you, when joined with the vigor of life, for this task; and I should with great pleasure, not only give you the perusal of all my papers, but any oral information of circumstances, which cannot be obtained from the former, that my memory will furnish: and I can with great truth add that my house would not only be at your service during the period of your preparing this work, but (and without an unmeaning compliment I say it) I should be exceedingly happy if you would make it your home. You might have an apartment to yourself, in which you could command your own time; you wou'd be considered and treated as one of the family; and meet with that cordial reception and entertainment which are characteristic of the sincerest friendship.

To reverberate European news would be idle, and we have little of domestic kind worthy of attention: We have held treaties indeed, with the Indians; but they were so unseasonably delayed, that these people by our last accounts from the westward, are in a discontented mood, supposed by many to be instigated thereto by our late enemies, now, to be sure, *fast friends*; who from any thing I can learn, under the indefinite expression of the treaty hold, and seem resolved to retain possession of our western Posts. Congress have also, after a long and tedious deliberation, passed an ordinance for laying off the Western Territory into States, and for disposing of the land; but in a manner and on terms which few people (in the Southern States) conceive can be accomplished: Both sides are sure, and the event is appealed to, let time decide it. It is however to be regretted that local politics and self-interested views obtrude themselves into every measure of public utility: but to such characters be the consequences.

My attention is more immediately engaged in a project which I think big with great political, as well as commercial consequences to these States, especially the middle ones: it is, by removing the obstructions, and extending the inland navigation of our rivers, to bring the States on the Atlantic in close connexion with those forming to the westward, by a short and easy transportation: without this, I can easily conceive they will have different views, separate interests and other connexions. I may be singular in my ideas; but they are these, that to open a door to, and make easy the way for those Settlers to the westward (which ought to progress regularly and compactly) before we make any stir about the navigation of the Mississippi, and before our settlements are far advanced towards that river, would be our true line of policy. It can, I think, be demonstrated, that the produce of the western Territory (if the navigations which are now in hand succeed, and of which I have no doubt) as low down the Ohio as the Great Kanhawa, I *believe* to the Falls, and between the parts above and the Lakes, may be brought either to the highest shipping port on this or James river, at a less expence, with more ease, (including the return) and in a much shorter time, than it can be carried to New Orleans if the Spaniards instead of restricting, were to throw open their ports and invite our trade. But if the commerce of that country should embrace this channel, and connexions be formed; experience has taught us (and there is a very recent proof with G:Britain) how next to impracticable it is to divert it; and if that should be the case, the Atlantic States (especially as those to the westward will in a great degree fill with foreigners) will be no more to the present union, except to excite perhaps very justly our fears, than the Country of California which is still more to the westward, and belonging to another power.

Mrs. Washington presents her compliments to you, and with every wish for your happiness, I am etc.

Ever the gentleman, Washington found time to salute Benjamin Franklin on his return to his native shores.

Mount Vernon, September 25, 1785.
DEAR SIR: Amid the public gratulations on your safe return to America, after a long absence and the many eminent services you have rendered it, for which as a benefited person I feel the obligation, permit an individual to join the public voice in expressing a

sense of them; and to assure you, that, as no one entertains more respect for your character, so none can salute you with more sincerity, or with greater pleasure, than I do on the occasion. With the highest regard and greatest consideration, I am, &c.

Death now began to winnow many of the Revolution stalwarts. One of the best was Jonathan Trumbull, wartime governor of Connecticut. His departure drew a letter of sympathy from Washington to his ex-aide, Jonathan Trumbull, Jr.

Mount Vernon, October 1, 1785.

MY DEAR SIR: It has so happened, that your letter of the first of last month did not reach me until Saturdays Post. You know, too well, the sincere respect and regard I entertained for your venerable fathers public and private character, to require assurances of the concern I felt for his death; or of that sympathy in your feelings for the loss of him, which is prompted by friendship. Under this loss however, great as your pangs may have been at the first shock, you have every thing to console you. A long and well spent life in the Service of his Country, placed Govr. Trumbull amongst the first of Patriots. In the social duties he yielded to none. and his Lamp, from the common course of Nature, being nearly extinguished, worn down with age and cares, but retaining his mental faculties in perfection, are blessings which rarely attend advanced life. All these combining, have secured to his memory universal respect and love here, and no doubt immeasurable happiness hereafter.

I am sensible that none of these observations can have escaped you, and that I can offer nothing which your own reason has not already suggested on this occasion; and being of Sterne's opinion, that "Before an affliction is digested, consolation comes too soon; and after it is digested, it comes too late: there is but a mark between these two, as fine almost as a hair, for a comforter to take aim at." I rarely attempt it, nor shall I add more on this subject to you, as it would only be a renewal of sorrow, by recalling a fresh to your remembrance things which had better be forgotten.

My principal pursuits are of a rural nature, in which I have great delight, especially as I am blessed with the enjoyment of good health. Mrs. Washington on the contrary is hardly ever well, but thankful for your kind remembrance of her, and joins me in every good wish for you, Mrs. Trumbull and your family. Be assured that with sentiments of the purest, esteem etc.

Another old friend from war days, Robert Morris, the financier who kept the army going, engaged Washington in a discussion of slavery and the activity of certain societies in the north who favored emancipation.

Mount Vernon,. April 12, 1786.

DEAR SIR: I give you the trouble of this letter at the instance of Mr. Dalby of Alexandria; who is called to Philadelphia to attend what he conceives to be a vexatious lawsuit respecting a slave of his, which a Society of Quakers in the city (formed for such purposes) have attempted to liberate; the merits of this case will no doubt appear upon trial. but from Mr. Dalby's state of the matter, it should seem that this Society is not only acting repugnant to justice so far as its conduct concerns strangers, but, in my opinion extremely impolitickly with respect to the State, the City in particular; and without being able, (but by acts of tyranny and oppression) to accomplish their own ends. He says the conduct of this society is not sanctioned by Law: had the case been otherwise, whatever my opinion of the Law might have been, my respect for the policy of the State would on this occasion have appeared in my silence; because against the penalties of promulgated Laws one may guard; but there is no avoiding the snares of individuals, or of private societies. And if the practice of this Society of which Mr. Dalby speaks, is not discountenanced, none of those whose *misfortune* it is to have slaves as attendants, will visit the City if they can possibly avoid it; because by so doing they hazard their property; or they must be at the expence (and this will not always succeed) of providing servants of another description for the trip.

I hope it will not be conceived from these observations, that it is my wish to hold the unhappy people, who are the subject of this letter, in slavery. I can only say that there is not a man living who wishes more sincerely than I do, to see a plan adopted for the abolition of it; but there is only one proper and effectual mode by which it can be accomplished, and that is by Legislative authority; and this, as far as my suffrage will go, shall never be wanting. But when slaves who are happy and contented with their present masters, are tampered with and seduced to leave them; when masters are taken unawares by these practices; when a conduct of this sort begets discontent on one side and resentment on the other, and when it happens to fall on a man, whose purse will not measure with that of the Society, and he looses his property for want of means to defend it; it is oppression in the latter case, and not humanity in any; because it introduces more evils than it can cure.

I will make no apology for writing to you on this subject; for if Mr. Dalby has not misconceived the matter, an evil exists which requires a remedy; if he has, my intentions have been good, though I may have been too precipitate in this address. Mrs. Washington joins me in every good and kind wish for Mrs. Morris and your family, and I am, &c.

Sometimes a note on a very slight matter gives a glimpse of the great man that otherwise would be missed. The following to Bushrod Washington is this sort of letter. Royal Gift was one of two jackasses sent to Washington by the King of Spain.

Mount Vernon, April 13, 1786.
DEAR BUSHROD: If Royal gift will administer, he shall be at the Service of your Mares, but at present he seems too full of Royalty, to have any thing to do with a plebean race; perhaps his Stomach may come to him, if not, I shall wish he had never come from his Most Catholic Majesty's Stables.

Your Papa has not been here yet. I am just come in from a Ride, the Dinner bell rings, and your Man says he must go off after it. So offer me affectionately to all, and believe me to be sincerely . . .

Washington wrote a few letters to Theodorick Bland, a Virginian who served with distinction throughout the Revolutionary War. This one is interesting because it gives additional evidence that Washington was by no means the resolutely solemn graybeard some biographers have painted him.

Mount Vernon, August 15, 1786.

DEAR SIR: By Colo. Fitzhugh I had the satisfaction to receive the humorous accot. you were pleased to give me of your nocturnal journey to Fredericksburg. I recollect very well, the Lady whom you mention to have had for a fellow traveller, and if you should chance to be in her company again, I should be much obliged by your presenting my compliments to her. The even tenor of my life (in which I can expect to meet with few extraordinary adventures) as well as my long seclusion in a great measure, from the exhilirating scenes of mixed society, must be an apology for my not attempting (with such provocatives to gaiety) to say some more sprightly things in reply to the brilliancy of her dialogue; or the vivacity with which you have reported it. I commend you, however, for passing the time in as merry a manner as you possibly could; it is assuredly better to go laughing than crying thro' the rough journey of life.

I have mentioned your request to Colo. Humphreys, who is still at Mt. Vernon and who has put a copy of his last poem into my hands to be forwarded with his compliments to you. He has farther desired me to inform you, in answer to the civil things you have said of it, that he feels himself singularly happy whenever he finds that his works are honored with the approbation of men of taste and liberallity. He regrets that he cannot send you the copy of a former poem, which after being several times reprinted in Europe, has lately been translated by the Marqs. de Chastelleux, and received with a great deal of applause at Paris.

I shall always be happy to give and receive communications on improvements in farming, and the various branches of agriculture. This is in my opinion, an object of infinite importance to the country; I consider it to be the proper source of American wealth and happiness. Whose streams might become more copious and diffusive, if gentlemen of leisure and capacity would turn their attention to it, and bring the result of their experiments together? Nothing but cultivation is wanting. Our lot has certainly destined a good country for our inheritance. We begin already to attract the notice of foreigners of distinction. A French general officer whose name is Du Plessis is now at Mount Vernon on his way to Georgia, with a design to settle there as a farmer.

Sequestered as I am, from the bustlings and intrigues of the world, in the calm walks of private life; I can hardly flatter myself with being able to give much light or assistance, to those who may be engag'd in passing thro' the dark and thorny paths of politics. I can only repeat what I have formerly told my countrymen in a very serious manner "that honesty will be found, on every experiment, the best policy". How far arguments deduced from this *topic*, and from the *present alarming* troubles in Rhode Island, can with pertinancy and force be made use of against any attempts to procure a paper currency in the State, I leave to your judgment to decide. The advantages which are to be derived from Seminaries of learning, from the improvement of our roads, a proper establishment of our Militia, the extension of inland navigation &c. must have struck you in too forcible a manner to need a remembrancer.

My sentiments respecting foederal measures, in general, are so well known that it is unnecessary to reiterate them. The two Mrs. Washingtons and my nephew join in compliments with me to Mrs. Bland and yourself, and I am, etc.

The "alarming troubles" in Rhode Island to which Washington refers were a riot at Newport and a partial famine in Providence as a result of that state's attempt to pay its debts by issuing its own paper money. Growing social and political unrest in other states only reinforced Washington's conviction that the Articles of Confederation, under which the Americans were attempting to govern themselves, were inadequate and should be replaced by a strong federal government. In numerous letters Washington practically made a slogan out of the phrase, "Sufficient powers to Congress for general purposes." Other prominent Americans had, in four years of peace, come to the same conclusion, and on May 25, 1787, a Constitutional Convention met in Philadelphia. The chairman of the Convention was George Washington. The Constitution hammered out by this group of brilliant compromisers was, in Washington's opinion, imperfect—but he was equally certain it was the best that could be achieved at the time. He therefore lent all his enormous prestige to the fight for ratification. This letter, to one of his old major generals, Benjamin Lincoln of Massachusetts, reports on the victory of the Federalist forces in Virginia.

Mount Vernon, June 29, 1788.

MY DEAR SIR: I beg you will accept my thanks for the communications handed to me in your letter of the 3d. instant, and my congratulations on the encreasing good dispositions of the Citizens of your State of which the late elections are strongly indicative. No one *can* rejoice more than I do at every step the people of this great Country take to preserve the Union, establish good order and government, and to render the Nation happy at home and respectable abroad. No Country upon Earth ever had it more in its power to attain these blessings than United America. Wondrously strange then, and much to be regretted indeed would it be, were we to neglect the means, and to depart from the road which Providence has pointed us to, so plainly; I cannot believe it will ever come to pass. The great Governor of the Universe has led us too long and too far on the road to happiness and glory, to forsake us in the midst of it. By folly and improper conduct, proceeding from a variety of causes, we may now and then get bewildered; but I hope and trust that there is good sense and virtue enough left to recover the right path before we shall be entirely lost.

You will, before this letter can have reached you, have heard of the Ratification of the new Government by this State. The final question without previous amendments was taken the 25th. Ayes, 89. Noes, 79; but something recommendatory, or declaratory of the rights, (accompanied) the ultimate decision. This account and the news of the adoption by New Hampshire arrived in Alexandria nearly about the same time on Friday evening; and, as you will suppose, was cause for great rejoicing among the Inhabitants who have not I believe an Antifederalist among them. Our Accounts from Richmond are, that the debates, through all the different Stages of the business, though (brisk) and animated, have been conducted with great dignity and temper; that the final decision exhibited an awful and solemn scene, and that there is every reason to expect a perfect acquiescence therein by the minority; not only from the declaration of Mr. Henry, the great leader of it, who has signified that though he can never be reconciled to the Constitution in its present form, and shall give it every *constitutional* opposition in his power yet that he will submit to it peaceably, as he thinks every good Citizen ought to do when it is in exercise and that he will both by precept and example inculcate this doctrine to all around him.

There is little doubt entertained here *now* of the ratification of the proposed Constitution by North Carolina; and however great the opposition to it may be in New York the leaders thereof will, I should conceive, consider well the consequences before they reject it. With respect to Rhode Island, the power that governs there has so far baffled all calculation on this question that no man would chuse to hazard an opinion lest he might be suspected of participating in its phrensy. You have every good wish of this family and the sincere regard of your affectionate &c.

Politics did not absorb all of Washington's attention during this period. He still found time to maintain by mail the friendships he had made in war days. Here he congratulates one of his favorite Frenchmen, the Marquis de Chastellux, on his recent marriage.

Mount Vernon, April 25 (–May 1), 1788.
MY DEAR MARQUIS: In reading your very friendly and acceptable letter of 21st. December 1787, which came to hand by the last mail, I was, as you may well suppose, not less delighted than surprised to come across that plain American word "my wife." A wife!

well my dear Marquis, I can hardly refrain from smiling to find you are caught at last. I saw, by the eulogium you often made on the happiness of domestic life in America, that you had swallowed the bait and that you would as surely be taken (one day or another) as you was a Philosopher and a Soldier. So your day has, at length, come. I am glad of it with all my heart and soul. It is quite good enough for you. Now you are well served for coming to fight in favor of the American Rebels, all the way across the Atlantic Ocean, by catching that terrible Contagion, domestic felicity, which time like the small pox or the plague, a man can have only once in his life: because it commonly lasts him (at least with us in America, I dont know how you manage these matters in France) for his whole life time. And yet after all the maledictions you so richly merit on the subject, the worst wish which I can find in my heart to make against Madame de Chastellux and yourself is, that you may neither of you ever get the better of this same domestic felicity during the entire course of your mortal existence.

If so wonderful an event should have occasioned me, my dear Marquis, to have written in a strange style, you will understand me as clearly as if I had said (what in plain English, is the simple truth) do me the justice to believe that I take a heartfelt interest in whatever concerns your happiness. And in this view, I sincerely congratulate you on your auspicious Matrimonial connection. I am happy to find that Madame de Chastellux is so intimately connected with the Dutchess of Orleans, as I have always understood that this noble lady was an illustrious pattern of connubial love, as well as an excellent model of virtue in general. . . .

The letter ends with a brief discussion of European and American politics. At home, Washington continued to be a generous friend to those close to him, such as Dr. James Craik, whose son, George Washington Craik, he was sending through school.

Mount Vernon, August 4, 1788.

DEAR SIR: With this letter you will receive the Horse I promised you; And which I now beg your acceptance of. He is not in such good order as I could wish, but as good as my means would place him.

I also send you Thirty pounds Cash for one years allowance for the Schooling of your Son G.W. I wish it was in my power to send the like sum for the other year, which is now about, or near due; and that could discharge your account for attendance and ministrens to the Sick of my family; but it really is not; for with much truth I can say, I never felt the want of money so sensibly since I was a boy of 15 years old as I have done for the last 12 months and probably shall do for 12 Months more to come. Sincerely and affectly. etc.

During these same straitened years Washington was support-ing no fewer than twenty-two nieces and nephews. Some of them were troublesome, notably George Steptoe Washington, sixteen, and his brother Lawrence, thirteen, the sons of his brother Samuel. Here Washington, who was paying their tuition, reprimands them for obstreperous conduct at school.

Mount Vernon, August 6, 1788.

DEAR GEORGE: It was with equal pain and surprise that I was in-formed by Colo. Hanson on Monday last, of your unjustifiable be-haviour in rescuing your brother from that chastisement, which was due to his improper conduct; and which you know, because you have been told it in explicit language, he was authorized to admin-ister whensoever he should deserve it. Such refractory behaviour on your part, I consider as an insult equally offered to myself after the above communications and I shall continue to view it in that light, till you have made satisfactory acknowledgments to Colo. Hanson for the offence given him.

It is as much my wish and intention to see justice done to you and your Brother as it is to punish either when it is merited; but there are proper modes by which this is to be obtained, and it is to be sought by a fair and candid representation of facts whch. can be supported, and not by vague complaints, disobedience, perverse-ness, or disobliging conduct, which make enemies without produc-ing the smallest good. So often, and strenuously have I endeavored to inculcate this advice, and to shew you the advantages, which are to be expected from close application to your studies, that it is unnecessary to repeat it. If the admonitions of friendship are lost other methods must be tried which cannot be more disagreeable to you than it would be to one, who wishes to avoid it, who is solicitous to see you and your Brother (the only remaining Sons of your father) turn out well, and who is very desirous of continuing your affectionate uncle.

Washington was delighted when a majority of the states speedily ratified the Constitution. But he was far less pleased when the leaders in the fight for ratification, notably Alexander Hamilton of New York, made it clear that they expected Washington to become the nation's first President. When Hamilton first broached the subject, Washington refused even to discuss it, maintaining it was an event which might not happen. But as letters from leaders in other states confirmed Hamilton's confident assertion, Washington had to face what was for him the unpleasant truth. Everyone believed that if the new government was to succeed it needed George Washington to preside at its launching. In the following letter to Hamilton he discusses the subject at some length, without attempting to hide his real feelings.

Mount Vernon, October 3, 1788.

DEAR SIR: In acknowledging the receipt of your candid and kind letter by the last Post; little more is incumbent upon me, than to thank you sincerely for the frankness with which you communicated your sentiments, and to assure you that the same manly tone of intercourse will always be more than barely welcome, indeed it will be highly acceptable to me. I am particularly glad in the present instance, that you have dealt thus freely and like a friend.

Although I could not help observing, from several publications and letters that my name had been sometimes spoken of, and that it was possible the *Contingency* which is the subject of your letter might happen; yet I thought it best to maintain a guarded silence and to seek the counsel of my best friends (which I certainly hold in the highest estimation) rather than to hazard an imputation unfriendly to the delicacy of my feelings. For, situated as I am, I could hardly bring the question into the slightest discussion, or ask an opinion even in the most confidential manner, without betraying, in my judgment, some impropriety of conduct, or without feeling an apprehension, that a premature display of anxiety might be construed into a vain-glorious desire of pushing myself into notice as a candidate. Now, if I am not grossly deceived in myself, I should unfeignedly rejoice, in case the Electors, by giving their votes in favor of some other person, would save me from the dreaded Dilemma of being forced to accept or refuse.

If that may not be, I am, in the next place, earnestly desirous of searching out the truth, and of knowing whether there does not exist a probability that the government would be just as happily and effectually carried into execution without my aid, as with it. I am *truly* solicitous to obtain all the previous information which the circumstances will afford, and to determine (when the determination can with propriety be no longer postponed) according to the principles of right reason, and the dictates of a clear conscience; without too great a reference to the unforeseen consequences, which may affect my person or reputation. Untill that period, I may fairly hold myself open to conviction; though I allow your sentiments to have weight in them; and I shall not pass by your arguments without giving them as dispassionate a consideration, as I can possibly bestow upon them.

In taking a survey of the subject, in whatever point of light I have been able to place it, I will not suppress the acknowledgment, my Dr. Sir that I have always felt a kind of gloom upon my mind, as often as I have been taught to expect, I might, and perhaps must ere long, be called to make a decision. You will, I am well assured, believe the assertion (though I have little expectation it would gain credit from those who are less acquainted with me) that if I should receive the appointment and if I should be prevailed upon to accept it, the acceptance would be attended with more diffidence and reluctance that I ever experienced before in my life. It would be, however, with a fixed and sole determination of lending whatever assistance might be in my power to promote the public weal, in hopes that at a convenient and early period my services might be dispensed with, and that I might be permitted once more to retire, to pass an unclouded evening after the stormy day of life, in the bosom of domestic tranquility.

But why these anticipations? if the friends to the Constitution conceive that my administering the government will be a means of its acceleration and strength, is it not probable that the adversaries of it may entertain the same ideas, and of course make it an object of opposition? That many of this description will become Electors, I can have no doubt of, any more than that their opposition will extend to any character who (from whatever cause) would be likely to thwart their measures. It might be impolitic in them to make this declaration *previous* to the Election; but I shall be out in my conjectures if they do not act conformably thereto, and that the seeming moderation by which they appear to be actuated at present is neither more or less than a finesse to lull and deceive. Their plan of opposition is systematized, and a regular intercourse, I have much reason to believe between the Leaders of it in the several States is formed to render is more effectual. With sentiments of sincere regard &c.

This and other subjects preoccupied Washington as he wrote to Lafayette.

Mount Vernon, January 29, 1789.
MY DEAR MARQUIS: By the last post I was favored with the receipt of your letter, dated the 5th of September last. Notwithstanding the distance of its date, it was peculiarly welcome to me: for I had not in the mean time received any satisfactory advices respecting yourself or your country. By that letter, my mind was placed much more at its ease, on both those subjects, than it had been for many months.

The last letter, which I had the pleasure of writing to you, was forwarded by Mr. Gouverneur Morris. Since his departure from America, nothing very material has occurred. The minds of men, however, have not been in a stagnant State. But patriotism, instead of faction, has generally agitated them. It is not a matter of wonder, that, in proportion as we approach to the time fixed for the organization and operation of the new government, their anxiety should have been encreased, rather than diminished.

The choice of Senators, Representatives, and Electors, which (excepting in that of the last description) took place at different times, in the different States, has afforded abundant topics for domestic News, since the beginning of Autumn. I need not enumerate the several particulars, as I imagine you see most of them detailed, in the American Gazettes. I will content myself with only saying, that the elections have been hitherto vastly more favorable than we could have expected, that federal sentiments seem to be growing with uncommon rapidity, and that this encreasing unanimity is not less indicative of the good disposition than the good sense of the Americans. Did it not savour so much of partiality for my Countrymen I might add, that I cannot help flattering myself the new Congress on account of the self-created respectability and various talents of its Members, will not be inferior to any Assembly in the world. From these and some other circumstances, I really entertain greater hopes, that America will not finally disappoint the expectations of her Friends, than I have at almost any former period. Still however, in such a fickle state of existence I would not be too sanguine in indulging myself with the contemplation of scenes of uninterrupted prosperity; lest some unforeseen mischance or perverseness should occasion the greater mortification, by blasting the enjoyment in the very bud.

I can say little or nothing new, in consequence of the repetition of your opinion, on the expediency there will be, for my accepting the office [the Presidency] to which you refer. Your sentiments, indeed, coincide much more nearly with those of my other friends, than with my own feelings. In truth my difficulties encrease and magnify as I draw towards the period, when, according to the common belief, it will be necessary for me to give a definitive answer, in one way or another. Should the circumstances render it, in a manner inevitably necessary, to be in the affirmative:

be assured, my dear Sir, I shall assume the task with the most unfeigned reluctance, and with a real diffidence for which I shall
probably receive no credit from the world. If I know my own heart,
nothing short of a conviction of duty will induce me again to take
an active part in public affairs; and, in that case, if I can form a
plan for my own conduct, my endeavours shall be unremittingly
exerted (even at the hazard of former fame or present popularity)
to extricate my country from the embarrassments in which it is en-
tangled, through want of credit; and to establish a general system
of policy, which if pursued will ensure permanent felicity to the
Commonwealth. I think I see a *path*, as clear and as direct as a ray
of light, which leads to the attainment of that object. Nothing but
harmony, honesty, industry and frugality are necessary to make us a
great and happy people. Happily the present posture of affairs and
the prevailing disposition of my countrymen promise to co-operate
in establishing those four great and essential pillars of public
felicity.

What has been considered at the moment as a disadvantage,
will probably turn out for our good. While our commerce has been
considerably curtailed, for want of that extensive credit formerly
given in Europe, and for default of remittance; the useful arts have
been almost imperceptibly pushed to a considerable degree of perfection.

Though I would not force the introduction of manufactures,
by extravagant encouragements, and to the prejudice of agriculture;
yet, I conceive much might be done in that way by women, children and others; without taking one really necessary hand from
tilling the earth. Certain it is, great savings are already made in
many articles of apparel, furniture and consumption. Equally certain it is, that no diminution in agriculture has taken place, at the
time when greater and more substantial improvements in manufacturers were making, than were ever before known in America. In
Pennsylvania they have attended particularly to the fabrication of
cotton cloths, hats, and all articles in leather. In Massachusetts
they are establishing factories of Duck, Cordage, Glass, and several
other extensive and useful branches. The number of shoes made in

one town and nails in another is incredible. In that State and Connecticut are also factories of superfine and other broad cloths. I have been writing to our friend Genl. Knox this day, to procure me homespun broad cloth, of the Hartford fabric, to make a suit of cloaths for myself. I hope it will not be a great while, before it will be unfashionable for a gentleman to appear in any other dress. Indeed we have already been too long subject to British prejudices. I use no porter or cheese in my family, but such as is made in America: both those articles may now be purchased of an excellent quality.

While you are quarrelling among yourselves in Europe; while one King is running mad, and others acting as if they were already so, by cutting the throats of the subjects of their neighbours, I think you need not doubt, my dear Marquis, we shall continue in tranquility here. And that population will be progressive so long as there shall continue to be so many easy means for obtaining a subsistence, and so ample a field for the exertion of talents and industry. All my family join in Compliments to Madame la Fayette and yours. Adieu.

His troublesome nephews were also on his mind. By now Washington has accepted the fact that he would be the first President. Before he departed for his inauguration he wrote a kind of farewell letter to young George Steptoe Washington in which he tried to condense many of the things a father might tell a son.

Mount Vernon, March 23, 1789.
DEAR GEORGE: As it is probable I shall soon be under the necessity of quitting this place, and entering once more into the bustle of public life, in conformity to the voice of my Country, and the earnest entreaties of my friends, however contrary it is to my own desires or inclinations, I think it incumbent on me as your uncle and friend, to give you some advisory hints, which, if properly attended to, will, I conceive, be found very useful to you in regulating your conduct and giving you respectability, not only at present, but thro' every period of life. You have now arrived to that age when you must quit the trifling amusements of a boy, and assume

the more dignified manners of a man.

At this crisis your conduct will attract the notice of those who are about you, and as the first impressions are generally the most lasting, your doings now may mark the leading traits of your character through life. It is therefore absolutely necessary if you mean to make any figure upon the stage, that you should take the first steps right. What these steps are, and what general line is to be pursued to lay the foundation of an honorable and happy progress, is the part of age and experience to point out. This I shall do, as far as in my power with the utmost chearfulness; and, I trust, that your own good sense will shew you the necessity of following it. The first and great object with you at present is to acquire, by industry, and application, such knowledge as your situation enables you to obtain, as will be useful to you in life. In doing this two other important advantages will be gained besides the acquisition of knowledge: namely, a habit of industry, and a disrelish of that profusion of money and dissipation of time which are ever attendant upon idleness. I do not mean by a close application to your studies that you should never enter into those amusements which are suited to your age and station: they can be made to go hand in hand with each other, and, used in their proper seasons, will ever be found to be a mutual assistance to one another. But what amusements, and when they are to be taken, is the great matter to be attended to. Your own judgement, with the advice of your *real* friends who may have an opportunity of a personal intercourse with you, can point out the particular manner in which you may best spend your moments of relaxation, better than I can at a distance. One thing, however, I would strongly impress upon you, vizt. that when you have leisure to go into company that it should always be of the best kind that the place you are in will afford; by this means you will be constantly improving your manners and cultivating your mind while you are relaxing from your books; and good company will always be found much less expensive than bad. You cannot offer, as an excuse for not using it, that you cannot gain admission there; or that you have not a proper attention paid you in it: this is an apology made only by those whose manners are disgusting, or whose character is exceptionable; neither of which I hope will ever be said of you. I cannot enjoin too strongly upon you a due observance of oeconomy and frugality, as you well know yourself, the present state of your property and finances will not admit of any unnecessary expense. The article of clothing is now one of the chief expences, you will incur, and in this, I fear, you are not so oeconomical as you should be. Decency and cleanliness will always be the first object in the dress of a judicious and sensible man; a conformity to the prevailing fashion in a certain degree is necessary; but it does not from thence follow that a man should always get a new Coat, or other clothes, upon every trifling change in the mode, when perhaps he has two or three very good ones by him. A person who is anxious to be a leader of the fashion, or one of the first to follow it will certainly appear in the eyes of judicious men, to have nothing better than a frequent change of dress to recomend him to notice. I would always wish you to appear sufficiently decent to entitle you to admission into any company where you may be; but I cannot too strongly enjoin it upon you, and your own knowledge must convince you of the truth of it, that you should be as little expensive in this respect as you properly can. You should always keep some clothes to wear to Church, or on particular occasions, which should not be worn everyday; this can be done without any additional expence; for whenever it is necessary to get new clothes, those which have been kept for particular occasions will then come in as every-day ones, unless they should be of a superior quality to the new. What I have said with respect to clothes will apply perhaps more pointedly to Lawrence than to you; and as you are much older than he is, and more capable of judging of the propriety of what I have here observed, you must pay attention to him in this respect, and see that he does not wear his Clothes improperly or extravagantly. Much more might be said to you, as a young man, upon the necessity of paying due attention to the moral virtues; but this may, perhaps, more properly be the subject of a future letter when you may be about to enter into the world. If you comply with the advice herein given to pay a diligent attention to your studies, and employ your time of relaxation in proper company, you will find but few opportunities and little inclination, while you continue at an Acadimy, to enter into those scenes of vice and dissipation which too often present themselves to youth in every place, and particularly in towns. If you are determined to neglect your books, and plunge into extravagance and dissipation, nothing I could say now would prevent it; for you must be employed, and if it is not in pursuit of those things which are profitable, it must be in pursuit of those which are destructive. As your time of continuing with Mr. Hanson will expire the last of this month and I understand Dr. Craik has expressed an inclination to take you and Lawrence to board with him, I shall know his determination respecting the matter; and if it is agreeable to him and Mrs. Craik to take you, I shall be pleased with it, for I am certain that nothing will be wanting on their parts to make your situation agreeable and useful to you. Should you live with the Doctor I shall request him to take you both under his peculiar care; provide such clothes for you, from time to time, as he shall judge necessary, and do by you in the same manner as he would if you were his own children. Which if he will undertake, I am sensible, from knowledge which I have of him, and the very amiable character and disposition of Mrs. Craik, that they will spare no proper exertions to make your situation pleasing and profitable to you. Should you or Lawrence therefore behave in such a manner as to occasion any complaint being made to me, you may depend upon losing that place which you now have in my affections, and any future hopes you may have from me. But if, on the contrary, your conduct is such as to merit my regard, you may always depend upon the warmest attachment, and sincere affection of Your friend and Uncle.

Both George Steptoe and his brother Lawrence turned out to be the solid middle-class citizens that Washington aimed at producing. Both went to Philadelphia College, now the University of Pennsylvania, at their uncle's expense and were satisfactory students. Young George inherited his father's plantation, Harewood, in Jefferson County, Virginia, and Washington, in his will, wiped out all moneys owed to him from the estate, as well as cost of both boys' education, which he estimated at one point to be $5,000.

CHAPTER EIGHT

President and Paterfamilias

On April 30, 1789, Washington took the oath of office and became President of the United States. Once more he ceased to be a private person and became a public man. *His letters were largely concerned with the multiple problems of the Presidency, how he should conduct his social life, the proper relation between the President and Congress, between the President and foreign ambassadors. All this was complicated by a serious illness, a kind of abscess [sometimes described as a tumor] in his thigh which produced a raging fever and incapacitated him for six weeks. Here he writes to his old friend Dr. Craik about his illness and about his nephews, who were boarding with Craik.*

New York, September 8, 1789.

DEAR SIR: The letter with which you favored me on the 24th ultimo came duly to hand, and for the friendly sentiments contained in it, you have my sincere and hearty thanks.

My disorder was of long and painful continuance, and though now freed from the latter, the wound given by the incision is not yet closed. Persuaded as I am that the case has been treated with skill, and with as much tenderness as the nature of the complaint would admit, yet I confess I often wished for your inspection of it. During the paroxysm, the distance rendered this impracticable, and after the paroxysm had passed I had no conception of being confined to a lying posture on one side six weeks, and that I should feel the remains of it more than twelve. The part affected is now reduced to the size of a barley corn, and by Saturday next (which will complete the thirteenth week) I expect it will be skinned over. Upon the whole, I have more reason to be thankful that it is no worse than to repine at the confinement.

The want of regular exercise, with the cares of office, will, I have no doubt hasten my departure for that country from whence no Traveller returns; but a faithful discharge of whatsoever trust I accept, as it ever has, so it always will be the primary consideration in every transaction of my life be the consequences what they may. Mrs. Washington has, I think, better health than usual, and the children are well and in the way of improvement.

I always expected, that the Gentleman, whose name you have mentioned would mark his opposition to the new government with consistency. Pride on the one hand, and want of manly candor on the other, will not I am certain let him acknowledge an error in his opinions respecting it though conviction should flash on his mind as strongly as a ray of light. If certain characters which you have also mentioned, should tread *blindfold* in his steps it would be matter of no wonder to me. They are in the habit of thinking that everything he says and does is right, and (if capable) they will not judge for themselves.

It gives me pleasure to hear, and I wish you to express it to them that my Nephews George and Lawrence Washington are attentive to their studies, and obedient to your orders and amonition. That kind of learning which is to fit them for the most useful and necessary purposes of life, among which writing well, arithmetic, and the less abstruse branches of the mathematics are certainly to be comprehended, ought to be particularly attended to, and it is my earnest wish that it should be so.

The Gazettes are so full of the occurrences of public, and indeed a private nature, which happen in this place that it is unnecessary (if I had more leisure than falls to my lot) to attempt a repetition: I shall therefore refer you to them or to the Alexandria paper, through which they may, if pains is taken, be retailed. Mrs. Washington and the rest of the family join me in every good and friendly wish for Mrs. Craik, yourself and the rest of your family; and with sentiments of sincere regard and friendship, I am &c.

A letter from the dying Benjamin Franklin stirred Washington deeply. Seldom has one great man written to another more affectingly than this.

New York, September 23, 1789.

DEAR SIR: The affectionate congratulations on the recovery of my health, and the warm expressions of personal friendship which were contained in your favor of the 16th instant, claim my gratitude. And the consideration that it was written when you were afflicted with a painful malady, greatly increased my obligation for it.

Would to God, my dear Sir, that I could congratulate you upon the removal of that excruciating pain under which you labour! and that your existence might close with as much ease to yourself, as its continuance has been beneficial to our Country and useful to mankind! Or, if the United wishes of a free people, joined with the earnest prayers of every friend to Science and humanity could relieve the body from pains or infirmities, you could claim an exemption on this score. But this cannot be, and you have within yourself the only resource to which we can confidently apply for relief: a *philosophic mind.*

If to be venerated for benevolence: If to be admired for talents: If to be esteemed for patriotism: if to be beloved for philanthropy, can gratify the human mind, you must have the pleasing consolation to know that you have not lived in vain; grateful occurrences of your life to be assured that so long as I retain my memory, you will be thought on with respect, veneration and Affection by Your sincere friend etc.

Washington had little time now to write long friendly epistles to Lafayette. What follows is rather brisk and might be said to come more from President Washington than father George. In the letter he refers to another reason for his reticence: the French Revolution has begun.

New York, October 14, 1789.

This is the first time I have written to you, my dear Marquis, since I have been in this place, and I have not received a line from you in the same space of time. This has been a long interval of silence between two persons whose habits of correspondence have been so uniterruptedly kept up as ours; but the new and arduous scenes in which we have both been lately engaged will afford a mutual excuse.

I wrote to you very fully in my last letters from Mount Vernon, and since that time the gazettes, which I know you receive, have given a pretty ample detail of our public proceedings. I therefore take the advantage of the politeness of the Comte de Moustier, (who is about returning to France) more with a view of assuring you that you are still remembered by me with affection, than with an intent to convey any political intelligence. I will only observe, generally, that the prospect is favorable to the political happiness of this country.

The revolution, which has taken place with you, is of such magnitude and of so momentous a nature that we hardly yet dare to form a conjecture about it. We however trust, and fervently pray that its consequences may prove happy to a nation, in whose fate we have so much cause to be interested and that its influence may be felt with pleasure by future generations.

Mrs. Washington joins me in best wishes to you and your amiable Partner. I am etc.

France was much on Washington's mind. This time he writes of the situation there to his old friend Rochambeau.

New York, August 10, 1790.

The little anecdote which you recall to mind, My dear Count, of your Countrymen at Rhode Island who burnt their mouths with the hot soup, while mine waited leisurely for it to cool, perhaps, when politically applied in the manner you have done, has not less truth than pleasantry in its resemblance of national characters. But if there shall be no worse consequence resulting from too great eagerness in swallowing something so delightful as liberty, than that of suffering a momentary pain or making a ridiculous figure with a scalled mouth; upon the whole it may be said you Frenchmen have come off well, considering how immoderately you thirsted for the cup of liberty. And no wonder as you drank it to the bottom, that some licentiousness should have been mingled with the dregs.

To view your Resolution in another and more serious point of light. It was impossible, in such a Country, and during such a struggle, but that disagreeable things, and even great enormities in some instances must have happened. Too many doubtless have occurred. Not so many, however, have existed as the English News-Papers have attempted to make us believe. For had we credited all the evil stories we have seen in them, we should almost have set it down for granted that the race of Frenchmen were about becoming extinct, and their Country a desert. So many of you, on different occasions, have they killed. Happily for you, we remembered how our own armies, after having been all slain to a man in the English News Papers, came to life again and even performed prodigies of valour against that very Nation whose News-papers had so unmercifully destroyed them. Mr. Jefferson, Mr. Trumbull and some others have taught us to believe more cautiously and more correctly on these points.

Now I will conclude by saying a word about ourselves, as I am certain your friendship is not less interested in our fate, than ours is in that of your Nation. We have a good government in Theory, and are carrying it pretty happily into practice. In a government which depends so much in its first stages on public opinion, much circumspection is still necessary for those who are engaged in its administration. Fortunately the current of public sentiment runs with us, and all things hitherto seem to succeed according to our wishes. In the meantime population increases, land is cleared, commerce extended, manufactories, and Heaven smiles upon us with favorable seasons and abundant crops.

As the news from France turned ugly, Washington's next letter to Lafayette shows a growing concern—and doubt—about the future of the French Revolution.

Philadelphia, July 28, 1791.

I have, my dear Sir, to acknowledge the receipt of your favors of the 7 of March and 3 of May, and to thank you for the communications which they contain relative to your public affairs. I assure you I have often contemplated, with great anxiety, the danger to which you are personally exposed by your peculiar and delicate situation in the tumult of the times, and your letters are far from quieting that friendly concern. But to one, who engaged in hazardous enterprises for the good of his country, and who is guided by pure and upright views, (as I am sure is the case with you) life is but a secondary consideration.

To a philanthropic mind the happiness of 24 millions of people cannot be indifferent; and by an American, whose country in the hour of distress received such liberal aid from the french, the disorders and incertitude of that Nation are to be peculiarly lamented. We must, however, place a confidence in that Providence who rules great events, trusting that out of confusion he will produce order, and, notwithstanding the dark clouds, which may threaten at present, that right will ultimately be established.

The tumultous populace of large cities are ever to be dreaded. Their indiscriminate violence prostrates for the time all public authority, and its consequences are sometimes extensive and terrible. In Paris we may suppose these tumults are peculiarly disastrous at this time, when the public mind is in a ferment, and when (as is always the case on such occasions) there are not wanting wicked and designing men, whose element is confusion, and who will not hesitate in destroying the public tranquillity to gain a favorite point. But until your Constitution is fixed, your government organized, and your representative Body renovated, much tranquillity cannot be expected; for, until these things are done, those who are unfriendly to the revolution, will not quit the hope of bringing matters back to their former state.

The decrees of the National Assembly respecting our tobacco and oil do not appear to be very pleasing to the people of this country; but I do not presume that any hasty measures will be adopted in consequence thereof; for we have never entertained a doubt of the friendly disposition of the french Nation toward us, and are therefore persuaded that if they have done any thing which seems to bear hard upon us, at a time when the Assembly must have been occupied in very important matters, and which perhaps would not allow time for a due consideration of the subject, they will, in the moment of calm deliberation, alter it and do what is right.

I readily perceive, my dear Sir, the critical situation in which you stand, and never can you have greater occasion to show your prudence, judgment, and magnanimity.

On the 6 of this month I returned from a tour through the southern States, which had employed me for more than three months. In the course of this journey I have been highly gratified in observing the flourishing state of the Country, and the good dispositions of the people. Industry and economy have become very fashionable in these parts, which were formerly noted for the opposite qualities, and the labours of man are assisted by the blessings of Providence. The attachment of all Classes of citizens to the general Government seems to be a pleasing presage of their future happiness and respectability.

The complete establishment of our public credit is a strong mark of the confidence of the people in the virtue of their Representatives, and the wisdom of their measures; and, while in Europe, wars or commotions seem to agitate almost every nation, peace and tranquillity prevail among us, except on some parts of our western frontiers, where the Indians have been troublesome, to reclaim or chastise whom proper measures are now pursuing. This contrast between the situation of the people of the United States, and those of Europe is too striking to be passed over, even by the most superficial observer, and may, I believe, be considered as one great cause of leading the people here to reflect more attentively on their own prosperous state, and to examine more minutely, and consequently approve more fully of the government under which they live, than they otherwise would have done. But we do not wish to be the only people who may taste the sweets of an equal and good government; we look with an anxious eye to the time, when happiness and tranquillity shall prevail in your country, and when all Europe shall be freed from commotions, tumults, and alarms.

Your friends in this country often express their great attachment to you by their anxiety for your safety. Knox, Jay, Hamilton, Jefferson remember you with affection; but none with more sincerity and true attachment than etc.

Between affairs of state Washington still found time to think of home. One of his chief worries was his niece Harriet, his brother Samuel's daughter, who was apparently on the verge of running wild.

Philadelphia, October 30, 1791.

DEAR HARRIOT: I have received your letter of the 21st. instant, and shall always be glad to hear from you. When my business will permit inclination will not be wanting in me to acknowledge the receipt of your letters, and this I shall do more cheerfully as it will afford me opportunities at those times of giving you such occasional advice, as your situation may require.

At present I could plead a better excuse for curtailing my letter to you than you had for shortening of yours to me, having a multitude of business before me while you have nothing to do, consequently you might, with equal convenience to yourself, have set down to write your letter an hour or two, or even a day sooner, as to have delayed it until your Cousin was on the point of sending to the Post-Office. I make this remark for no other reason than to shew you it is better to offer no excuse than a bad one, if at any time you should happen to fall into an error.

Occupied as my time now is, and must be during the sitting of Congress, I nevertheless will endeavor to inculcate upon your mind the delicacy and danger of that period, to which you are now arrived under peculiar circumstances. You are just entering into the state of womanhood, without the watchful eye of a Mother to admonish, or the protecting aid of a Father to advise and defend you; you may not be sensible that you are at this moment about to be stamped with that character which will adhere to you through life; the consequence of which you have not perhaps attended to, but be assured it is of the utmost importance that you should.

Your cousins, with whom you live are well qualified to give you advice, and I am sure they will if you are disposed to receive it. But if you are disobliging, self-willed, and untowardly it is hardly to be expected that they will engage themselves in unpleasant disputes with you, especially Fanny, whose mild and placid temper will not permit her to exceed the limits of wholesome admonition or gentle rebuke. Think then to what dangers a giddy girl of 15 or 16 must be exposed in circumstances like these. To be under but little or no controul may be pleasing to a mind that does not reflect, but this pleasure cannot be of long duration, and reason, too late perhaps, may convince you of the folly of mis-spending time. You are not to learn, I am certain, that your fortune is small; supply the want of it then with a well cultivated mind; with dispositions to industry and frugality; with gentleness of manners, obliging temper, and such qualifications as will attract notice, and recommend you to a happy establishment for life.

You might instead of associating with those from whom you can derive nothing that is good, but may have observed every thing that is deceitful, lying, and bad, become the intimate companion of and aid to your Cousin in the domestic concerns of the family. Many Girls before they have arrived at your age have been found so trustworthy as to take the whole trouble of a family from their Mothers; but it is by a steady and rigid attention to the rules of propriety that such confidence is obtained, and nothing would give me more pleasure than to hear that you had acquired it. The merits and benefits of it would redound more to your advantage in your progress thro' life, and to the person with whom you may in due time form a matrimonial connexion than to any others; but to none would such a circumstance afford more real satisfaction, than to Your affectionate Uncle.

Washington's fondness for the brilliant but eccentric Gouverneur Morris was not shared by many other Americans. When he nominated Morris to be ambassador to France, he wrote to him as one friend to another urging some mild alterations in his personality.

Philadelphia, January 28, 1792.

MY DEAR SIR: . . . . The official communications from the Secretary of State, accompanying this letter, will convey to you the evidence of my *nomination*, and *appointment* of you to Minister Plenipotentiary for the United States at the Court of France; and my assurance, that both were made with *all my heart*, will, I am persuaded, satisfy you as to that fact. I wish I could add that the *advice* and *consent* flowed from a similar source. Candour forbids it, and friendship requires, that I should assign the causes, as far as they have come to my knowledge.

Whilst your abilities, knowledge in the affairs of this Country, and disposition to serve it, were adduced and asserted on one hand; you were charged on the other hand, with levity and imprudence of conversation and conduct. It was urged that your habits of expression indicated a *hauteur* disgusting to those, who happen to differ from you in sentiment; and among a people, who study civility and politeness more than any other nation, it must be displeasing; that in France you were considered as a favorer of Aristocracy, and unfriendly to its Revolution (I suppose they meant constitution). That under this impression, you could not be an acceptable public character, of consequence would not be able, however willing, to promote the interest of this Country in an essential degree. That in England you indiscreetly communicated the purport of your Mission in the first instance, to the Minister of France, at that Court, who availing himself in the same moment of the occasion, gave it the appearance of a movement through his Court. This, and other circumstances of a similar nature, added to a close intercourse with the opposition Members, occasioned distrust, and gave displeasure to the Ministry; which was the cause, it is said, of that reserve which you experienced in negotiating the business which had been intrusted to you.

But not to go further into detail, I will place the ideas of your political adversaries, in the light which their arguments have presented them to me; vizt. That the promptitude, with which your lively and brilliant imagination is displayed, allows too little time for deliberation and correction; and is the primary cause of those sallies, which too often offend, and of that ridicule of characters, which begets enmity not easy to be forgotten, but which might easily be avoided, if it was under the control of more caution and prudence. In a word, that it is indispensably necessary, that more circumspection should be observed by our representatives abroad, than they conceive you are inclined to adopt.

In this statement you have the pros and cons; by reciting them, I give you a proof of my friendship if I give none of my policy or judgment. I do it on the presumption, that a mind conscious of its own rectitude fears not what is said of it, but will bid defiance to and despise shafts that are not barbed with accusations against honor or integrity. And because I have the fullest confidence (supposing the allegations to be founded in whole or part) that you would find no difficulty, being apprized of the exceptionable light in which they are viewed, and considering yourself as the representative of this Country, to effect a change, and thereby silence, in the most unequivocal and satisfactory manner, your political opponents.

Of my good opinion, and of my friendship and regard, you may be assured, and that I am etc.

By now Washington's first term was drawing to a close and he began mentioning to many friends, such as James Madison, his wish to retire to Mount Vernon. At the same time, his continuing concern for Lafayette and the future of the French Revolution play an ironic counterpart in his letters. The aggressive conduct of Republican France would soon make Washington's retirement impossible. On July 11, 1789, Lafayette was appointed colonel general of the new National Guard of Paris, and in April 1791 he suppressed

an uprising. *Promoted to lieutenant general, he suppressed an-*
other uprising after the proclamation of the Constitution, on Sep-
tember 18, 1791. Soon thereafter, disenchanted with the violent
tendencies of the revolution, he retired but was recalled a few
months later to resist the threat of an Austrian invasion. Washing-
ton can do little more, by mail, than assure his adopted son that his
American friends are rooting for him.

Philadelphia, June 10, 1792.
MY DEAR SIR: In the revolution of a great Nation we must not be
surprized at the vicissitudes to which individuals are liable; and the
changes they experience will always be in proportion to the weight
of their public character; I was therefore not surprised, my dear Sir,
at receiving your letter dated at Metz which you had the goodness
to write me on the 22d of January. That personal ease and private
enjoyment is not your primary object I well know, and until peace
and tranquillity are restored to your Country upon permanent and
honorable grounds I was fully persuaded, in my own mind, that
you could not be permitted long to enjoy that domestic retirement,
into which you had fondly entered.

Since the commencement of your revolution our attention has
been drawn, with no small anxiety, almost to France alone; but at
this moment Europe in general seems pregnant with great events,
and to whatever nation we turn our eyes there appears to be more
or less cause to believe, that an important change will take place at
no very distant period. Those philanthropic spirits who regard the
happiness of mankind are now watching the progress of things with
the greatest solicitude, and consider the event of the present crisis
as fixing the fate of man. How great! How important, therefore, is
the part, which the actors in this momentous scene have to perform! Not only the fate of millions of the present day depends
upon them, but the happiness of posterity is involved in their deci-
sions.

You who are on the spot cannot, I presume, determine when
or where these great beginnings will terminate, and for us, at this
distance to pretend to give an opinion to that effect would at least

be deemed presumptuous. We are however, anxious that the horrors of war may be avoided, if possible, and the rights of man so well understood and so permanently fixed, as while despotic oppression is avoided on the one hand, licentiousness may not be substituted for liberty nor confusion take place of order on the other. The just medium cannot be expected to be found in a moment, the first vibrations always go to the extremes, and cool reason, which can alone establish a permanent and equal government, is as little to be expected in the tumults of popular commotion, as an attention to the liberties of the people is to be found in the dark Divan of a despotic tyrant.

I assure you, my dear Sir, I have not been a little anxious for your personal safety, and I have yet no grounds for removing that anxiety; but I have the consolation of believing that, if you should fall it will be in defence of that cause which your heart tells you is just. And to the care of that Providence, whose interposition and protection we have so often experienced, do I chearfully commit you and your nation, trusting that he will bring order out of confusion, and finally place things upon the ground on which they ought to stand.

The affairs of the United States still go on in a prosperous train. We encrease daily in numbers and riches, and the people are blessed with the enjoyment of those rights which can alone give security and happiness to a Nation. The War with the Indians on our western frontier will, I hope, be terminated in the course of the present season without further effusion of blood; but, in case the measures taken to promote a pacification should fail, such steps are pursued as must, I think, render the issue by the sword very unfavorable to them.

Soon after the rising of Congress I made a journey to Mount Vernon, from whence I returned but a few days ago, and expect, (if nothing of a public nature should occur to detain me here) to go there again some time next month with Mrs. Washington and her two little grand children, where we shall continue 'till near the next meeting of Congress.

Your friends in this Country are interested in your welfare, and frequently enquire about you with an anxiety that bespeaks a warm affection. I am afraid my Nephew George, your old Aid, will never have his health perfectly re-established, he has lately been attacked with the alarming symptom of spitting large quantities of blood, and the Physicians give no hopes of a restoration unless it can be effected by a change of air, and a total dereliction of business, to which he is too anxiously attentive. (He will, if he should be taken from his family and friends leave three fine childn. viz. two Sons and a daughter, the eldest of the boys he has given the name of Fayette to and a fine looking child he is.)

Hamilton Knox Jay and Jefferson are well and remember you with affection. Mrs. Washington desires to be presented to you in terms of friendship and warm regard, to which I add my most affectionate wishes and sincere prayers for your health and happiness, and request you to make the same acceptable to Madm. le Fayette and your children. (I am &c.)

Meanwhile there was Harriet. A letter to his sister Betty Lewis discusses her problems.

Mount Vernon, October 7, 1792.
MY DR. SISTER: As Mrs. Washington and myself expect to set out tomorrow for Philadelphia, and the Major and Fanny the day after, if the vessel which is to carry him to Colo. Bassets, arrives in time, I have taken the advantage of the good opportunity afforded by Mr. Robert Lewis of sending Harriet to Fredericksburg. It is done at this time (notwithstanding your proposed visit to Albemarle), 1st. because it would be improper to leave her here after we are all gone; 2d. because there would be no person to accompany her down afterwards; and 3d. because it might be inconvenient for her to travel alone.

She comes, as Mrs. Washington informs me, very well provided with everything proper for a girl in her situation; this much I know, that she costs me enough to place her in it. I do not however want you, (or any one else) to do more by her than merely to admit her into your family whilst this House is uninhabited by a female white woman, and thereby rendered an unfit place for her to remain at. I shall continue to do for her what I have already done for seven years past; and that is to furnish her with such reasonable and proper necessaries as she may stand in need of, notwithstanding I have had both her brothers upon my hands, and I have been obliged to pay several hundred pounds out of my own pocket, for their boards, schooling, clothing, &c.&c. of them, for more than the period aforementioned; their father's estate being unable to discharge the Executions as fast as they are issued against it.

Harriet has sense enough, but no disposition to industry, nor to be careful of her clothes. Your example and admonition, with proper restraints may overcome the two last; and to that end I wish you would examine her clothes and direct her in their use and application of them; for without this they will be, I am told, dabbed about in every hole and corner, and her best things always in use. Fanny was too easy, too much of her own indolent disposition and had too little authority to cause, either by precept or example, any change in this for the better and Mrs. Washington's absence has been injurious to her in many respects: but she is young, and with good advice may yet make a fine woman. If, notwithstanding the suggestion that she is well provided with everything (except a Cloak which may not be had in Alexandria, and may be got at Fredericksburgh) a deficiency is found and you wish to supply it, there will be no occasion for your laying in advance more than ten days; as I could at any time remit a bank note in a letter, to you in four days after I was made acquainted with the amount. I do not mean by this to launch into expensiveness; she has no pretensions to it, nor would the state of my finances enable me to indulge her in that if she had.

Mrs. Washington joins me in best wishes for the perfect restoration of your health, and every other blessing, I am etc.

George Augustine Washington had, during Washington's first term, served as manager of Mount Vernon, but the family scourge, tuberculosis, returned to plague him and he had to resign. Washington writes a gentle letter of condolence to a man he knows is near death, a death which undoubtedly recalled the tragic death of his beloved brother Lawrence, almost a half century before.

Philadelphia, January 27, 1793.

MY DEAR GEORGE: I do not write you often, because I have no business to write upon; because all the News I could communicate is contained in the Papers which I forward every week; because I conceive it unnecessary to repeat the assurances of sincere regard and friendship I have always professed for you, or the disposition I feel to render every Service in my power to you and yours; and lastly because I conceive the more undisturbed you are, the better it is for you.

It has given your friends much pain to find that change of Air has not been productive of that favorable change in your health, which was the wishes of them all. But the will of Heaven is not to be controverted or scrutinized by the children of this world. It therefore becomes the Creatures of it to submit with patience and resignation to the will of the Creator whether it be to prolong, or to shorten the number of our days. To bless them with health, or afflict them with pain.

My fervent wishes attend you, in which I am heartily joined by your aunt, and these are extended with equal sincerity to Fanny and the children. I am always your Affect. uncle.

Lafayette, meanwhile, had seen his worst forebodings about the French Revolution come true. When he tried to block the advancement of the extremist Jacobins he was declared a traitor, and in August 1792 he fled to Liege, where he was held prisoner by the Austrians for the next five years. Washington, stubbornly loyal, writes to his friend's wife, assuring her of his support.

Philadelphia, January 31, 1793.

MADAM: If I had words that could convey to you an adequate idea of my feelings on the present situation of the Mr. de la Fayette, this letter would appear to you in a different garb. The sole object in writing to you now, is to inform you that I have deposited in the hands of Mr. Nicholas Van Staphorst of Amsterdam, Two thousand three hundred and ten guilders holland currency, equal to two hundred guineas subject to your orders.

This sum is, I am certain, the least I am indebted for services rendered me by Mr. de la Fayette, of which I never yet have received the account. I could add much, but it is best perhaps that I should say little on this subject. Your goodness will supply my deficiency.

The uncertainty of your situation (after all the enquiries I have made) has occasioned a delay in this address and remittance; and even now, the measure adopted is more the effect of a desire to find where you are, than from any knowledge I have obtained of your residence.

At all times, and under all circumstances, you, and yours, will possess the regard of him, who has the honor &c.

Not long after, the President received word of George Augustine's death. He offers not only his condolences but the hospitality of Mount Vernon to the widow.

Philadelphia, February 24, 1793.
MY DEAR FANNY: To you, who so well know the affectionate regard I had for our departed friend, it is unnecessary to describe the sorrow with which I was afflicted at the news of his death, although it was an event I had expected many weeks before it happened. To express this sorrow with the force I feel it, would answer no other purpose than to revive, in your breast, that poignancy of anguish, which, by this time, I hope is abated. Reason and resignation to the divine will, which is just, and wise in all its dispensations, cannot, in such a mind as yours, fail to produce this effect.

The object of the present letter is to convey to your mind the warmest assurances of my love, friendship, and disposition to serve you; These also I profess to have in an eminent degree, for your Children.

What plan you have contemplated, or whether in so short a time you have contemplated any, is unknown to me; and therefore

I add, that the one which strikes me most favorably, by being best calculated to promote the interest of yourself and Children, is to return to your old habitation at Mount Vernon. You can go to no place where you will be more welcome, nor to any where you can live at less expence, or trouble; matters at Mount Vernn. are now so arranged as to be under the care of responsible persons, and so they may continue; which would ease you of that anxiety, which the care of so large a family, otherwise, would naturally involve you in. It is unnecessary to observe to you that Housekeeping, under *any* circumstances, and with the best oeconomy, is expensive; and, where provision for it is to be made, will be found, I fear, beyond your means.

You might bring my niece, Harriet Washington with you for a Companion; whose conduct, I hear with pleasure, has given much satisfaction to my sister. I shall, under my present view of things, be at Mount Vernon about the first of April for, perhaps, a fortnight; But your Aunt and family will not, I expect, be there before the middle of July. My Affectionate regards attend you and your Children; and I shall always be your sincere friend.

Sometimes Washington's fondness for old friends got him into trouble. Witness this correspondence with Bryan Fairfax.

Philadelphia, March 6, 1793.
DEAR SIR: I have been favored with your Letter of the 17 Ulto: and beg you to be assured that nothing was ever farther from my thoughts than taking amiss your not coming to the road to see me the day I passed by your House on my return to this City; as an unequivocal proof of this fact, I have only to assure you that I should not have been found there, had you come out to it; for it was not until I was opposite to your House, that I sent the Servant in, without making any halt myself, being in a hurry to meet and do some business with the Commissioners of the Federal District, at George Town, before Mrs. Washington should come up, that we might proceed some miles on our journey (which we accordingly did) that afternoon. Motives of friendship and respect was all I

had in view by sending in to know how you did as I was about to leave the Country and had it not in my power, for the reason just mentioned, to call upon you myself for that purpose.

I thank you for your kind condolence on the Death of my Nephew. It is a loss I sincerely regret, but as it is the will of Heaven, whose decrees are always just and wise, I submit to it without a murmur. . . .

The letter ends with a brief discussion of a complicated estate, for which Washington was serving as one of the executors. Meanwhile, Lafayette, in prison and in imminent danger of death, was much on Washington's mind. Even as he wrote to the Marquis, vowing his support, Lafayette's troubles were becoming Washington's troubles. The French Revolution exploded in all directions and war broke out between Great Britain and Republican France. Vowing neutrality, Washington was buffeted on both sides by pro-English and pro-French Americans. In the midst of this turmoil, Thomas Jefferson, his pro-French Secretary of State, resigned. A lesser man might have looked upon this gesture as hostile, or at least as a desertion of the ship of state when a man of genius was badly needed. Instead, Washington's farewell letter to him is full of friendship.

Philadelphia, January 1, 1794.

DEAR SIR: I yesterday received, with sincere regret your resignation of the office of Secretary of State. Since it has been impossible to prevail upon you, to forego any longer the indulgence of your desire for private life; the event, however anxious I am to avert it, must be submitted to.

But I cannot suffer you to leave your Station, without assuring you, that the opinion, which I had formed, of your integrity and talents, and which dictated your original nomination, has been confirmed by the fullest experience; and that both have been eminently displayed in the discharge of your duties.

Let a conviction of my most earnest prayers for your happiness accompany you in your retirement; and while I accept with the warmest thanks your solicitude for my welfare, I beg you to believe that I always am &c.

International affairs as much as personality problems forced Washington to recall Gouverneur Morris from France. To prove that his friendship remained firm, however, he wrote the following note while en route to Mount Vernon.

Baltimore, June 19, 1794.

MY DEAR SIR: The difficulty (under existing circumstances) of knowing what to write to you, had determined me to write nothing, but to let the matter rest altogether upon the public communications from The Secretary of State. Coming to this place, however, (on a flying trip to Mount Vernon) and finding the Vessel in which Mr. Monroe [James Monroe, the new Ambassador] is on board, had not left the River, I have so far departed from my determination as to be seated in order to assure you that my confidence in, and friendship and regard for you, remains undiminished. To time, and your own observations, if you should return immediately to this country, I commit the rest; and It will be nothing new to assure you that I am always and very sincerely Yours etc.

The problems of the younger generation, particularly romantic ones, continued to hold Washington's interest. The following letter to Elizabeth Parke Custis, another of Martha's granddaughters, reveals Washington's sharp thoughts on love and sound thinking on marriage.

German Town, September 14, 1794.

MY DEAR BETCY: Shall I, in answer to your letter of the 7th. instant say, when you are as near the *Pinnacle* of happiness as your Sister Patcy conceives herself to be; or when your candour shines more conspicuously than it does in *that* letter, that I will *then*, comply with the request you have made, for my Picture?

No: I will grant it without either: for if the latter was to be a preliminary, it would be sometime I apprehend before *that* Picture would be found pendant *at* your breast; it not being within the bounds or probability that the contemplation of an inanimate thing, whatever might be the reflections arising from the possession of it, can be the *only* wish of your heart.

Respect may place it among the desirable objects of it, but there are emotions of a softer kind, to wch. the heart of a girl turned of eighteen, is susceptible, that must have generated much warmer ideas, although the fruition of them may, apparently, be more distant than those of your Sister's.

Having (by way of a hint) delivered a sentiment to Patty, which may be useful to her (if it be remembered after the change that is contemplated, is consummated) I will suggest another, more applicable to yourself.

Do not then in your contemplation of the marriage state, look for perfect felicity before you consent to wed. Nor conceive, from the fine tales of Poets and lovers of old have told us, of the transports of mutual love, that heaven has taken its abode on earth: Nor do not deceive yourself in supposing, that the only mean by which these are to be obtained, is to drink deep of the cup, and revel in an ocean of love. Love is a mighty pretty thing; but like all other delicious things, it is cloying; and when the first transports of the passion begins to subside, which it assuredly will do, and yield, oftentimes too late, to more sober reflections, it serves to evince, that love is too dainty a food to live upon *alone*, and ought not to be considered farther than as a necessary ingredient for that matrimonial happiness which results from a combination of causes; none of which are of greater importance, than that the object on whom it is placed, should possess good sense, good dispositions, and the means of supporting you in the way you have been brought up. Such qualifications cannot fail to attract (after marriage) your esteem and regard, into wch. or into disgust, sooner or later, love naturally resolves itself; and who at the same time, has a claim to the respect, and esteem of the circle he moves in. Without these, whatever may be your first impressions of the man, they will end in disappointment; for be assured, and experience will convince you, that there is no truth more certain, than that all our enjoyments fall short of our expectations; and to none does it apply with more force, than to the gratification of the passions. You may believe me to be always, and sincerely Your Affectionate.

Of all Martha's granddaughters, by far Washington's favorite was Eleanor Parke Custis, known affectionately to her grandparents as Nellie. She was raised at Mount Vernon with her younger brother, George, and as far as Washington was concerned, she could do no wrong. As Nellie grew into a beautiful young woman, suitors thronged from all directions. She apparently felt that no one approached the awesome stature of the man she admired most and declared herself immune to their charms. This remark produced from Washington a letter in which fondness and wisdom are equally mixed.

Philadelphia, January 16, 1795.
DEAR NELLIE: Your letter, the receipt of which I am now acknowledging, is written correctly and in fair characters, which is an evidence that you command, when you please, a fair hand. Possessed of these advantages, it will be your own fault if you do not avail yourself of them, and attention being paid to the choice of your subjects, you can have nothing to fear from the malignancy of criticism, as your ideas are lively, and your descriptions agreeable. Let me touch a little now on your Georgetown ball, and happy, thrice happy, for the fair who were assembled on the occasion, that there was a man to spare; for had there been 79 ladies and only 78 gentlemen, there might, in the course of the evening, have been some disorder among the caps; notwithstanding the apathy which *one* of the company entertains for the *"youth"* of the present day, and her determination "never to give herself a moment's uneasiness on account of any of them." A hint here: men and women feel the same inclinations to each other *now* that they always have done, and which they will continue to do until there is a new order of things, and *you*, as others have done, may find, perhaps, that the passions of your sex are easier raised than allayed. Do not therefore boast too soon or too strongly of your insensibility to, or resistance of, its

powers. In the composition of the human frame there is a good deal of inflammable matter, however dormant it may lie for a time, and like an intimate acquaintance of yours, when the torch is put to it, *that* which is *within you* may burst into a blaze; for which reason and especially too, as I have entered upon the chapter of advices, I will read you a lecture drawn from this text.

Love is said to be an involuntary passion, and it is, therefore, contended that it cannot be resisted. This is true in part only, for like all things else, when nourished and supplied plentifully with aliment, it is rapid in its progress; but let these be withdrawn and it may be stifled in its birth or much stinted in its growth. For example, a woman (the same may be said of the other sex) all beautiful and accomplished, will, while her hand and heart are undisposed of, turn the heads and set the circle in which she moves on fire. Let her marry, and what is the consequence? The madness *ceases* and all is quiet again. Why? not because there is any diminution in the charms of the lady, but because there is an end of hope. Hence it follows, that love may and therefore ought to be under the guidance of reason, for although we cannot avoid first impressions, we may assuredly place them under guard; and my motives for treating on this subject are to show you, while you remain Eleanor Parke Custis, spinster, and retain the resolution to love with moderation, the propriety of adhering to the latter resolution, at least until you have secured your game, and the way by which it may be accomplished.

When the fire is beginning to kindle, and your heart growing warm, propound these questions to it. Who is this invader? Have I a competent knowledge of him? Is he a man of good character; a man of sense? For, be assured, a sensible woman can never be happy with a fool. What has been his walk in life? Is he a gambler, a spendthrift, or drunkard? Is his fortune sufficient to maintain me in the manner I have been accustomed to live, and my sisters do live, and is he one to whom my friends can have no reasonable objection? If these interrogatories can be satisfactorily answered, there will remain but one more to be asked, that, however, is an important one. Have I sufficient ground to conclude that his affections are engaged by me? Without this the heart of sensibility will struggle against a passion that is not reciprocated; delicacy, custom, or call it by what epithet you will, having precluded all advances on your part. The declaration, without the *most indirect* invitation of yours, must proceed from the man, to render it permanent and valuable, and nothing short of good sense and an easy unaffected conduct can draw the line between prudery and coquetry. It would be no great departure from truth to say, that it rarely happens otherwise than that a thorough-paced coquette dies in celibacy, as a punishment for her attempts to mislead others, by encouraging looks, words, or actions, given for no other purpose than to draw men on to make overtures that they may be rejected.

This day, according to our information, gives a husband to your elder sister, and consummates, it is to be presumed, her fondest desires. The dawn with us is bright, and propitious, I hope, of her future happiness, for a full measure of which she and Mr. Law * have my earnest wishes. Compliments and congratulations on this occasion, and best regards are presented to your mamma, Dr. Stuart and family; and every blessing, among which a good husband when you want and deserve one, is bestowed on you by yours, affectionately.

On the job, meanwhile, another stalwart had deserted Washington. Alexander Hamilton withdrew from the government to pursue a private career. Washington saluted his departure with another warm testimonial.

Philadelphia, February 2, 1795.
DEAR SIR: After so long an experience of your public services, I am naturally led, at this moment of your departure from office, which it has always been my wish to prevent, to review them. In every relation, which you have borne to me, I have found that my confidence in your talents, exertions and integrity, has been well placed.

---

* This should be Mr. Peter, as Martha Parke Custis married Thomas Peter. Perhaps the error was made in copying the letter for George Washington Parke Custis's book, *Recollections of Washington,* or the busy President may have gotten his grandchildren's marital plans confused.

I the more freely render this testimony of my approbation, because I speak from opportunities of information wch. cannot deceive me, and which furnish satisfactory proof of your title to public regard.

My most earnest wishes for your happiness will attend you in your retirement, and you may assure yourself of the sincere esteem, regard and friendship of, dear Sir, your affectionate, &c.

Not long after, the Lafayette problem appeared in a new guise. The marquis's son, George Washington Lafayette, appeared in Boston accompanied by a tutor, announcing his intention to study in the United States. Washington, struggling to maintain the precarious neutrality between France and England, decided he could not, as President, see the lad. But he made sure that young Lafayette was protected and entertained by friends in Boston. Two months after the lad's arrival, Washington finally decided it was safe to communicate with him, and welcomed him in the following letter.

Philadelphia, November 22, 1795

MY DEAR YOUNG FRIEND: It was with sincere pleasure I received your letter from Boston, and with the heart of affection I welcome you to this City.

Considerations of a political nature added to those which were assigned by yourself, or Mr. Frestal of a sort more private, but not less interesting to your friends left no doubt in my mind of the propriety of your remaining incog until some plan advantageous to *yourself* and eligible for *all* parties could be devised for bringing you forwd. under more favorable auspices.

These considerations, and a journey which I was in the act of commencing when I received your letter (and from which I have not long since been returned to this city) restrained me from writing to you at that time, but I imposed upon Mr. Cabot a gentleman of character and one in whose discretion I could place entire confidence, the agreeable office of assuring you, in my name, of my warmest affection and support; of my determination to stand in the place of a father and friend to you undr. all cirs; requesting him at the sametime to make arrangemts. with Mr. Frestal for supplying your immediate wants, and moreover that he would add thereto every thing consolatory on my part. All of which I now renew to you in the most unequivocal terms; for you may be assured, that the sincere, and affectionate attachment which I had to your unfortunate father, my friend and compatriot in arms will extend with not less warmth to you, his son; do not therefore ascribe my silence from the period of your interview with Mr. Cabot to a wrong cause.

The causes, which have imposed this conduct on us both, not being entirely removed, it is my desire, that you, and Mr. Frestal would repair to Colo Hamilton, in the City of New York, who is authorised by me to fix with you on the most eligable plan for your present accommodation. This gentleman was always in habits of great intimacy with, and is warmly attached to, Mr. de la Fayette; you may rely therefore on his friendship and the efficacy of his advice.

How long the causes wch. have withheld you from me may continue, I am not able, at this moment to decide but be assured of my wishes to embrace you so soon as they shall have ceased and that whenever the period arrives I shall do it with fervency. In the meantime let me begin with fatherly advice to you to apply closely to your studies that the season of your youth may be improved to the utmost; that you may be found the deserving Son of a meritorious father. Adieu; believe me to be as you will always find me Your Affecte. friend.

A more cheerful letter goes to Elizabeth Parke Custis a few months later, on the announcement of her engagement to Mr. Law.

Philadelphia, February 10, 1796.
MY DEAR BETSEY: I have obeyed your injunction in not acknowledging the receipt of your letter of the first instant until I should hear from Mr. Law. This happened yesterday; I therefore proceed to assure you, if Mr. Law is the man of your choice, of wch. there can be no doubt, as he has merits to engage your affections, and

you have declared that he has not only done so, but that you find, after a careful examination of your heart, you cannot be happy without him; that your alliance with him meets my approbation. *Yes*, Betsey, and this approbation is accompanied with my fervent wishes that you may be as happy in this important event as your most Sanguine imagination has ever presented to your view. Along with these wishes, I bestow on you my choicest blessings.

Nothing contained in your letter, in Mrs. Laws, or in any other from our friends intimate *when* you are to taste the sweets of Matrimony; I therefore call upon *you*, who have more honesty than disguise, to give me the details. Nay more, that you will relate all your feelings to *me* on this occasion: or as a Quaker would say "all the workings of the spirit within."

This, I have a right to expect in return for my blessing, so promptly bestowed, after you had concealed the matter from me so long. Being entitled therefore to this confidence, and to a compliance with my requests, I shall look forward to the fulfilment of it.

If after marriage Mr. Laws business should call him to this City, the same room which Mr. Peter and your sister occupied will accomodate you two; and it will be equally at your service.

You know how much I love you, how much I have been gratified by your attentions to those things which you had reason to believe were grateful to my feelings. And having *no* doubt of your continuing the *same* conduct, as the effect will be pleasing to *me*, and unattended with any disadvantage to *yourself*, I shall remain with the sincerest friendship, and the most Affectionate regard, etc.

Finally, Washington's affection overcame his caution and he decided to see young Lafayette, come what may. He invites him to join him at Philadelphia.

Philadelphia, March 31, 1796.
MY DEAR SIR: Your letter of the 28th instt. was received yesterday. The enclosures which accompanied it, evidence much discretion; and your conduct therein meets my entire approbation.

In the early part of this month, I put a letter into the hands of Colo. Hamilton, inviting you to this place; and expected, until your letter of the above date was received, to have embraced you, under my own roof, tomorrow or next day.

As the period for this, seems to be more distant, from the purport of your enquiries; I again repeat my former request; and wish that without delay, you and Mr. Frestel, with your baggage &ca. would proceed immediately to this City, and to my house; where a room is prepared for you and him.

Under expectation of your doing this, it is as unnecessary, as it might be improper, to go more into detail until I have the pleasure of seeing you; and to render every service in my power to the Son of my friend, for whom I have always entertained the purest Affections. These are too strong not to extend themselves to you. Therefore believe me to be, as I really am, Sincerly and Affectionately Yours, &c.

At the same time Washington was never too busy to worry about the romantic problems of his nieces and nephews. Harriet Washington was still one of his most troublesome charges. He discusses her sudden decision to marry in the following letter to his sister Betty.

Philadelphia, April 7, 1796.

MY DEAR SISTER: Your letter of the 27th. Ulto. was enclosed to me by Mr. Parks, in one from himself, dated the 1st instt. on the same subject.

Harriot having very little fortune herself, has no *right* to expect a great one in the man she marry's; but if he has not a competency to support her in the way she has lived, in the circle of her friends, she will not find the matrimonial state so comfortable as she may have expected when a family is looking up to her and but scanty means to support it.

Altho' she has no right to expect a man of fortune, she certainly has just pretentions to expect one whose connexions are respectable, and whose relations she could have no objection to associate with. How far this is, or is not the case with Mr. Parks, I know not, for neither his own letter, or yours give any acct. of his family nor whether he is a native or a foreigner; and we have his own word only for his possessing *any* property at all altho' he estimates his fortune at £3000. A precarious dependence this when applied to a man in Trade.

I do not wish to thwart Harriots inclination if her affects. are placed on Mr. Parks and if upon the enquiries I shall make or cause to be made into his family and connexions, there shall be found nothing exceptionable in them; that he is, as you say "very much respected by all his acquaintance, sober, sedate, and attentive to business;" and is moreover in good business; I shall throw no impedimt. in the way of their Marriage: altho' I should have preferred, if a *good* match had not offer'd in the meanwhile that she shd. have remained single until I was once more settled at Mt. Vernon and she a resident there which, if life is spared to us, will certainly happen to me in ten or eleven Months; because then she would have been in the way of seeing much company, and would have had a much fairer prospect of matching respectably than with one who is little known, and of whose circumstances few or none can know much about.

Having had no business to write to you upon, and being very much occupied by my public duties, are the only reasons why I have been silent. I am persuaded you will enjoy more ease and quiet, and meet with fewer vexations where you now are, than where you did live. It is my sincere wish that you should do so and that your days may be happy; in these Mrs. Washington joins with Your most Affecte. Brother.

Now in his last year of the Presidency, Washington obviously longed for retirement. Already he looked forward to enjoying Mount Vernon and was attempting to lure favorite friends there. The following letter to David Humphreys, whom he had just appointed Minister to Spain, reveals these feelings, along with the Gibraltarlike integrity that enabled Washington to ignore scurrilous personal attacks on him from pro-French Americans.

Philadelphia, June 12, 1796.

MY DR. HUMPHREY: I could not suffer Captain O'Brien to return without carrying along with him this evidence of my continued regard and friendship for you. In expressing of which, I shall be concise; for a long and interesting session, closed only the first day of this month; many laws wch. require immediate attention and execution; added to a preparation for a journey to Mount Vernon (to morrow) for a little relaxation from the unpleasant scenes which have been, and are continually presenting themselves to my view, will not, however well disposed I might otherwise be, permit me to be profuse.

From the Office of State you will receive every thing that relates to business; and the gazettes, which I presume accompany the dispatches, will bring you pretty well acquainted with the state of politics and of parties in this country; and shew you in what manner I am attacked for a steady opposition to every measure which has a tendency to disturb the peace and tranquillity of it. But these attacks, unjust and unpleasant as they are, will occasion no change in my conduct; nor will they work any other effect in my mind, than to increase the anxious desire which has long possessed my breast, to enjoy in the shades of retirement the consolation of having rendered my Country every service my abilities were competent to, uninfluenced by pecuniary or ambitious considerations as they respected myself, and without any attempt to provide for my friends farther than their merits, abstractedly, entitle them to; nor an attempt in *any* instance to bring a relation of mine into Office. Malignity therefore may dart her shafts; but no earthly power can deprive me of the consolation of knowing that I have not in the course of my administration been guilty of a *wilful* error, however numerous they may have been from other causes. When you shall think with the poet that "the post of honor is a private station," and may be inclined to enjoy yourself in my shades (I do not mean the shades below, where, if you put it off long, I may be) I can only tell you that you will meet with the same cordial reception at Mount Vernon that you have always experienced at that place, and that I am, &c.

During this same year Washington began a correspondence with George Washington Parke Custis, who was then at the College of New Jersey, later known as Princeton. Washington was as eager to give him a good education as he had been with his father, but the boy's indolent nature proved to be even more intractable.

Philadelphia, November 15, 1796.

DEAR WASHINGTON: Yesterday's mail brought me your letter of the 12th instant, and under cover of this letter you will receive a ten-dollar bill, to purchase a gown, &c., if proper. But as the classes may be distinguished by a different insignia, I advise you not to provide these without first obtaining the approbation of your tutors; otherwise you may be distinguished more by folly, than by the dress.

It affords me pleasure to hear that you are agreeably fixed; and I receive still more from the assurance you give of attending closely to your studies. It is you yourself who is to derive immediate benefit from these. Your country may do it hereafter. The more knowledge you acquire, the greater will be the probability of your succeeding in both, and the greater will be your thirst for more.

I rejoice to hear you went through your examination with propriety, and have no doubt but that the president has placed you in the class which he conceived best adapted to the present state of your improvement. The more there are above you, the greater your exertions should be to ascend; but let your promotion result from your own application, and from intrinsic merit, not from the labors of others. The last would prove fallacious, and expose you to the reproach of the daw in borrowed feathers. This would be inexcusable in you, because there is no occasion for it; forasmuch, as you need nothing but the exertion of the talents you possess, with proper directions, to acquire all that is necessary; and the hours allotted for study, if properly improved, will enable you to do this. Although the confinement may feel irksome at first, the advantages resulting from it, to a reflecting mind, will soon overcome it.

Endeavor to conciliate the good will of *all* your fellow-students, rendering them every act of kindness in your power. Be particularly obliging and attentive to your chamber-mate, Mr.

Forsyth; who, from the account I have of him, is an admirable young man, and strongly impressed with the importance of a liberal and finished education. But above all, be obedient to your tutors, and in a particular manner respect the president of the seminary who is both learned and good.

For any particular advantage you may derive from the attention and aid of Mr. Forsyth, I shall have a disposition to reward. One thing more and I will close this letter. Never let an indigent person ask, without receiving *something*, if you have the means; always recollecting in what light the widow's mite was viewed.

Your grandmother, sister, and all here are well, and feeling a strong interest in your welfare, join most cordially with me in every good wish for it. Affectionately, I am your sincere friend.

Like his father before him, young Custis was adept at making large resolutions and failing to fulfill them. But Washington's fondness for the boy remained unshaken. Here he tries to maintain the proper balance between supervision and benevolence.

Philadelphia, January 11, 1797.
DEAR WASHINGTON: I hasten to acknowledge the receipt of your letter, dated the 7th instant, but which did not get to my hands until yesterday, and to express to you the sincere pleasure I feel in finding that I had interpreted some parts of your letter erroneously. As you have the best and most unequivocal evidence the case is susceptible of, that I have no other object in view by extending my cares and advice to you than what will redound to your own respectability, honor, and future happiness in life, so be assured, that while you give me reasons to expect a ready submission to my counsels, and while I hear that you are diligent in pursuing the means which are to acquire these advantages, it will afford me infinite gratification. Your last letter is replete with assurances of this nature; I place entire confidence in them. They have removed all the doubts which were expressed in my last letter to you, and let me repeat it again, have conveyed very pleasing sensations to my mind.

It was not my wish to check your correspondences, very far from it; for with proper characters (and none can be more desirable than with your papa and Mr. Lear) [Tobias Lear, Washington's secretary] and on proper subjects, it will give you a habit of expressing your ideas upon all occasions with facility and correctness. I meant no more, by telling you we should be content with hearing from you once a week, than that these correspondences were not to be considered as an injunction or an imposition, thereby interfering with your studies or concerns of a more important nature. So far am I from discountenancing writing of any kind (except upon the principle above mentioned) that I should be pleased to hear, and you yourself might derive advantages from a short diary (recorded in a book) of the occurances which happen to you within your sphere. Trifling as this may appear at first view, it may become an introduction to more interesting matters. At any rate, by carefully preserving these, it would afford you more satisfaction in a retrospective view, that what you may conceive at present.

Another thing I would recommend to you, not because I want to know how you spend your money, and that is, to keep an account book, and enter therein every farthing of your receipts and expenditures. The doing of which would initiate you into a habit, from which considerable advantages would result. Where no account of this sort is kept, there can be no investigation; no corrections of errors; no discovery from a recurrence thereto, wherein too much, or too little, had been appropriated to particular uses. From an early attention to these matters, important and lasting benefits may follow.

We are well, and all unite in best wishes for you; and with sincere affection, etc.

One of Washington's last letters as President was this generous advice to the incoming chief executive, John Adams, on how to handle the problem of advancing his son, John Quincy Adams, who had already distinguished himself in the diplomatic corps and was currently serving as United States Minister to Holland.

Monday, February 20, 1797.

DEAR SIR: I thank you for giving me the perusal of the enclosed, The sentimts. do honor to the head and heart of the writer, and if my wishes would be of any avail they should go to you in a *strong hope* that you will not withhold merited promotion for Mr. John Adams because he is your Son. For without intending to compliment the father or the mother, or to censure any others, I give it as my decided opinion that Mr. Adams is the most valuable public character we have abroad, and that he will prove himself to be the ablest of all our Diplomatic Corps.

If he was now to be brought into *that* line, or into any other public walk, I could not, upon the principle which has regulated my own conduct, disapprove the caution which is hinted at in the letter. But he is already entered; the public more and more, as he is known, are appreciating his talents and worth; and his country would sustain a loss if these are checked by over delicacy on your part. With sincere esteem and affectionate regard I am etc.

As the time for his retirement drew closer, Washington became more sentimental about his friends. Henry Knox, who had served him long and faithfully, stood high on any list of Washington's favorites.

Philadelphia, March 2, 1797.

MY DEAR SIR: Amongst the last Acts of my political life, and before I go hence into retirement, *profound*, will be the acknowledgment of your kind and affectionate letter from Boston, dated the 15th. of January.

From the friendship I have always borne you, and from the interest I have ever taken in whatever relates to your prosperity and happiness, I participated in the sorrows which I know you must have felt for your late heavy losses [three of Knox's children had recently died]. But it is not for man to scan the wisdom of Providence. The best he can do, is to submit to its decrees. Reason, religion and Philosophy, teaches us to do this, but 'tis time alone that can ameliorate the pangs of humanity, and soften its woes.

To the wearied traveller who sees a resting place, and is bending his body to lean thereon, I now compare myself; but to be suffered to do *this* in peace, is I perceive too much, to be endured by *some*. To misrepresent my motives; to reprobate my politics; and to weaken the confidence which has been reposed in my administration, are objects which cannot be relinquished by those who, will be satisfied with nothing short of a change in our political System. The consolation however, which results from conscious rectitude, and the approving voice of my Country, unequivocally expressed by its Representatives, deprives their sting of its poison, and places in the same point of view both the weakness, and malignity of their efforts.

Although the prospect of retirement is most grateful to my soul, and I have not a wish to mix again in the great world, or to partake in its politics, yet, I am not without my regrets at parting with (perhaps never more to meet) the few intimates whom I love, among these, be assured you are one.

The account given by Mr. Bingham and others, of your agreeable Situation and prospects at St. George's, gave me infinite pleasure; and no one wishes more sincerely than I do, that they may increase with your years. The remainder of my life (which in the course of nature cannot be long) will be occupied in rural amusements, and though I shall seclude myself as much as possible from the noisy and bustling crowd, none more than myself, would be regaled by the company of those I esteem, at Mount Vernon: more than 20 Miles from which, after I arrive there, it is not likely I ever shall be.

As early in next week as I can make arrangements for it, I shall commence my journey for Mount Vernon. To morrow, at dinner, I shall, as a servant of the public, take my leave of the President Elect, of the foreign characters, heads of Departments, &ca. And the day following, with pleasure, I shall witness the inauguration of my Successor to the Chair of government.

On the subject of Politics I shall say nothing; you will have an opportunity of seeing and conversing with many of the Legislators;

from whom, so far as it relates to the proceedings of their own body, they can give you the details. The Gazettes will furnish the rest.

Mrs. Washington unites with me in every good wish for you, Mrs. Knox and family, and with unfeigned truth, I am yours always, and affectionately.

CHAPTER NINE

Mount Vernon Once More

At last Washington returned to Mount Vernon. One of his first letters from there went to George Washington Parke Custis, a chatty note that tells us more about his homecoming than anything else.

Mount Vernon, April 3, 1797.

DEAR WASHINGTON: Your letter of the 25th ultimo has been duly received, and as your grandmamma or sister will write to you by this post, I shall leave it to them to furnish you with the details of our journey, and the occurrences since our arrival.

It gives me singular pleasure to hear that your time has been so well employed during the last winter, and that you are so sensible of the good effects of it yourself. If your improvement in other matters is equal to that which is visible in your writing, it can not but be pleasing to your friends; for the change there, both in the characters and diction is considerably for the better. A perseverance in such a course will redound much to your own benefit and reputation, and will make you at all times a welcome guest at Mount Vernon.

I have nothing to do in which you could be usefully employed in Philadelphia, and approve your determination to delay no time at that or any other place on the road, that you may have the more of it to spend among your friends in this quarter, who are very anxious to see you.

We are all in a litter and dirt, occasioned by joiners, masons, and painters, working in the house, all parts of which, as well as the out-buildings, I find upon examination, to be exceedingly out of repairs. I am etc.

Though visitors found him as vigorous as ever, Washington himself could feel old age coming on. He shows signs of it in this letter to Lawrence Augustine Washington, son of his brother Samuel, congratulating him on his forthcoming wedding.

Mount Vernon, September 3, 1797.

DEAR LAWRENCE: Your letter of 23d of the last, was received on the first day of the present month.

In the interesting event which you have announced, I sincerely wish you and the lady who is to be the partner of your future fortunes, all imaginable happiness. To attain which, depends very much upon the parties themselves: and from the character you have drawn of Miss Wood, and from what I have heard of it from others, I think your prospects are fair and pleasing.

If any substantial good could result from my becoming a guest at your Wedding, I would make exertions to be there; but as wedding Assemblies are better calculated for those who are *coming in to,* than to those who are *going out of* life, you must accept the good wishes of your Aunt and myself in place of personal attendance, for I think it not likely that either of us will ever be more than 25 miles from Mount Vernon again, while we are inhabitants of this Terrestrial Globe.

We offer our respects to the family with whom you are going to connect yourself, and in a particular manner I desire to be presented to the old lady, Grandmother of Miss Wood; for whom I have, and always had, a very high esteem and regard; present us also to your brother and his family. I remain, etc.

Washington's devotion to Lafayette remained green until the end of his days. Here he writes to him as a kind of stepfather to his son. After spending almost a year at Mount Vernon, young Lafayette had departed for France. In his pocket was a check from Washington for three hundred dollars. Earlier, Washington's accounts showed a check for a hundred dollars given to the young man to buy things he might hesitate to ask for.

Mount Vernon, October 8, 1797.

MY DEAR SIR: This letter will, I hope and expect, be presented to you by your Son, who is highly deserving of such Parents as you and your amiable Lady.

He can relate, much better than I can describe, my participation in your sufferings, my solicitude for your relief, the measures I adopted (though ineffectually) to facilitate your liberation from an unjust and cruel imprisonment, and the joy I experienced at the news of its accomplishment. I shall hasten therefore to congratulate you, and be assured no one can do it with more cordiality, with more sincerity, or with greater affection, on the restoration of that liberty which every act of your life entitles you to the enjoyment of; and I hope I may add, to the uninterrupted possession of your Estates, and the confidence of your Country. The re-possession of these things, though they cannot compensate for the hardships you have endured, may, nevertheless soften the painful remembrance of them.

From the delicate and responsible situation in which I stood as a public officer, but more especially from a misconception of the manner in which your son had left France (till explained in a personal interview with himself) he did not come immediately into my family on his arrival in America, tho' he was assured in the first moments of it, of my protection and support. His conduct, since he first set his feet on American ground, has been exemplary in every point of view, such as has gained him the esteem, affection and confidence of all who have had the pleasure of his acquaintance. His filial affection and duty, and his ardent desire to embrace his parents and Sisters in the first moments of their releasement, would not allow him to await the authentic account of this much desired event; but at the same time that I suggested the propriety of this, I could not withhold my assent to the gratification of his wishes, to fly to the Arms of those whom he holds most dear; persuaded as he is, from the information he has received, that he shall find you all in Paris.

M. Frestal has been a true Mentor to George. No Parent could have been more attentive to a favourite Son; and he richly merits all that can be said of his virtues, of his good sense, and of his prudence. Both your son and him carry with them the vows, and regrets of this family, and of all who know them. And you may be assured that you yourself never stood higher in the affections of the People of this country than at the present moment.

With what concerns myself, personally, I shall not take up your time; further than to add, that I have once more retreated to the shades of my own Vine and Fig tree, where I shall remain with best vows for the prosperity of that country for whose happiness I have toiled many years, to establish its Independence, Constitution, and Laws, and for the good of mankind in general, until the days of my sojournment, whh. cannot be many, are accomplished.

Having bid a final adieu to the walks of public life, and meaning to withdraw myself from the Politics thereof, I shall refer you to Mr. Frestal and George, who (at the sametime that they have, from prudential considerations, avoided all interference in the Politics of the Country) cannot have been inattentive observers of what was passing among us, to give you a general view of our situation, and of the party, which in my opinion, has disturbed the Peace and tranquillity of it. And with sentiments of the highest regard for you, your lady and daughters, and with assurances that, if inclination or events, should induce you, or any of them, to visit America, no person in it would receive you with more cordiality and affection, than . . .

Washington's warm feelings for Lafayette's son are evident in this bon voyage letter. As always with friends who have shared Mount Vernon with him, Washington adds some chatty news of the neighborhood.

Mount Vernon, December 5, 1797.
MY DEAR GEORGE: With that pleasure which I shall always feel at hearing from you, or of any thing which may contribute to your happiness, I received your several letters from New York, dated in October and that of the 2d. of November from Sea, by Mr. Latimer. If my best vows would have contributed to a prosperous Voy-

age, and a happy meeting with your Parents and Sisters in France, both must have happened to the utmost extent of your wishes 'ere this, for they were offered on the Altar of Sincerity; and are now followed with assurances that, if you should ever return to America again, that you will find the same cordial reception within the Walls of this Mansion, as you have heretofore experienced.

Great as my wishes are that you may have met with your Parents in France, I am not without fear, from our late accounts that you have been disappointed. How far the event [the coup d'etat of Fructidor] which took place in Paris, on the 4th. of September, may have effected their prospects in that Country, is not for me (who knows so little of the principles which governed on that occasion) to express any opinion thereon; but as I have seen an official report from the American Consul at Hamburgh, of the terms on which the Prisoners at Olmutz were released, the proceedings of your Parents after their arrival at Hamburgh, is rendered equivocal with us.

Few things have occurred, since you left us which merit attention, except an earlier Winter than has almost ever been known; for since the beginning of November we have scarcely experienced a moderate day; and at this moment the Mercury in Fahrenht. is standing at 10° only above o. The Creeks and smaller Waters are all shut up, and the navigation of the River is much impeded by Ice.

Mrs. Peter has added another daughter to the family and both mother and child are well, as are Mr. and Mrs. Law and their child, who are now here on a visit before their departure for Philadelphia, at which place they propose to spend the Winter. The younger parts of this family are also in good health, and unite most cordially with me in tendering you their best wishes, to which I add assurances of the sincere friendship and affectionate regard of Yours, etc.

P.S. As you noticed in one of your letters from New York Christopher's [Washington's Negro valet] excursion to Bethleham, I have pleasure in informing you, that he derived so much aid from the medicine he took as to have remained perfectly well ever since; and has placed such confidence in his Doctrs. skill, that he wou'd not again dispair of being cured of the bite of a mad dog; if the Hydrophoby was strong upon him.

In February, 1798, George Washington Lafayette rejoined his mother and father, who had been released from prison. The next year he enlisted in the Dutch army to fight the Russians and English. In March 1800 George was given a commission as a second lieutenant in the French Hussars and took part in the battle of Marengo. He served gallantly throughout the early years of Napoleon's campaigns, but was never promoted because his father remained hostile to the Corsican's dictatorship. George finally resigned from the army, but after Napoleon's fall he became active in French politics and remained a prominent though by no means dominant figure for the rest of his life.

Much as he enjoyed his visit, Washington was no doubt relieved to see young Lafayette depart. The retired President had his hands full with George Washington Parke Custis, who had flunked out of Princeton and returned to Mount Vernon. Here Washington writes to the boy's stepfather, Doctor David Stuart, with a note of desperation, if not despair, in his plea for help.

Mount Vernon, January 22, 1798.
DEAR SIR: Washington leaves this today, on a visit to Hope Park [the Stuart estate], which will afford you an opportunity to examine the progress he has made in the studies he was directed to pursue.

I can, and I believe do, keep him in his room a certain portion of the 24 hours, but it will be impossible for me to make him attend to his Books, if inclination, on his part, is wanting; nor while I am out, if he chuses to be so too, is it in my power to prevent it. I will not say this is the case, nor will I run the hazard of doing him injustice by saying he does not apply, as he ought, to what has been prescribed; but no risk will be run, and candour requires I declare it as my opinion, that he will not derive much benefit in any course which can be marked out for him at this place, without an *able*

Preceptor always with him, nor then, for reasons, which do not require to be detailed.

What is best to be done with him, I know not. My opinion always has been that the University of Massachusetts would have been the most eligible Seminary to have sent him to, 1st, because it is on a larger Scale than any other; and 2nd, because I believe that the habits of the youth there, whether from the discipline of the School. or from the greater attention of the People, generally, to morals and a more regular course of life, are less prone to dissipation and debauchery than they are at the Colleges South of it. It may be asked, if this was my opinion, why did I not send him there? the answer is as short, as to me it was weighty; being the only male of his family and knowing (although it would have been submitted to) that it would have proved a heart rending stroke to have him at that distance. I was disposed to try a nearer Seminary, of good repute; which from some cause, or combinations of causes, has not, after the experiment of a year, been found to answer the end that was contemplated. Whether to send him there *now*, or indeed to any other public School, is at least problematical, and to suffer him to mispend his time at this place, will be disgraceful to himself and me.

If I was to propose to him, to go to the University at Cambridge (in Massachusetts) [Harvard] he might, as has been usual for him on like occasions, say he would go whereever I chose to send him; but if he should go contrary to his inclination, and without a disposition to apply his time properly, an expense without any benefit would result from the measure. Knowing how much I have been disappointed, and my mind disturbed by his conduct, he would not, I am sure, make a candid disclosure of his sentiments to me on this or any other plan I might propose for the completion of his education; for which reason I would pray that you (or perhaps Mrs. Stuart cd. succeed better than any other) would draw ———— [mutilated] and explicit disclosure ———— [mutilated] wishes and views are: for if they are absolutely fixed, an attempt to counteract them by absolute controul would be as idle as the endeavour to stop a rivulet that is constantly running. Its progress while mound upon mound is erected, may be arrested; but this must have an end, and everything would be swept with the torrent.

The more I think of his entering at William and Mary, (unless he could be placed in the Bishop's family) the more doubtful I am of its utility, on many accounts; which had better be the subject or oral communications than by letter. I shall wish to hear from you on the subject of this letter. On occasion of severe reprimand, I found it necessary to give Washington sometime ago, I received the enclosed from him. I have little doubt of his meaning well, but he has not resolution, or exertion enough to act well. Our best wishes attend Mrs. Stuart and the family, I am, etc.

Pleading letters from relatives were part of Washington's daily routine. Here he writes to a young cousin on his mother's side of the family, Sally Ball Haynie, dispensing charity and advice without much enthusiasm.

Mount Vernon, February 11, 1798.
MISS SALLEY: I have received your letter of the 28th. of last month, and without enquiry at this time why you left Mr. Lewis's family or how you employ your time, I have requested him to furnish you with ten pounds to supply you with such necessaries as you may be in immediate want.

But as you have no fortune to support you, Industry, oeconomy, and a virtuous conduct are your surest resort, and best dependance. In every station of life, these are commendable. In the one in which it has pleased Providence to place you, it is indispensably necessary that they should mark all your footsteps. It is no disparagement to the first lady in the Land to be constantly employed, at some work or another; to you, it would prove, in addition to a chaste and unsullied reputation the surest means of attracting the notice of some man with whom your future fortune will be united in a Matrimonial bond and without which it would be in vain to expect a person of worth. I wish you well and am Your friend.

Young Custis had by this time transferred to the college at Annapolis. As usual, he was bursting with new resolutions and at least the appearance of energy. Ever hopeful, Washington responds with encouragement.

Mount Vernon, March 19, 1798.

DEAR WASHINGTON: Your letter of the 12th instant has been received; and it gives me and your friends here much pleasure to find that you are agreeably fixed and disposed to prosecute your studies with zeal and alacrity.

Let these continue to be your primary objects and pursuits; all other matters at your time of life are of secondary consideration. For it is on a well-grounded knowledge of these, your respectability in maturer age, your usefulness to your country, and indeed, your own private gratification, when you come seriously to reflect upon the importance of them, will depend. The wise man, you know, has told us (and a more useful lesson never was taught) that there is a *time for all things*; and now is the time for laying in such a stock of erudition as will effect the purposes I have mentioned. And above all things, I exhort you to pursue the *course* of studies that Mr. Mc-Dowell, of whom every one, as well as yourself, speaks highly, has or shall mark out as the most eligible path to accomplish the end. It is from the experience and knowledge of preceptors that youth is to be advantageously instructed. If the latter are to mark out their own course, there would be little or no occasion for the former, and what would be the consequence it is not difficult to predict.

One or other of the family will expect to receive a letter from you once a fortnight, that we may know how you are in health; in addition to which, I shall expect to hear how you are progressing in your studies, as time advances. All here join in best wishes for you, among whom, your sister Peter is of the number; and you may be assured of the friendship of your affectionate etc.

Now comes one of the most significant letters in Washington's life. A farewell to youth, and to the woman who had made that youth memorable—Sally Fairfax. She had remained in Eng-

land during all the intervening years and was now a widow. Her husband had never won the title she pursued so ardently. It had passed instead to his brother Bryan Fairfax, who still lived in Virginia, only a few miles from Mount Vernon.

Mount Vernon, May 16, 1798.

MY DEAR MADAM: Five and twenty years, nearly, have passed away since I have considered myself as the permanent resident of this place; or have been in a situation to endulge myself in a familiar intercourse with my friends, by letter or otherwise.

During this period, so many important events have occurred, and such changes in men and things have taken place, as the compass of a letter would give you but an inadequate idea of. None of which events, however, nor all of them together, have been able to eradicate from my mind, the recollection of those happy moments, the happiest in my life, which I have enjoyed in your company.

Worn out in a manner by the toils of my past labour, I am again seated under my Vine and Fig tree, and wish I could add that, there are none to make us affraid; but those whom we have been accustomed to call our good friends and Allies, are endeavouring, if not to make us affraid, yet to despoil us of our property; and are provoking us to Acts of self-defence, which may lead to War. What will be the result of such measures, time, that faithful expositor of all things, must disclose. My wish is, to spend the remainder of my days (which cannot be many) in rural amusements; free from those cares [from] which public responsibility is never exempt.

Before the War, and even while it existed, altho' I was eight years from home at one stretch, (except the *en passant visits* made to it on my March to and from the Siege of Yorktown) I made considerable additions to my dwelling house, and alterations in my Offices, and Gardens; but the dilapidation occasioned by time, and those neglects which are co-extensive with the absence of Proprietors, have occupied as much of my time, within the last twelve months in repairing them, as at any former period in the same space. and it is matter of sore regret, when I cast my eyes towards

Belvoir, which I often do, to reflect that the former Inhabitants of it, with whom we lived in such harmony and friendship, no longer reside there; and that the ruins can only be viewed as the memento of former pleasures; and permit me to add, that I have wondered often, (your nearest relations being in this Country), that you should not prefer spending the evening of your life among them rather than close the sublunary Scene in a foreign Country, numerous as your acquaintances may be, and sincere, as the friendships you may have formed.

A Century hence, if this Country keeps united (and it is surely its policy and Interest to do so) will produce a City, though not as large as London, yet of a magnitude inferior to few others in Europe, on the Banks of the Potomack; where one is now establishing for the permanent Seat of the Government of the United States (between Alexandria and Georgetown, on the Maryland side of the River). A situation not excelled for commanding prospect, good water, salubrious air, and safe harbour by any in the world; and where elegant buildings are erecting and in forwardness, for the reception of Congress in the year 1800.

Alexandria, within the last seven years, (since the establishment of the General Government) has increased in buildings, in population, in the improvement of its Streets by well executed pavements, and in the extension of its Wharves, in a manner, of which you can have very little idea. This shew of prosperity, you will readily conceive, is owing to its commerce, the extension of *that trade* is occasioned in (a great degree) by opening of the Inland navigation of the Potomack River; now cleared to Fort Cumberland, upwards of 200 miles, and by a similar attempt to accomplish the like up the Shenandoah, 150 miles more. In a word, if this Country can steer clear of European politics, stand firm on its bottom, and be wise and temperate in its government, it bids fair to be one of the greatest and happiest nations in the world. . . .

The rest of the letter is illegible. Sally did not take Washington's advice. She remained in England and died at Bath at a very advanced age. Washington, meanwhile, went back to berating his grandson.

> *Mount Vernon, June 13, 1798.*
> DEAR WASHINGTON: It is now near five weeks since any person of this family has heard from you, though you were requested to write once a fortnight. Knowing how apt your grandmamma is to suspect that you are sick, or that some accident has happened to you, how could you omit this?
>
> I have said that none of us have heard from you, but it behooves me to add, that from persons in Alexandria, lately from Annapolis, I have, with much surprise, been informed of your devoting much time, and paying much attention, to a certain young lady of that place. Knowing that conjectures are often substituted for facts, and idle reports are circulated without foundation, we are not disposed to give greater credence to *these* than what arises from a fear that your application to books is not such as it ought to be, and that the hours that might be more profitably employed at your studies are mispent in this manner.
>
> Recollect again the saying of the wise man, "There is a time for all things," and sure I am this is not a time for *a boy of your age* to enter into engagements which might end in sorrow and repentance. Yours affectionately.

Washington's correspondence with young Custis achieves total despair in the following letter. His grandson had flunked out of still another school and was coming home.

> *Mount Vernon, July 24, 1798.*
> DEAR WASHINGTON: Your letter of the 21st was received last night. The question, "I would thank you to inform me whether I leave it entirely, or not, so that I may pack up accordingly," really astonishes me! for it would seem as if *nothing* I could say to you made more than a *momentary* impression. Did I not, before you went to that seminary, and since by letter, endeavor to fix indelibly on your

mind, that the object for which you were sent there was to finish a course of education which you yourself were to derive the benefit of hereafter, and for pressing which upon you, you would be the first to thank your friends so soon as reason has its proper sway in the direction of your thoughts?

As there is a regular stage between Annapolis and the federal city, embrace that as the easiest and most convenient way of getting to the latter, from whence Mr. Law or Mr. Peter will, I have no doubt, send you hither; or a horse might meet you there, or at Alexandria, at an appointed time.

The family are well; and I am, as usual, your etc.

Though Washington was no longer an active politician, he was very much still father of his country. The members of President John Adams' cabinet wrote him regularly. While he replied to them in private, Washington scrupulously avoided making any public statement on the delicate international situation. England and France were still at war and were jockeying for influence in the young United States. A pro-French faction, led by Thomas Jefferson, was already launching a political campaign to unseat President Adams. In this context, Washington naturally dealt carefully with a letter from a certain John Langhorn asking for his opinion on the current political situation. Only later did he learn that no such person existed and that his letter had been called for at the local post office by a servant of Thomas Jefferson. Here Washington writes to his nephew Bushrod, telling him in no uncertain terms what he thought of such tactics.

Mount Vernon, August 12, 1798.

MY DEAR SIR: I have received your letter of the 7th. instant, giving an extract of Mr. Nicholas's letter to you. With respect to the request contained in it, I leave the matter *entirely* to his own *discretion*, with your advise, to advance or halt, according to the tenableness of his ground, and circumstances.

If he could prove, indubitably, that the letter addressed to me, with the signature of Jno. Langhorne, was a forgery, no doubt would remain in the mind of any one that it was written with a view to effect some nefarious purpose. and if the person he suspects, is the *real* Author or abetter, it would be a pity not to expose him to Public execration; for attempting, in so dishonorable a way, to obtain a disclosure of Sentiments of which some advantage could be taken. But Mr. Nicholas will unquestionably know, that if the proofs fail, the matter will recoil, and that the statement must be *full*, and not a partial one that is given to the Public; not only as the most satisfactory mode of bringing it before the tribunal, but shortest in the result: for he will have a persevering phalanx to contend against.

It seems to me that he would be obligd to disclose the *manner*, in which his correspondence and mine began, and the *motives* wch. led to it; for until the discovery was made, and communicated by him to me, that *Jno. Langhorne* was a fictitious name, I had not the smallest suspicion thereof; but, on the contrary, viewed the production as that of a Pedagogue, who was desirous of exhibiting a few of his flowers. and after returning a civil, but short answer, I never thought more of him, or his letter, until the history of the business was developed by Mr. Nicholas. All this must appear; or contrivance would be retorted. I will only add that, as Mr. Nicholas has made you a confidant in this business, I shall acquiesce with pleasure in any steps he may take, that will bring me forward, with your concurrence. If a *trick* so dirty and shabby as this is supposed to be, could be *clearly proved*, it would, in my opinion, be attended with a happy effect at this time; but, on the other hand, if it should be attempted and fail, the reverse would be the consequence.

I little thought when I retired to the Shades of Private life, last year, that any event would happen, *in my day*, that could bring me again, on the Public theatre; but so it is; and the remnent of a life which required ease and tranquility, will end more than probably in toil and responsibility.

Your Mother left us on friday; for your Brother Corbins, after giving us the pleasure of her's, and Nancy Washington's Company, eight or ten days. Corbins wife is much better, and hopes are entertained of her being perfectly restored.

Your Aunt and the family unite with me in best wishes for yourself and Mrs. Washington; and I am etc.

Back at his most unfavorite task, Washington here writes to David Stuart, again seeking some glimmer of advice on what to do about George Washington Custis.

Mount Vernon, August 13, 1798.

DEAR SIR: If you, or Mrs. Stuart could, by indirect means, discover the State of Washington Custis's mind, it would be to be wished. He appears to me to be moped and Stupid. says nothing, and is always in some hole or corner excluded from Company. Before he left Annapolis, he wrote to me desiring to know whether he was to return there, or not, that he might pack up accordingly; I answered, that I was astonished at the question! and that it appeared to me that nothing that could be said to him had the least effect, or left an impression beyond the moment. Whether this, by thwarting his views, is the cause of his present behavior, I know not. Enclosed is his letter and my answer. To be returned when read. We are as usual; and unite in best regards for you, Mrs. Stuart and the family. I am etc.

The problem of George Washington Parke Custis was one that Washington never solved. His later life was undistinguished. In 1806 he married Mary Lee Fitzhugh and built a handsome house, Arlington, where he lived as a gentleman farmer and dilettante, basking in the reflection of Washington's glory. He imported Merino sheep, wrote a play, Pocahontas, which ran for twelve nights in Philadelphia, and made numerous notes for a book on Washington which he never wrote. They were later published and though some glimpses of Washington at home are undoubtedly authentic and valuable, historians have come to regard the book as grossly inaccurate.

World affairs suddenly distracted Washington from his wayward grandson. Diplomatic relations with France worsened until war looked inevitable. To his own amazement, Washington found himself once more involved in commanding an army. Here he tells about it in a chatty letter to George Washington Lafayette. He mentions along the way that Nellie Custis has become engaged to his nephew Lawrence Lewis, a match that delighted Washington immensely. He showed his pleasure by giving the young couple twenty-five hundred acres of the Mount Vernon estate as a wedding present.

Mount Vernon, December 25, 1798.

MY DEAR GEORGE: —Having written a long letter to General La Fayette I shall write a short one to you; and it shall relate principally, if not altogether, to domestic concerns.

At the time you left this country you would not, less than I did, believe that in the course of events any occurrence could arise, which would again take me from the walks of Mount Vernon. But the injuries we have received, and are threatened with, have induced me once more (if occasion should require it) to tread the thorny path of public life, and for this purpose I have accepted a Commission to command the Armies of the United States, if, unfortunately, we should be forced to a War.

Your acquaintance Lawrence Lewis is appointed Captain of a Troop of Light Dragoons; but intends, before he enters the Camp of Mars to engage in that of Venus; Eleanor Custis and he having entered into a contract of marriage; which, I understand, is to be fulfilled on my birthday (the 22d. of Feby). Washington Custis prefering a Military career to literary pursuits, is appointed Cornet in Lewis's Troop, and Washington Craik a Lieutenancy. Young Carroll of Carrolton, will be a Volunteer Aid of mine, and Mr. Lear is my Secretary.

Young gentlemen of the first families, fortunes and expectations in the United States, are offering their Services; but I hope, and most ardently pray, that the Directory in your Country will not, by a perseverence in the insults and injuries which they have heaped on this, make it necessary to resort to Arms to repel an Invasion, or to do ourselves justice. I can undertake to affirm, that necessity *only* will drive us to it, although I am but just returned from a six weeks visit in Philadelphia to make arrangements there for it, eventually.

Mrs. and Mr. Law and their pet Eliza, Mr. and Mrs. Peter and their two children, and Doctr. Stuart and family (whom I ought to have mentioned first) are all well; and would, if they knew I was writing to you, request to be remembered to you in the most affectionate terms. I recollect no material change that has taken place in men or things since you left America. Alexandria continues to thrive, and the Public buildings in the federal City go on well: and many private ones are commencing for the accommodation of the Members of Congress, and Officers of Government, preparatory to the removal of the Government to that place.

Mrs. Washington holds you in constant remembrance, and offers you every good wish, which she prays you to extend to your amiable mother and Sisters whenever it may be in your Power. Nelly, Washington and Lewis would, I am sure, unite heartily in these, were they at home; but all of them are absent, the first at Hope Park, and the other two beyond the Mountains. When the clouds which at present overcast the Political horrison are dispelled, it would give all your friends great pleasure to see you in your old walks, and to none more than to your Sincere and affectionate friend.

PS. If Mr. Frestal should be with you, or you should have occasion to write to him, be so good as to present him with the best wishes of this family.

The war scare dwindled almost as quickly as it loomed and Washington returned to the life of a gentleman farmer, glad to drop politics and military matters once more.

The last year of the century trickled slowly away and with it came news of the death of Charles Washington, the youngest and least successful of the brothers. For most of his later life he was an alcoholic. Washington's letter to kinsman Burgess Ball, though brief, has much of the man in it.

Mount Vernon, September 22, 1799.

DEAR SIR: Your letter of the 16th. instt. has been received, informing me of the death of my brother.

The death of near relations always produces awful and affecting emotions, under whatsoever circumstances it may happen. That of my brother's has been so long expected, and his latter days so uncomfortable to himself, must have prepared all around him for the stroke; though painful in the effect.

I was the *first*, and am now the *last*, of my fathers Children by the second marriage who remain. When I shall be called upon to follow them, is known only to the giver of life. When the summons comes I shall endeavour to obey it with a good grace.

Mrs. Washington has been, and still is, very much indisposed, but unites with me in best wishes for you, Mrs. Ball and family. With great esteem, &c.

Less than two months later, the call came for Washington and he was as good as his word. On December 9, 1799, Washington said farewell to a brace of nephews who had been visiting at Mount Vernon. "It was a bright frosty morning," one of them later recalled. "He had taken his usual ride and the clear, healthy flush on his cheek and his spritely manner brought the remark from both of us that we had never seen the General look so well. I have sometimes thought him decidedly the handsomest man I ever saw; and when in lively mood, so full of pleasantry, so agreeable to all with whom he associated, that I could hardly realize that he was the same Washington whose dignity awed all who approached him."

On Wednesday, the eleventh, Washington had dinner with Bryan Fairfax, his son, and daughter, who was said to have a remarkable resemblance to the Sally Fairfax Washington knew and loved. The next day he was on horseback, as usual, riding around Mount Vernon's farms. The weather turned nasty, a cold, sleeting rain. He ignored it, and stayed on his horse for the better part of five hours. Later that night, as he sat by the fire reading aloud items of interest from the local paper, his secretary, Tobias Lear, noticed he was hoarse and suggested that he take something for his cold. Washington said he preferred "to let it go as it came."

About 3 A.M. the following morning, Washington awoke with his throat so swollen he could scarcely breathe or speak. His discomfiture woke Martha, but he refused to let her get out of bed in the icy cold to send for help. He suffered stoically until dawn, when a servant arrived as usual to light the fire.

His old friend, Dr. James Craik, rushed to Mount Vernon and summoned two other doctors for consultation. But the limited medical knowledge of 1799 could do nothing for Washington, who was probably suffering from a streptococcus infection in his throat. Throughout the day he sank slowly. In the early evening he spoke to the doctors in a low, strained voice. "I feel myself going. I thank you for your attention. You had better not take any more trouble about me; but let me go off quietly. I cannot last long."

About ten o'clock, Washington gestured to Tobias Lear, who leaned close to catch the broken voice as it whispered: "I am just going. Have me decently buried and do not let my body be put into the vault in less than two days after I am dead." The grief-stricken Lear nodded. Washington looked directly at him, and said, "Do you understand me? "

"Yes, sir," choked Lear.

With a sigh, George Washington spoke his last words. " 'Tis well."

Lear remained by his side, holding his hand. Suddenly Washington withdrew it and took his own pulse. Lear called to Dr. Craik, who hurried to the bedside as the big hand slipped off the wrist to fall helplessly on the counterpane. Craik laid his hand gently over Washington's eyes as he died, in Lear's words, "without a struggle or a sigh."

A wave of grief engulfed the Nation. Orators mounted pulpits and stages to praise the departed hero. Among the millions who mourned George Washington, the public servant, the first citizen of the world, a fortunate few mourned that rarest of human beings, a true friend.

INDEX